The Uncertain Promise of Retiree Health Benefits

An Evaluation of Corporate Obligations

Mark J. Warshawsky

The AEI Press

Publisher for the American Enterprise Institute
WASHINGTON, D.C.

1992

Distributed by arrangement with

University Press of America
4720 Boston Way
Lanham, Md. 20706

3 Henrietta Street
London WC2E 8LU England

Library of Congress Cataloging-in-Publication Data
Warshawsky, Mark J.
   The uncertain promise of retiree health benefits: an evaluation of
corporate obligations
       p.   cm. — (AEI studies: 552)
   Includes bibliographical references.
   ISBN 0-8447-7011-6
   1. Insurance. Health—United States. 2. Retirees—Medical
care—United States—Finance. 3. Retirees—United States—Insurance
requirements. 4. Retirees—Legal status, laws, etc.—United States.
5. Insurance. Health—Law and legislation—United States.
   I. Title. II. Series.
   HG9396.W37   1991

368.3'8—dc20   91-45391
                                                                         CIP

AEI Studies 552

The AEI PRESS
Publisher for the American Enterprise Institute
1150 17th Street, N.W., Washington, D.C. 20036

Printed in the United States of America

Acknowledgments

This book was written while I was a visiting scholar at the American Enterprise Institute in 1990, on leave from my position as a senior economist in the Capital Markets section at the Federal Reserve Board. My thanks go to Michael Prell and John Rea of the Federal Reserve and to Chris DeMuth of the American Enterprise Institute for making my visit possible. Any views expressed in this book, however, are my own and do not reflect the views of the governors or of the official staff of the Federal Reserve Board, or those of the staff of the American Enterprise Institute.

I received advice and assistance from many people in the course of conducting the research for this book. In particular, my wife, Laura B. Warshawsky, gave me considerable advice on chapter 3. The third section of chapter 9 is based on joint work conducted with Professor Fred Mittelstaedt of Arizona State University. Carolyn Weaver and Robert Helms of the American Enterprise Institute, Professor Mittelstaedt, several anonymous reviewers, and my wife also provided helpful suggestions and comments throughout the book.

Among those who gave me help with data sources, legal doctrines, institutional features, or more general advice were William Wiatrowski of the Bureau of Labor Statistics, John Turner, Dan Beller, and Joseph Applebaum of the Pension and Welfare Benefits Administration, Christine Nickerson of the Actuarial Standards Board, Jerry Hercenberg and Stephen Miller of McDermott, Will and Emery, Lawrence Bader of Salomon Brothers, Joseph Newhouse of Harvard University, Bruce Vander Els of A. Foster Higgins, John Gabel of the Health Insurance Association of America, Ken Leong, Sol Mussey, Daniel Waldo, and John Wandeshin of the Health Care Financing Administration, Clint McCulley of the Bureau of Economic Analysis, William Thompson of the Pension Benefit Guaranty Corporation, Kathleen Holness of American Telephone and Telegraph, Joe Moran of New York Life, Fred Ruebeck of Eli Lilly, Anna Rappaport of Mercer, Meidinger, Hansen, Stephen Meskin of Martin Segal, Stephen Stone of Allstate Insurance, Jerry Stein and William Matusz of Prudential Insurance, Sheila Zedlewski of the Urban Institute, Cynthia Fagnoni of the General Accounting Office, Alan Monheit of the Agency for Health Care Policy and Research, Christine Dolan of the Employee Benefits Research Institute, Diana Scott of the

ACKNOWLEDGMENTS

Financial Accounting Standards Board, Marvin Kosters of the American Enterprise Institute, Martha Scanlon of the Federal Reserve Board, Roger Thomas, and Sam Saltzberg.

I dedicate this book to my wife, Laura, and to my son, David, in appreciation and with love.

MARK J. WARSHAWSKY

About the Authors

MARK J. WARSHAWSKY is a senior economist in the Division of Research and Statistics of the Federal Reserve Board, where he has conducted research since 1984 in corporate finance, securities markets, and retiree benefits. Mr. Warshawsky was a visiting scholar at the American Enterprise Institute when he wrote this book. He served as a staff member of the Working Group on Financial Markets in 1988, worked as a health insurance actuary with Combined Insurance, and is the author of more than twenty publications.

WILLIAM J. DENNIS, JR., is a senior research fellow at the NFIB Foundation, an affiliate of the National Federation of Independent Business. He has written extensively on small business and is author or coauthor of several monographs.

OLIVIA MITCHELL is professor of labor economics at Cornell University's Industrial and Labor Relations School and is associate editor of the *Industrial and Labor Relations Review*. She is coauthor of *Retirement, Pensions, and Social Security*.

HERBERT NEHRLING is a former chairman of the Employee Benefits Committee and served on the board of directors of the ERISA Industry Committee and the Association of Private Pension and Welfare Plans. He is an active member of the investment committee of the state of Delaware's pension fund.

MARK PAULY is Bendheim Professor of Health Care Systems, Public Management Insurance, and Economics at the Wharton School, University of Pennsylvania. He is a member of the Institute of Medicine and principal investigator of an evaluation of the Pew National Dental Foundation Program for the Pew Foundation.

ANNA RAPPAPORT is managing director of William M. Mercer, Inc., and has served as vice president of the Equitable Life Insurance Society of the United States and as senior vice president and chief actuary of the Standard Security Life Insurance Company of New York.

TIMOTHY RAY is a partner in the Washington, D.C., office of Coopers & Lybrand, overseeing the actuarial, benefits, and compensation consulting practice. He specializes in health care issues.

EUGENE STEUERLE is senior fellow at the Urban Institute and author of a weekly column, "Economic Perspective," for *Tax Notes* magazine. Between 1987 and 1989 he was the deputy assistant secretary of the treasury for tax analysis.

FRED VAN REMORTEL is managing director of the Retiree Health Care Group of Brown Bridgeman & Company and is responsible for the firm's relations with government agencies. He specializes in post-retirement medical benefit funding for Fortune 100 companies.

JOHN VINE is a partner in the Washington, D.C., law firm of Covington & Burling, specializing in employee benefits. He is counsel to the ERISA Industry Committee and cochairman of the Subcommittee on Executive Compensation of the Committee on Employee Benefits of the Tax Section, American Bar Association.

Contents

Foreword

The aging of the American population, especially of the "baby boom generation," underlies several important economic and social policy issues. The bulge in the postwar population, now in its productive middle age, will reach the traditional ages of retirement in the first two decades of the next century. As a result of this increase in the number of aged, combined with expected increases in life expectancy, those aged sixty-five and over are projected to increase from 12.6 percent of the population in 1990 to 17.5 percent in 2020. This means that in thirty years the United States will have approximately the same proportion of elderly as live in the state of Florida today.

This expected increase causes major concerns in health policy. The elderly are high users of health care products and services, and health care expenditures have been increasing at rates in excess of real economic growth. The Medicare Hospital Trust Fund is projected to run out of funds in 2005, some seven years before the baby boom generation begins to become eligible for Medicare. The growth in outpatient Medicare expenditures, currently 75 percent financed from general revenues, is expected to require an even larger proportion of tax revenues to maintain the current level of benefits.

This concern about the future of health policy is not restricted to the public sector. About 182 million of the population were covered by private insurance in 1989. Employer-provided insurance covered 153 million American workers and their dependents. Only a fraction of those covered in the private sector are now retired, but a large number of those now working expect to receive retiree health benefits when they retire.

How certain is this promise of retiree health benefits? This is the central issue that economist Mark Warshawsky addresses in this book. As his title indicates, what is perceived by many employees as a promise from their employer is far from ensured. In light of the aging of the working population and the rising cost of health care, employers are questioning their ability to continue offering retiree health benefits, at least on the terms they were offered in the past. This situation has been given increased public exposure by the Financial Accounting Standards Board's (FASB) requirement that companies show their accrued liabilities for retiree health benefits on their financial statements.

Mark Warshawsky's book gives us a complete look at the many ramifications of the economic and policy issues concerning retiree health benefits. He identifies the issues important to the policy and business communities, he presents data on these issues, he reviews the legal aspects of obligations to provide retiree benefits, he estimates the size of these future obligations, and he analyzes the implications of these issues for public policy. In short, he provides us with a careful analysis of what should be of interest to anyone who wants to understand why business managers, workers, and public policy officials are raising questions about the future of retiree health benefits.

This book also presents the views of several academic and business experts regarding the implications of changing business and policy conditions on the future availability of retiree health benefits. The presentations presented by these eight experts are based on a seminar held at the American Enterprise Institute in early 1991. Organized to explore the implications of Mark Warshawsky's estimates of future obligations, the seminar also covered the economic effects of the FASB rule, the pros and cons of accrual accounting, the effects of retiree health benefits on company pension obligations, the ways retiree health benefits will affect Medicare, and policy proposals that might give stronger incentives to private firms to provide retiree health benefits. The reader will encounter a variety of opinions on these topics—both in agreement and in disagreement with one another and with Mark Warshawsky—by a group of people selected for their knowledge of and involvement in retiree health benefits.

The American Enterprise Institute has been publishing research on both health policy and pension policy for over twenty years. We would like to thank Mark Warshawsky and those who participated in the seminar on retiree health benefits for helping to continue this tradition of careful analysis of important domestic policy issues.

ROBERT B. HELMS
Resident Scholar and Director of Health Policy Studies
American Enterprise Institute

1

The Problem of
Retiree Health Benefits

The provision of health care benefits to retired workers and their families by employers has become increasingly important, and even controversial, in recent years. The cost to employers of these benefits has risen rapidly. Retirees have lost promised benefits owing to the bankruptcy of plan sponsors or to the cancellation or severe contraction of benefit plans. With the passage of the Medicare Catastrophic Care Act of 1988, the federal government planned to increase the level of health benefits provided to the elderly by the Medicare program, thereby removing some of the burden for retiree health benefits from employers. Following repeal of the act, however, numerous proposals have sought to slow the growth of the Medicare program, potentially increasing the burden for employers.

Consciousness of the extent of the obligation of employers for retiree health benefits has been raised by the decision of the rule-making authority for financial accounting standards in the private sector to require corporations to record very sizable amounts for the accrued expense and largely unfunded liability for these benefits in financial statements. The issue of retiree health benefits is also important because it is a significant, although not currently dominant, part of the general problem of the provision and financing of health care in the United States.

This book characterizes retiree health benefits as a "problem." The benefits are a problem to financially ailing employers, who promised in happier times to provide these increasingly costly benefits to retirees. The benefits are a problem to retirees, particularly those under age sixty-five and therefore ineligible for Medicare coverage, who worry that their only source of affordable health insurance coverage may not be secure, or who already face reduced or canceled benefits and have decided to litigate in the federal courts. The benefits are a problem for the efficiency of the health care system because, especially for retirees eligible for Medicare, they may reduce the demand by the consumer for

1

FIGURE 1-1
NATIONAL HEALTH EXPENDITURES AS A PERCENTAGE OF GNP, 1959–1990

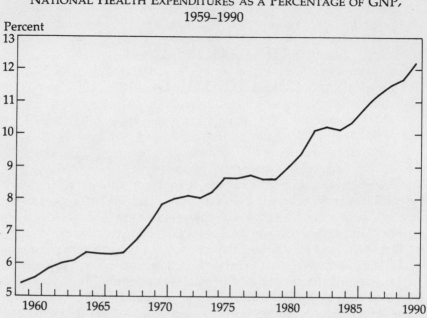

NOTE: 1990 is an estimate, in part.
SOURCE: National Income and Product Account.

economy in the delivery of health care and may reduce sensitivity to the prices charged for services rendered or commodities bought.

What is a relatively modest problem now may become a major problem in the future. As the population of the United States has aged and as medical care has become increasingly complex and costly in the past decades, the burden of providing health care has grown. As shown in figure 1-1, national expenditures on health care, as a percentage of the gross national product, have risen from 5.5 percent in 1960 to 12 percent in 1990.[1] And as the population continues to age in the decades ahead, the burden will continue to grow. Although the federal government tried to expand the coverage of the Medicare program in 1988, policy makers in 1990 sought, in an environment of huge budget deficits, to reduce the rate of growth in Medicare spending. Hence, it may fall to employers providing retiree health benefits to pick up the slack. Yet many employers are under financial pressure themselves and are often less able than the federal government to control the costs and utilization of health care. Furthermore, because retiree benefits are the subject of vaguely worded contracts and are largely unfunded, their security is not ensured.

2

Although retiree health benefits are a problem now and may represent a major problem in the future, the immediate cause for interest in the issue is the promulgation in December 1990 of a new financial accounting standard for private employers. The standard would move accounting for retiree health plans from a pay-as-you-go or cash basis to an accrual basis, thereby increasing significantly the expense recognized for these benefits and creating ex nihilo an accrued liability in financial statements. Discussion of the pending accounting standard itself has focused the attention of management, investors, unions, and policy makers on the economic significance of retiree health benefits. Furthermore, the creation of the accounting standard has occurred in the midst of an active legal environment, both in the courts and, to a lesser extent, in the Congress.

Because of the growing economic significance of retiree health benefits, because of the difficult legal issues encountered when companies try to cancel or reduce these benefits, and because of the major changes pending in the new standard of accounting for these benefits, it seems appropriate and timely to write a book describing these aspects of the issue. Furthermore, because retiree health benefits represent a current problem in several respects and because they may become an even larger problem in the future, some proposals to public policy makers of possible ways of dealing with the issue are discussed near the end of the book.

An Economic Framework

In order to provide some cohesion to the various parts of this book addressing the legal, accounting, and financial aspects of retiree health benefits and to provide some underpinnings to the policy suggestions, it is necessary to create a broad economic framework for discussion. Retiree health benefits, like pensions, are a form of deferred compensation. That is, in exchange for the labor services provided by active workers, some firms promise in addition to current wages and other benefits to provide their workers with free or highly subsidized health insurance benefits upon retirement. In a unionized context, this exchange is the conscious result of a collective bargaining agreement. In a nonunionized environment, it is the result of the workings of supply and demand in the labor market, manifest in written contracts and customs and practices in the workplace.

The advantages to workers of deferred compensation in the form of retiree health benefits are manifold. Like the receipt of current health insurance benefits, receipt of health benefits in future retirement years is, in essence, income exempt from the payment of federal and state

3

income taxes. Although pension benefits are also tax-favored income (howbeit tax-deferred and not tax-exempt), health benefits, as payment-in-kind, generally are not at risk from price inflation because they are essentially indexed to the cost of health care. For retirees younger than age sixty-five, and therefore ineligible for Medicare, health insurance coverage provided through the employer's group plan is nearly always more extensive and more economical than would be available from an insurance company or from Blue Cross–Blue Shield in the form of an individual health insurance policy. For retirees above age sixty-five, employer-provided health insurance supplements Medicare coverage, particularly for prescription drugs.

The provision of retiree health benefits also offers advantages to the sponsoring employer. It is possible that wages are somewhat lower than they would be without the provision of retiree health benefits. It is also possible that higher quality workers are attracted and retained because of the existence of a retiree health benefit plan, and especially in a unionized context, smoother management–labor relations may result. Because retiree health benefits generally are given only upon the attainment of retirement status with the sponsoring employer, the loyalty and perseverance of long-term service is rewarded, while costly turnover is penalized. Finally, having a retiree health plan may enable an employer to downsize rationally and humanely. It could encourage workers to retire prior to age sixty-five by guaranteeing these workers continued health insurance coverage prior to their eligibility for Medicare. Like other forms of compensation, the costs of retiree health benefits are tax-deductible expenses for the employer. The prefunding of these benefits, however, currently has only limited tax benefits, especially when compared with pension plans, and is not widely practiced by employers.

While retiree health benefits represent the result of a mutually beneficial exchange between workers and employers, ample room exists for problems and abuses in the exchange under current law. In particular, because retiree health benefits are not generally prefunded, this form of worker's deferred compensation depends almost entirely on the sponsoring employer's willingness and ability to pay benefits years and decades into the future. Court action may protect some workers against the outright cancellation of benefits, particularly when the terms of written contracts clearly intend the continuation of benefits. But in most cases, and particularly when written documents clearly reserve the employer's right to cancel or amend benefits unilaterally, workers are at the complete whim of employers' wishes. Furthermore, even when employers desire to fulfill their half of the exchange, as no doubt most do, workers are still at risk that the employer's possible future decline, bankruptcy, or restructuring will prevent the payment of retiree health benefits. And owing to the chaotic state of affairs in the panoply of master contract documents, summary plan descriptions, booklets, letters, and other written and oral communications, the exact nature of the promise made to workers is often left unclear.

Problems and abuses of these types in the area of pension benefits led to the passage of the Employee Retirement Income Security Act (ERISA) of 1974. The protections of ERISA, however, generally do not apply to retiree health plans. There are two practical explanations for the silence of ERISA on this subject. First, retiree health benefits were not a particularly costly item in 1974, and hence they were not of great importance either to employers or workers, especially in comparison with pensions. Second, because they are directly related to health care, retiree health insurance benefits are considerably more complicated and were thought to require more flexibility in design, unencumbered by law and regulation, than pension benefits. Owing to significant changes in the general economic environment since the early 1970s, and in particular owing to the explosion of health care costs, however, retiree health benefits have indeed become a significant item. Furthermore, dissatisfaction with the inefficiencies of the entire health care system is causing many to question its current organization and incentive structure.

Summary of the Book

The Institutional Environment. In the vast majority of cases, health benefits to retirees are provided through the same group health plan or plans as are benefits to active workers. Chapter 2 describes the features of typical group health plans offered by large- and medium-sized corporations, focusing on the most common type of plan offered in connection with retiree health benefits—a fee-for-service or indemnity plan. Retired workers under age sixty-five usually receive benefits identical to those of active workers. For retirees above age sixty-five and eligible for Medicare, benefits from employer-sponsored plans fill in and supplement some of the gaps in health care coverage left by the Medicare program. Coordination of benefits with Medicare can occur in several ways, generally covering at least part of the Medicare deductible and coinsurance payments for hospitalization and physician services, as well as prescription drugs. Typically, workers will receive lifetime health benefits upon retirement, provided they have worked at a company long enough also to receive benefits from the company's pension plan. In about half the cases, employers pay the full retiree health premium, while in most of the remainder of cases, employers pay at least some of the

5

premium. Employers, however, do not usually prefund these plans, owing in part to the absence of tax-favored funding options.

Although retiree health plans, as welfare benefit plans, are not subject to most of the strictures that the Employee Retirement Income Security Act of 1974 has imposed on pension plans, they must nevertheless operate within the limits of some rules and laws. Chapter 3 will discuss these rules. In particular, they include reporting and disclosure standards, fiduciary responsibilities, and the requirement to continue benefits, at cost to the employee, for a short period after separation from employment (Consolidated Omnibus Budget Reconciliation Act, so-called COBRA, coverage). In the special case of a bankrupt company, the Retiree Benefits Bankruptcy Protection Act of 1988, passed in response to the bankruptcy of LTV Corp., moves retiree health benefits up the creditor-priority ladder slightly. This act, however, does not ensure that there will necessarily be any assets available to pay for retiree benefits earned over the working lives of employees, and it does not address the issue of unilateral cancellation or amendment of benefit plans by viable employers.

Whether an employer may legally cancel or modify retiree health benefits generally depends on the language of the relevant plan documents. Chapter 4 examines the alternatives when the language of the documents is ambiguous or the documents do not exist. Current legal doctrine in some circuits of the federal court system holds that reference should be made to the intent of the parties as expressed in extrinsic evidence such as statements made at exit interviews, and to the reasonable inference that retirement benefits are intended to last for the length of retirees' lives. In other circuits, however, no such inference is made, and greater latitude to employer decisions is given. In all circuits, if the language of plan documents unambiguously reserves the right to the employer to cancel or amend benefits, courts will allow such actions. Moreover, all circuits would probably allow unilateral changes in future retiree health benefits promised to active workers, including those near retirement age.

Chapter 5 examines the financial accounting standards for retiree health benefits, which, like those for pensions, have been subject to considerable discussion and evolution during the past decade. Although the organization responsible for setting standards in the private sector, the Financial Accounting Standards Board (FASB), tentatively decided as early as 1982 that retiree health benefits were a form of deferred compensation and hence logically subject to accrual accounting, significant opposition stalled the evolution of actual standards in this direction. In 1984, the FASB required that companies should disclose at least the pay-as-you-go cost of their retiree health plans. In an exposure draft of a new standard in February 1989, the FASB finally proposed that full accrual accounting should be implemented in future years. The standard was approved, with some modifications, by the FASB in December 1990 and is described in some detail. The standard is a thorough statement of the method to be used in calculating the accrued expense and liability for retiree health (and other nonpension) benefits. A very few companies have already implemented the proposed standard—one example is given—and a field test of the standard for twenty-five large companies was performed in 1989.

The Economic Environment. Chapter 6 addresses the finding by various surveys that somewhat less than half of all retirees, or about 11 million people, were provided health benefits through employer-sponsored plans in the late 1980s. Of these covered retirees, about 30 percent received benefits because they are the spouses of workers who earned the benefit through their employment with a plan sponsor. Of covered retirees, about 40 percent are younger than sixty-five. Approximately one-quarter of covered retirees received benefits through former employment with a federal, state, or local governmental entity. The remainder of covered retirees received benefits from a private sector employer, typically a large company in the utilities, petroleum refining, primary metal, transportation equipment, or airlines and pipelines industries. In chapter 6, it is hypothesized that, because retiree health benefits are not prefunded, only larger employers heretofore have been trusted by workers to make good on retirement promises.

Retiree health benefits have become a costly benefit, and they will become more costly owing to several trends, as chapter 7 will discuss. Life expectancy has improved and is expected to continue to improve for men and, especially, for women. The proportion of the general population above age fifty-five is increasing. Indeed, this aging process is expected to accelerate in the coming decades. Moreover, the secular decline in the labor-force participation rate of men aged fifty-five and older has continued through the 1980s. Although the labor-force participation rate of women has generally increased, at older ages their participation rate has also declined slightly.

The cost of health care has been increasing rapidly in recent years, often at rates well in excess of the rate of general inflation. Although part of this "excess" price inflation may be explained by the statistical methods used in calculating the various components of the consumer price index, some prominent researchers contend that the increases are real and that the causes are institutional and economic in nature. In particular, the increase in insurance coverage and the improvement in benefits offered in the past decades have been cited as factors leading to inefficiencies and distortions in the market for health care. Cost-shifting by Medicare can also lead to increased costs for employer-sponsored health plans. Finally, the attitude of active workers and retirees toward employer-provided retiree health insurance is protective, as evidenced by their willingness to strike and to litigate to prevent the cancellation or reduction of benefits.

A simulation model is created in chapter 8 to give estimates of the pay-as-you-go cost and of the accrued expense and liability consistent with the new FASB standard (FASB-consistent), for a typical retiree health plan for several representative demographic groups. After making reasonable assumptions, choosing the appropriate parameter values, and basing the estimates on the earlier discussion in chapter 6 of the number of retirees covered by group health plans in the private sector, the simulation model is used to estimate in the aggregate the pay-as-you-go cost, the accrued expense, and the accrued liability for retiree health benefits provided in the private sector. The aggregate estimate for the pay-as-you-go cost in 1988 is $11.3 billion. The FASB-consistent accrued expense in 1988 is estimated at $58.9 billion, and the 1988 accrued liability is estimated at $332.1 billion. The 1989 accrued liability is estimated at $426.5 billion. The proposed FASB standard, if implemented in 1988, would have reduced profits in the aggregate by about 20 percent. The 1988 liability calculated under the standard represented more than 10 percent of the market value of equity.

In 1988, 676 companies in a sample of 2,215 large and medium-sized companies trading on the New York and American Stock Exchanges indicated in their financial statements that they provide health benefits to retirees. The pay-as-you-go cost reported under current accounting standards in 1988 statements for 548 of the 676 companies totaled $7.7 billion. This number is largely consistent with the aggregate estimate of the simulation model, when one takes into account the companies not reporting costs or the provision of retiree health benefits, the absence of reporting about multiemployer plans, and the companies not included in the sample. Basing figures at least in part on the reported costs and using the simulation model, companies are matched with some of the representative demographic groups, and the FASB-consistent estimates of accrued expense and liability for the 676 companies are calculated. As reported in chapter 9, in 1988, the accrued expense for these companies was $42.2 billion and the accrued liability was $255.5 billion. It should be noted that the estimate of accrued liability for these companies alone is larger than the estimates for the entire private sector made by other analysts.

Because not all companies offer retiree health benefits, the "incidence" of the accrual of benefits is more concentrated than estimates for the entire private sector would indicate. In particular, the new FASB standard, if implemented in 1989, would have reduced reported earnings of the 676 companies that indicated they provide retiree health benefits by about 30 percent; the accrued liability calculated for these companies represented about 17.5 percent of the market value of equity. The burden for some companies is higher still than these measures indicate. Numbers of this magnitude represent, of course, the extent of these companies' obligations for retiree health benefits to be paid in the future under reasonable assumptions about future conditions. Numbers of this magnitude would be especially worrisome if awareness of them came upon the financial markets all at once. Empirical evidence indicates that the stock market is generally aware of the obligations of firms and that estimates of the liabilities for retiree health benefits are included, but somewhat inaccurately and with somewhat of an understatement, in share prices. The incomplete extent of the market's recognition may owe to a lack of knowledge or to the belief that future actions by the government or by plan sponsors will reduce employers' obligations.

The Policy Environment. As chapter 10 points out, the passage and repeal of the Medicare Catastrophic Coverage Act of 1988 represent critical events for understanding the attitudes of the public and of Congress concerning the problem of health care for retirees. In particular, the retired elderly view health care from former employers as a vested benefit, and Congress is reluctant to challenge this presumption—and perhaps even agrees with it. As such, the events surrounding the Medicare act and subsequent events will inform the steps that public policy makers can or will take in dealing with retiree health care. Another recent example of the political difficulties arising from an attempt to deal with retiree health benefits is the failure of the Coal Commission, appointed after the bitter Pittston strike, to reach a consensus about steps to take to alleviate the financial problems of the health trust funds in the coal industry.

The growing realization of employers resulting from the new accounting standard of the extent of their obligation for retiree health benefits has already caused a few companies to cut back on benefits, or even to cancel plans entirely; it will likely cause many other companies to consider such actions in the near future. More litigation and employee dissatisfaction will result from such steps. When added to the concerns for benefit security resulting from the bankruptcies of major plan sponsors, a clearer and more permanent definition of the obligation for retiree health care becomes necessary. Moreover, because employee distrust has been and will be engendered, prefunding for the retiree benefits becomes logical. Current options for tax-favored prefunding are

9

poorly designed, however, as vehicles for adequate levels of funding, for containing excessive insurance coverage, or for consistency with other features of the tax code, particularly regarding pension plans.

I suggest fairly broad policy goals in order to enable the evaluation of practical policy options. Two policy options in particular are considered: the status quo and "ERISA-fication."

The appendix concludes the book with suggestions for further research and the collection of better and more easily accessible statistics. A better understanding is needed of the relationship between expenditures on health care and measures of well-being in order to better evaluate policy options. Information about the specific features of retiree health plans offered by specific employers to workers is needed in order to conduct studies of labor market behavior.

2

Description of Benefits
and Tax Considerations

Retiree health benefits are health care benefits provided to retirees, and often to their dependents and surviving spouses, through an employer's group health plan. In the vast majority of cases, benefits to retirees are provided through the same health plan or plans as benefits to active workers. Therefore, to gain an insight into retiree benefits it is necessary first to acquire some basic knowledge about group health plans. Because benefits for retirees above age sixty-five are coordinated in some fashion with the Medicare program, it is also useful to have an outline of the provisions of Medicare and of the five ways in which retiree health plans are coordinated with that federal program. Finally, basic information about eligibility criteria and cost-sharing arrangements of plans and tax considerations completes the description of retiree health plans that is necessary to engage in further discussions in later chapters about the legal, accounting, and economic aspects of the issue and suggestions for public policy.

Group Health Plans

Types of Plans. According to the 1988 survey of employee benefits of the Bureau of Labor Statistics (BLS), virtually all health care plans provided by medium and large private employers cover the major categories of health care: namely, hospital room and board, physician and surgeon care, laboratory services, prescription drugs, and private duty nursing.[1] Nearly all plans also cover mental health care, although coverage is generally subject to special limitations. Other common categories of covered care include alcohol and drug abuse treatment and dental care.

According to the BLS survey, about three-fourths of participants in group health plans were covered by a traditional indemnity or fee-for-service plan. These plans pay for specific medical procedures as expenses

11

are incurred. About 40 percent of indemnity plan participants were in self-insured plans, in which the plan sponsor bears the financial risk for making plan payments. About 35 percent of participants were in commercially insured plans, in which the plan sponsor pays premiums periodically to an insurance company and bears no further risk. About 20 percent were in Blue Cross–Blue Shield plans, in which the plan sponsor pays premiums to one of these nonprofit organizations. The remainder of participants were in plans with mixed funding arrangements.

Health maintenance organizations (HMOs) cover about 20 percent of participants in health plans. Participation in this type of health plan has grown rapidly in recent years. HMOs are prepaid plans that provide medical services to plan participants for a fixed fee. Participants in HMO plans, unlike those in indemnity plans, are generally required to use HMO physicians exclusively. These physicians are paid either a salary, a predetermined annual fee, or a negotiated, discounted fee for service to provide plan participants with any medical service deemed necessary. HMOs are divided into two categories: group and staff, in which medical services are provided in a central clinic; and individual practice association, in which HMO physicians work from their own offices. HMOs usually cover a wider range of categories of health care than indemnity plans, including hearing care, physical examinations, well-baby care, and immunizations and inoculations.

About 7 percent of plan participants were covered by preferred provider organizations (PPOs). PPOs pay a higher benefit to plan participants for services rendered by designated hospitals and physicians. Participants are free, however, to choose any physician or hospital.

Coverage Limitations. The BLS divides group health plans into four categories of coverage: full coverage, coverage with internal limitations only, coverage with comprehensive limitations only, and coverage with internal and comprehensive limitations. A plan provides full coverage if there are no restrictions on the number of days of care, no dollar maximums on benefits, and no required payments by the plan participant. Some HMOs may be considered full coverage plans. Internal limitations restrict the level of coverage for a particular type of service: for example, a maximum of sixty days of hospitalization per year, or a 50 percent coinsurance rate for mental health care. A comprehensive limitation can be an annual deductible, a coinsurance requirement, or a maximum annual or lifetime benefit amount that applies to all services covered by the plan. Typical examples of comprehensive limitations, which are ubiquitous in fee-for-service plans to control costs, include a $150 annual deductible, a requirement that participants pay 20 percent of covered expenses beyond the deductible (coinsurance), or a $1 million cap on lifetime plan payments per participant. In most plans with a coinsurance requirement, however, the plan begins to pay 100 percent of covered expenses after a maximum annual amount of out-of-pocket expenses is reached, generally $1,000 per individual and $2,500 per family. An example of a plan with internal and comprehensive limitations is one with an internal limit of 120 days of fully paid hospitalization, with benefits beyond that point subject to comprehensive limitations. Most indemnity plans have internal and comprehensive limitations of various types.

In addition to limitations, many plans have instituted other special features designed to contain costs, particularly for hospitalization and surgery. These features include coverage for less expensive alternatives to an extended hospital stay, such as treatment in an extended care facility, home health care, or hospice. A feature intended to eliminate unnecessary surgery and hospitalization is the payment of a higher level of benefits when the surgery or hospital stay is certified as necessary by a second physician.

About half of the plans require no premium payment by the active worker for individual coverage, and about a third require no payment for family coverage. The remainder of the plans require participant contributions of varying levels.

As mentioned above, nearly all retiree health plans are tied to the plans that provide benefits to active workers.[2] Hence, most retiree plans provide retired workers under age sixty-five with benefits identical to those of active workers. Retiree plans differ, however, in the way benefits for retirees above age sixty-five are coordinated with Medicare.[3] A brief description of the current provisions of the Medicare program and the way retiree health plans coordinate with Medicare will be given in the next two sections.

Medicare

Medicare is an entitlement program of the federal government, covering medical expenses for virtually all Americans above sixty-five years of age.[4] Spending in fiscal year 1990 was some $100 billion. The program was enacted in 1965 and is administered by the Health Care Financing Administration (HCFA), within the Department of Health and Human Services. Medicare is composed of two separate programs: hospital insurance (HI) and supplementary medical insurance (SMI).

Hospital Insurance. The HI program covers inpatient hospital care, posthospital care in skilled nursing facilities, home health agency

13

services, and hospice care for the terminally ill. The SMI program covers many types of medical services and supplies furnished by physicians and other health care professionals in connection with physicians' services, as well as certain types of outpatient treatments. Outpatient prescription drugs are not covered by either the HI or the SMI program. All persons aged sixty-five or older and some disabled persons of any age are eligible for Medicare if they are entitled to social security benefits. Those persons above age sixty-five but ineligible for Medicare may enroll if they pay a monthly premium representing the full actuarial cost of benefits under the HI program.

The rules governing the HI program limit coverage to an episode of illness. An episode begins with an enrollee's first day of hospitalization and ends when the enrollee has not been an inpatient for at least sixty days. HI covers up to ninety days of services in a hospital during a single episode. After an initial deductible for each episode, the patient is entitled to sixty days of hospitalization with no cost sharing. From the sixty-first through the ninetieth day of the episode, the patient is required to pay coinsurance equal to one-fourth of the deductible. HI enrollees also have a lifetime reserve of sixty additional hospital days which they may use if the benefit for ninety days allotted for the episode is exhausted. Lifetime reserve days require a coinsurance equal to one-half the deductible. In 1989, the deductible was $560.

Prior to 1983, the HI program was operated as a traditional fee-for-service plan, where fees were paid for the "reasonable cost" of hospital care. Since then, hospitals have been paid a fixed prospective payment for each diagnosis-related group (DRG). Hence, when a Medicare patient is admitted to the hospital, he is diagnosed and given a DRG designation. Based on the diagnosis at admission, the hospital generally receives a fixed payment for that DRG, regardless of the number of days the patient is actually hospitalized and regardless of the cost of the procedures eventually performed.[5]

Supplementary Medical Insurance. To enable an enrollee in the SMI program to be reimbursed for expenditures on medical services and supplies covered under the SMI program, those expenditures must exceed the SMI deductible during the calendar year. The SMI deductible in 1990 was $75. Under the Omnibus Budget Reconciliation Act of 1990, the deductible was increased to $100 beginning January 1, 1991. After the deductible is met, SMI pays 80 percent of the allowed reasonable charges for covered physicians' services. Physicians can accept or reject assignment of reasonable charges. If the physician accepts, he submits the bill to Medicare and agrees to receive from Medicare 80 percent of the reasonable charge. The patient is responsible for the deductible and the remaining 20 percent. If the physician rejects assignment, he bills the patient, who in turns submits a claim to Medicare. The patient is responsible for the difference between the physician's charge and the allowed charge, as well as the 20 percent coinsurance and deductible.

The HI program is financed through a tax on a portion of current employment earnings. The SMI program is financed by premiums paid by or on behalf of enrollees and by contributions from the federal government. The SMI premium is calculated by HCFA to cover one-fourth of the cost of the program for aged beneficiaries. In 1990, the monthly premium was $28.60; by 1995, the premium is scheduled to increase to $46.10, in order to maintain premium revenues as one-fourth of the program costs in the face of the expectation that the inflation rate for health care would continue to be high. Both HI and SMI are pay-as-you-go programs, with accumulations in the trust funds intended to cover short-term fluctuations in the costs of the programs.

Coordination of Benefits

There are five ways in which employer-sponsored health benefit plans coordinate with Medicare the payment of benefits to retirees above age sixty-five: through full coordination of benefits, through exclusion, through carve-out, through supplement, and through fixed allowance. Full coordination of benefits, the most costly option to employers, entails the payment to the plan participant of the difference between what Medicare pays and the actual cost of health services, up to what the plan would pay without Medicare. For example, suppose a physician who does not accept Medicare assignment performs a major procedure and charges the sixty-seven–year-old plan participant $3,000. Medicare will pay $1,600, or 80 percent of reasonable charges of $2,000, assuming the participant has already met the SMI deductible. Under full coordination of benefits, the plan will pay $1,400—that is, the difference between what Medicare pays and the actual cost of services. This difference, of course, is less than what the plan would have paid without Medicare—that is, $2,240, or 80 percent of $2,800 ($3,000 minus an assumed plan deductible of $200).

The exclusion option applies plan deductibles and coinsurance requirements after Medicare has made payment. In the example given above, the plan will pay $960. Again assuming a $200 plan deductible and a 20 percent rate of coinsurance, 80 percent of $1,200 ($1,400 minus $200), or $960, is paid by the plan.

Carve-out, the most common option used by employers, requires the payment of benefits at the level required by the plan reduced by the amount of the Medicare payment. In the example above, a plan under this option would pay $640—that is, $2,240, the plan's required payment without Medicare, minus $1,600, the payment by Medicare.

The supplement option mimics the type of benefit coverage given by some medigap policies sold by commercial insurance companies and Blue Cross–Blue Shield organizations to Medicare-eligible individuals. Under the supplement option, the plan fills in the gaps left by Medicare's deductible and coinsurance requirement. In the example above, the plan would pay $400 or the amount of coinsurance left to the plan participant by Medicare.

In the four options described thus far, if the group health plan covers services not paid by Medicare, such as prescription drugs, the plan will have to pay for the full cost of such benefits, subject to the plan's internal and comprehensive limitations. In the fixed allowance option, services not covered by Medicare and specifically enumerated in the plan are, in fact, the only benefits paid by the plan. In other words, in the above example of a medical procedure covered by Medicare, the plan with a fixed allowance option would have no further obligation, as it considers payment by Medicare as full payment for any procedure covered by Medicare.

Some notion of the distribution of retiree health plans by options for coordination of benefits can be gained by reference to a survey of plan sponsors conducted in 1988 by the Health Insurance Association of America (HIAA) and Johns Hopkins University.[6] The HIAA survey found that three-fourths of participants in retiree health plans were associated with companies sponsoring plans that employed the carve-out option. The full coordination of benefits option was used for 22 percent of plan participants, and the exclusion option was used for 11 percent. The supplement and fixed allowance options were each used for 8 percent of participants. (The above percentages total more than 100 percent because some survey respondents reported that they used different options for different plans they sponsored and HIAA was unable to assign the coordination options to plans exactly.) The HIAA survey notes that retiree health plans are more likely to be indemnity plans than is typical of group health plans in general. The survey also notes that about 40 percent of participants in retiree health plans have their SMI premiums paid for them by their former employers.

Eligibility Criteria and Cost-sharing Arrangements

Retiree health plans differ in the criteria used to determine eligibility for the continuation of subsidized benefits after retirement. In order to be eligible for retiree health benefits, most plans require that the employee be vested for pension benefits and be formally retired from the company.[7]

Because vesting for most pension plans occurs after five years of service, most, but not all, participants in health plans offering retiree benefits who retire at the normal retirement age, sixty-five, will be eligible for retiree benefits. Some plans, however, do not impose any service requirement. Moreover, many plans also offer entitlement following eligibility for early retirement—that is, after ten or fifteen years of service and attainment of age fifty-five or sixty.

Very few plans give benefits to long-term employees who leave the company (or are fired) prior to retirement. Hence, unlike pensions where vesting for some level of benefits generally occurs after five years, regardless of whether the employee formally retires or not, retiree health plans are given, albeit in full, only upon retirement. In essence, retiree health benefits are an all-or-nothing proposition to an employee and probably are intended by employers to serve as a reward to loyal employees who remain with the company until retirement.

Some companies have recently established a more gradual vesting schedule, while still maintaining retirement as the main eligibility criterion. For example, one bank holding corporation gave free lifetime health benefits to retirees for many years, but it recently began basing its contribution to the plan on each retiree's age and length of service at retirement. An employee who retires at age fifty-five with twenty-five years of service will have 42 percent of his retiree health premiums paid by the company. An employee who retires at age sixty-two with twenty-five years of service will receive reimbursement for 67 percent of premiums. An employee who retires at age sixty-five with thirty years of service will receive 100 percent reimbursement. An employee who leaves prior to retirement, however, still does not vest in any level of retiree health benefits. The company freezes its contribution at the retirement date, with the retiree paying for future increases in premiums, essentially making its plan a hybrid defined benefit–defined contribution plan. The plan is defined benefit to the time of retirement and defined contribution thereafter. While maintaining coverage for the same type of care and at the same level of benefits for retirees and active workers, this company also established separate premium levels based on the separate levels of utilization of benefits by the two groups.

According to the BLS survey, employers pay the full cost of retiree health premiums for about 55 percent of retiree plan participants. The remaining participants share costs with their former employers. According to the 1988 Current Population Survey, explained in more detail in chapter 6, at least 4 million of the approximately 10 to 11 million retirees receiving employer-sponsored health benefits did not have to pay any insurance premium for their coverage, as shown in tables 2–1 and 2–2. At least another 1.4 million retirees, paying less than $50 monthly, were

17

TABLE 2–1
CONTRIBUTION BY FORMER EMPLOYER FOR HEALTH INSURANCE OF RETIREES, BY TYPE OF COVERAGE
(millions of retirees)

Firm's Contribution toward Premium	Type of Coverage		
	Total	Self-only	Family
Firm pays all of premium	4.075	1.641	2.434
Firm pays some of premium	3.080	1.070	2.010
Firm pays none of premium	2.105	1.128	.977
Don't know	.383	.179	.204
No response	.512	.210	.302
Total retirees[a]	10.155	4.228	5.927

a. Excludes 28,000 retirees who did not report type of coverage.
SOURCE: Urban Institute tabulations based on August 1988 Current Population Survey, Supplement on Retiree Health Insurance Benefits.

given large subsidies by their former employers. More detailed information about the number of retirees covered by employer-sponsored health plans, according to various surveys, will be given in chapter 6.

Current Options for Tax-favored Prefunding

Although as a matter of prudent management practice or because of pressure from unions, a company might desire to set aside assets for (prefund) its obligation to provide retiree health benefits, very few companies, to date, have done so. Apparently some companies have felt that prefunding would indicate a firmer commitment to the continued provision of benefits than they care to make. Some other companies may feel that investing assets in their own businesses offers a higher rate of return than the after-tax return on any assets available in the market for investment in a retiree benefit trust. And many companies reportedly are dissatisfied with the current options available for tax-favored prefunding and are withholding the start of prefunding as a way of pressuring Congress to offer improved tax incentives similar to the type of incentives offered for pension funding.[8]

A company may currently get tax benefit for prefunding a retiree health benefit plan in essentially two ways.[9] A separate 401(h) account to provide retiree health benefits may be instituted in conjunction with an already established pension fund. Alternatively, an independent 501(c)(9) welfare benefit fund may be set up. Each of these methods, however, is circumscribed so that the tax benefits are limited, complete

TABLE 2-2
CONTRIBUTION BY RETIREE FOR EMPLOYER-PROVIDED HEALTH INSURANCE, BY TYPE
OF COVERAGE
(millions of retirees)

Retiree's Contribution toward Monthly Premium	Type of Coverage		
	Total	Self-only	Family
$0	4.075	1.641	2.434
$1—< $25	.669	.361	.308
$25—< $50	.765	.373	.392
$50—< $100	1.127	.543	.584
$100—< $200	.695	.208	.487
$200+	.306	.041	.265
No response	2.514	1.061	1.453
Total retirees[a]	10.155	4.228	5.927

a. Excludes 28,000 retirees who did not report type of coverage.
SOURCE: Urban Institute tabulations based on August 1988 Current Population Survey, Supplement on Retiree Health Insurance Benefits.

prefunding of the entire obligation to provide benefits is impossible, and in some situations, utilization of a prefunding method is simply not allowed.[10]

401(h) Accounts. Under the 401(h) method of prefunding retiree health plans, the income earned in the separate account is not taxable. Also, employer contributions to the account are deductible under the same rules as apply to contributions to pension funds. Several requirements and restrictions, however, are imposed on the utilization of this method and on the amount of deductible contributions allowed. The first requirement is that the medical benefits, when added to any life insurance provided by the plan, must be "incidental" to benefits provided by the pension plan. Medical benefits are considered incidental if the aggregate of employer contributions to provide medical and life insurance benefits does not exceed 25 percent of the aggregate contributions made to provide medical, life insurance, and pension benefits.

The Internal Revenue Service (IRS) had interpreted this requirement in early 1989 as allowing companies making no contributions to their overfunded defined-benefit pension plans to make contributions to a 401(h) account, up to the rate of 33 percent of the contributions the companies would have made for their pension plans had the plans not been overfunded (the actuarial normal cost). Congress, however, explicitly disallowed this interpretation, in legislation passed later in that year.

19

Because many large companies have overfunded pension plans, this legislation effectively prevented these companies, which generally offer retiree health plans also, from currently setting up 401(h) accounts. Any transfer of excess pension assets to a 401(h) account had also been prevented because the IRS explicitly stated in 1987 that any transfer from the pension fund to a 401(h) account would disqualify the pension plan as a tax-favored entity. Such transfers will be permitted in the future under certain conditions, however, as is explained below.

The second requirement for using the 401(h) funding method is that assets in the 401(h) account must be used only to satisfy the obligation to provide retiree health benefits. Upon the satisfaction of the obligation, however, any remaining assets in the account are to revert to the employer and not to the retirees. The third substantive requirement is that the employer's contributions to the separate account are to be "reasonable and ascertainable." As a related matter, to be deductible the contributions may not exceed the total cost of providing the medical benefits, as determined by any generally accepted actuarial cost method. In addition, the annual contribution may not exceed the greater of the following amounts: the level amount, or level percentage, of compensation that would allocate the unfunded obligation over the remaining future service of each employee; or 10 percent of the unfunded obligation.

In the Omnibus Budget Reconciliation Act of 1990, five annual transfers of excess pension assets to a 401(h) account are permitted. The transfers became permissible beginning in 1991, with a special rule applying in 1990. The transferred assets are not includable in the employer's gross income and are not subject to the excise tax generally leveled on reversions of pension assets. The annual transfers do not cause the disqualification of the pension plan or violate the requirement for subordination of health benefits. In order to qualify for the favorable treatment, however, the annual transfers are restricted to the amount of retiree health benefits that would have been deductible by the employer during the year, determined on a cash basis. In other words, no prefunding is allowed with transferred assets. Furthermore, the amount of allowable transfers are reduced, on a pro rata basis, to the extent that the employer has previously made contributions to a 401(h) or to a voluntary employees' beneficiary association (VEBA) account relating to the benefits to be paid during the year. And the employer is not entitled to a deduction for the provision of retiree health benefits, except to the extent that the total of such payments exceeds the amount transferred to the 401(h) account.

Another requirement that must be satisfied prior to the transfer is that accrued retirement benefits under the pension plan must be nonforfeitable, as if the plan terminated on the date of transfer. In other words, active workers not yet vested in their pension benefits must become immediately vested in their accrued benefits if the transfer option is utilized. A further requirement for the transfer is that the level of retiree benefits provided must at least equal (in per capita terms) the higher of the dollar amounts expended in the two years preceding the year of the transfer.[11]

In November 1990, an employee stock ownership plan (ESOP) established by Procter and Gamble to defease its obligation for retiree health benefits issued securities worth $1 billion. Under the arrangement (dubbed by the legal and benefit consultant communities as an HSOP), a 401(h) account was put alongside a money purchase pension plan, which itself was placed in the ESOP. The ESOP would pay health benefits to retirees through the 401(h) account, thereby ensuring that these distributions are tax-free to recipients (unlike usual ESOP distributions). The assets of the ESOP, Proctor and Gamble stock, were purchased with the proceeds of the security issues, and they will be used to prefund the retiree health obligation. Proctor and Gamble would pay tax-exempt dividends and interest to the ESOP or on its behalf, essentially financing its retiree health liability in a tax-favored manner. Although it initially approved the HSOP, the IRS reportedly is having second thoughts on the entire matter, owing to the concern that many employers will copy the example of Proctor and Gamble and billions in federal tax revenues will be lost.

VEBA Accounts. The second tax-favored method of prefunding retiree health benefits is the establishment of a welfare benefit fund. In general, to receive tax-favored treatment, the fund is required to be a VEBA—that is, a 501(c)(9) account. Although employer contributions to a VEBA, within the very strict limits described below, are deductible, earnings of the VEBA are taxable to the plan sponsor as unrelated business taxable income (UBTI).[12] In addition, to qualify as a VEBA, certain rules must be satisfied prohibiting the provision of benefits on a basis favorable to highly compensated employees. A separate VEBA account must be established for medical benefits that are to be provided to a retiree who is a "key" employee, and contributions into these accounts count against the limitations on employer contributions to the pension fund for that employee.

Contributions to VEBA are deductible as long as they do not exceed the sum of the following: (1) the direct (pay-as-you-go) cost of providing benefits, and (2) the addition to the account's reserve allowed by the tax code, reduced by (3) the after-tax earnings of the account. The reserve allowed in the account may be accumulated no more rapidly than on a level basis over the working lives of employees. In other words, a funding

21

method that front-loads the accumulation of the reserve to the first years of employment would presumably not be acceptable. In addition, deductible contributions are to be made on the assumption that there will be no medical inflation, increase in utilization, or improvement in benefits. These last limitations, of course, severely restrict a company's ability to fully fund its retiree health benefit obligation (at least as calculated on an FASB-consistent basis) in a tax-favored manner through a VEBA account.

Most of the limitations on funding and nondiscrimination rules for VEBA accounts were imposed in the Deficit Reduction Act of 1984 because of Congress's concern that VEBAs were being used as tax shelters by small corporations. Under the Tax Reform Act of 1986, however, these limits do not apply to a VEBA account established under a collective bargaining agreement.

3

Statutory Requirements

The statutory requirements for retiree health benefit plans are explained in this chapter. Although an employer is not required by law to provide health benefits for its retired employees, if the employer chooses to do so it must comply with the rules and laws that generally govern employer-provided welfare benefits. The first section of this chapter will describe the enacted laws that govern welfare (including retiree health) benefits, particularly the reporting and disclosure requirements. The second section will examine the special law that applies to the provision of retiree benefits once an employer has entered bankruptcy proceedings.

Although the reporting requirements were enacted to help protect workers and retirees by clarifying their rights to promised benefits, the chaotic state of affairs in plan documentation has, in fact, failed to provide much clarification or protection, as will be noted in the next chapter and at the end of chapter 5. Similarly, although the special bankruptcy law relating to retiree health benefits was intended to improve the security of retiree benefits, the results of cases brought under the law have been disappointing to retirees.

ERISA Requirements

The Employee Retirement Income Security Act of 1974 (ERISA) requires employers whose activities affect commerce and who provide welfare benefits to their employees to comply with three types of requirements to protect participants' interests. These three types include: (1) reporting and disclosure standards, (2) fiduciary responsibility, and (3) continuation of certain benefits—that is, COBRA coverage. Sponsors of welfare benefit plans, however, are excluded from the complex funding, vesting, and participation requirements imposed by ERISA on sponsors of pension plans.

Definition of an ERISA Welfare Benefit Plan. The definition of a welfare benefit plan is any "plan, fund, or program . . . established or maintained

23

by an employer or by an employee organization, or by both, to the extent that such plan, fund, or program was established or is maintained for the purpose of providing for its participants or their beneficiaries, through the purchase of insurance or otherwise, . . . medical, surgical, or hospital care or benefits, or benefits in the event of sickness, accident, disability, death, or unemployment. . . ."[1] Retiree health benefits are treated like any other type of employer-provided welfare benefits. If the employer establishes or maintains a program of health benefits for its retired employees, that program is a welfare benefit plan for purposes of ERISA and, as such, is subject to ERISA requirements. Certain plans are exempted from ERISA requirements. These include plans maintained by churches or by local, state, and federal governmental entities.

Reporting and Disclosure Requirements. An employer who sponsors a plan that is subject to ERISA must provide to each participant and beneficiary under the plan a summary plan description, written in a manner calculated to be understood by the average plan participant and sufficiently accurate and comprehensive to reasonably let such participants and beneficiaries know their rights and obligations under the plan. The summary plan description should include the following information:

- the name and type of administration of the plan
- the name and address of the administrator
- the name and address of the person designated as agent for the service of legal process, if such person is not the administrator
- names and addresses of the trustees, if any
- a description of the benefits provided
- a description of the relevant provisions of any applicable collective bargaining agreement
- the plan's requirements respecting eligibility for participation and benefits
- circumstances that may result in disqualification, ineligibility, or denial or loss of benefits
- the source of financing of the plan and the identity of any organization through which benefits are provided
- the procedures to be followed in presenting claims for benefits under the plan and the remedies available under the plan for the redress of claims that are denied in whole or in part

In addition, the employer must provide each participant with a summary of any material modification in the terms of the plan or any change in the information set forth in the summary plan description.

The employer has a duty of reporting to the Department of Labor (DOL) and the IRS in addition to his duty of providing the participants with information. The employer must file a copy of each summary plan description and each summary of material modifications with the DOL. The employer must also complete and file a Form 5500-series annual report with the IRS, which is also reviewed by the DOL. The annual report contains the following information:

- financial statements regarding the plan's funding, if any, including a statement of assets and liabilities, a statement of changes in fund balance, and a statement of changes in financial position
- a schedule of transactions involving parties in interest
- the number of employees (active and retired) covered by the plan
- the name and address of each fiduciary
- the name of each person who received compensation from the plan for services rendered to the plan or its participants
- an explanation of the reason for any change in appointment of trustee, accountant, insurance carrier, enrolled actuary, administrator, investment manager, or custodian
- the premium rate or subscription charges paid to any insurance carrier, plus certain information about the amount of premiums received, the number of persons covered by each class of benefits, and the number of claims paid

Welfare benefit plans that have fewer than 100 participants on the first day of the plan year are exempt from the reporting requirements if the benefits are provided either through an insurance company or from the general assets of the employer. (Thus, a small plan where benefits were paid out of a trust or other fund established by the employer would not be exempt under this provision.)

Fiduciary Responsibility. ERISA also imposes fiduciary responsibility on employers. Because of such responsibility, an employee benefit plan must be established and maintained pursuant to a written instrument—that is, an official plan document—that shall provide for one or more named fiduciaries who jointly or severally have authority to control and manage the operation and administration of the plan.[2] Each employee benefit plan must provide a procedure for amending and terminating the plan, and it must specify the basis on which payments are to be made to and from the plan.[3]

If a plan has assets (other than a plan that consists of individual retirement accounts, or to the extent that a plan's assets consist of insurance contracts or policies), such assets must be held in trust by one or more trustees. These trustees either must be named in the trust document or the plan document, or they must be appointed by a named fiduciary.[4] The assets of a plan must be held for the exclusive purposes of providing benefits to plan participants and defraying reasonable expenses of plan administration.[5] Plan fiduciaries are subject to civil and criminal liability for failure to comply with the various requirements of ERISA.

Continuation (COBRA) Coverage. The third requirement that ERISA imposes on employers who have twenty or more employees and who sponsor group health plans is to provide continuation-coverage under health plans to certain qualified beneficiaries, including employees who terminate employment and their dependents, who would otherwise no longer be eligible for benefits. This duty was added by the Consolidated Omnibus Budget Reconciliation Act of 1985, and it is generally referred to as COBRA coverage. The statutory language also appears in §4980B of the Internal Revenue Code, which imposes a tax on employers who fail to comply with the COBRA coverage notification and provision rules.

Continuation coverage must be made available to each covered employee and to any other qualified beneficiary who has been entitled to benefits under the employer's plan by virtue of the employment of the covered employee. Qualified beneficiaries include the covered employee and the spouse and dependent children of the employee.

Continuation coverage consists of the right of the qualified beneficiary to elect to maintain coverage under the employer's health plan for a period of time, at the beneficiary's expense. The employer is required to notify each participant of his future right to COBRA coverage upon the participant's entry into the plan.

The right to elect continuation coverage itself is triggered by a qualifying event. Qualifying events for an employee include: the voluntary or involuntary termination of employment for any reason (including early retirement) other than gross misconduct; a reduction in employment hours, which would result in loss of coverage; and a bankruptcy proceeding under Chapter 11, with respect to an employer from whose employment a covered employee retired. Retirement at the age of Medicare eligibility is not a qualifying event for the employee, except in the case of bankruptcy. Qualifying events for a covered employee's beneficiaries include:

- the death of a covered employee
- the termination or reduction in hours of a covered employee
- the divorce or legal separation of the qualified beneficiary from the covered employee
- the covered employee's becoming entitled to Medicare benefits

- the cessation of dependent status for a child of a covered employee
- a bankruptcy proceeding under Chapter 11, with respect to an employer from whose employment a covered employee retired

If the qualified beneficiary elects to receive COBRA coverage, he is required to pay the premium for his coverage to the employer. The employer may charge up to 102 percent of the applicable premium that is charged for the same type of coverage for similarly situated active employees. The employer may charge up to 150 percent of the applicable premium if the period of COBRA coverage is extended beyond eighteen months for a disabled qualified beneficiary.

The period of COBRA coverage begins on the date of the qualifying event and ends not earlier than the earliest to occur of the following:

- generally thirty-six months, except where the qualifying event is a termination or reduction in the employee's hours or the bankruptcy of the employer
- in the case of a termination or reduction in hours, eighteen months, unless another qualifying event occurs that extends the coverage period to a maximum of thirty-six months
- in the case of bankruptcy of the employer, COBRA coverage continues until the date of death of the retiree, or thirty-six months after the death of the retiree in the case of the surviving spouse or dependent child of the retiree
- the termination of the plan sponsored by the employer
- the failure of the qualified beneficiary to pay the premium for COBRA coverage
- the eligibility of the qualified beneficiary for coverage under another health plan, except where a preexisting condition is not covered by the new plan
- the eligibility of the qualified beneficiary for coverage under Medicare—except that this does not apply to retirees, spouses, or surviving spouses of retirees, or dependent children of retirees if bankruptcy of the employer was the qualifying event

A conversion option to an individual policy is required to be provided during the 180-day period ending on the expiration date of COBRA coverage, if a conversion option is otherwise generally available under the plan.

Special COBRA Rules in Bankruptcy. If retiree coverage would be substantially eliminated within one year of the date of the commencement of the bankruptcy proceeding, then the term "qualified beneficiary"

27

includes retirees who retire on or before the date of substantial loss of coverage, plus the spouse, surviving spouse, or dependent child of the retiree. The retiree's or other beneficiary's subsequent eligibility for Medicare does not terminate continuation-coverage in this instance; rather, the coverage appears to be guaranteed for life or until the plan is terminated.

Retiree Health Benefits in Bankruptcy

The most significant instance, to date, of a bankrupt company's unilaterally canceling health benefits to retirees occurred when LTV Corp. filed for bankruptcy and reorganization under Chapter 11 of the Bankruptcy Code on July 17, 1986. LTV asserted that it was prohibited from continuing to pay premiums for health and life insurance policies covering some 78,000 union and nonunion retirees because such payments were made from general revenues and represented prepetition obligations. A prepetition obligation is a liability of the firm incurred prior to the petition for protection from creditors under Chapter 11. The payment of any prepetition obligation is frozen so as not to infringe on the rights of other creditors, and because its immediate payment is not considered necessary to the continued operation of the company while the bankruptcy proceedings continue. Immediately upon LTV's termination of retiree health coverage the Steelworkers Union struck, and a bill was passed by the Senate on July 30, 1986, ordering LTV to reinstate the benefits. In response to these pressures, LTV requested and received a bankruptcy court order allowing it to resume making premium payments.

The Retiree Benefits Bankruptcy Protection Act of 1988. Congress passed a series of stopgap measures requiring LTV to continue paying retiree health benefits, while it deliberated on a more permanent solution to the problem. On June 16, 1988, the Retiree Benefits Bankruptcy Protection Act of 1988 was enacted, amending the Bankruptcy Code. In essence, the act accomplished two things. It moved the liability for retiree health benefits up the priority ladder slightly, by requiring the continued timely payment of benefits, perhaps at a modified level. And the act placed retiree health benefits among the first issues that must be dealt with by the bankruptcy court. In many cases, retirees were often last in the creditor queue for the determination of the amount allotted to the continued payment of benefits. The act did not, however, resolve the legal question of the vesting rights of retirees to benefits; if the company denied it had an obligation to retirees, that issue would still have to be decided by the bankruptcy court under legal doctrines to be explained in the next chapter. The act also did not ensure that assets would necessarily be available for the payment of benefits, even if it were determined that the bankrupt company indeed had an obligation to pay lifetime benefits.[6]

The Retiree Benefits Act requires that health benefits provided to retirees pursuant to a welfare benefit plan that was in effect at the time of the bankruptcy filing should be continued, until a modification is agreed to by the retirees and the company or is ordered by the court. Contributions by the bankrupt company to a multiemployer welfare plan are considered retiree benefits for the purposes of the act. The act makes retiree benefits equivalent to administrative expenses, which have a priority status in bankruptcy. When the bankrupt company attempts to modify the retiree benefits, representatives of the retiree group are to be appointed to negotiate the modification. The union may represent the class of union retirees, if the court deems it appropriate. If good faith bargaining between the company and the retirees' representatives produces no agreement, the bankruptcy court may allow a modification in retiree benefit payments, provided the modification is necessary to permit the reorganization of the bankrupt company and to ensure fair treatment of all creditors. According to the act, the modification need not be a one-time occurrence; subsequent modifications (favorable or unfavorable to retirees) may be warranted by the (improving or deteriorating) financial condition of the bankrupt company. The act provides that retiree benefits paid between the time of the filing for bankruptcy and the time a reorganization plan is confirmed should not be deducted from claims for benefits that remain unpaid.

Finally, the act provides that a reorganization plan can not be approved unless retiree benefits continue to be paid, at least at the modified level, for "the duration of the period the debtor [employer] has obligated itself to provide such benefits." This last phrase indicates the act's recognition that an employer has a right, according to the terms of the plan document and to relevant law outside of the bankruptcy code, to modify or terminate retiree benefits. Indeed, the committee report accompanying the act notes that "the broader issues associated with retiree benefits remain to be addressed by other committees of appropriate jurisdiction."[7]

Some Recent Court Cases. At least two very recent court cases have been decided in which the Retiree Benefits Bankruptcy Protection Act has been invoked. In both cases, somewhat ironically, retirees received little relief owing to the act. In *GF Corporation*, the Bankruptcy Court for the Northern District of Ohio sustained a motion filed by the Steelworkers Union seeking the continued payment of retiree health benefits by a bankrupt manufacturer of office furniture.[8] The court agreed that the application of the Retiree Benefits Act was clearly appropriate in this case. The court claimed, however, that it was faced with desultory remedial choices. Because the company had no disposable assets from which to make retiree health payments, to force the company to comply with the act, the court could either compel the conversion of the bankruptcy into a Chapter 7 liquidation or appoint a trustee.

Either choice, however, would actually worsen the position of retirees. The protection given by the Retiree Benefits Act would no longer be available outside of Chapter 11 proceedings, and the appointment of a trustee unfamiliar with the company's business would make reorganization more difficult and costly and hence would lower the value of assets available for the eventual payment of retiree benefits and other obligations. The court further concluded that it could not require the company to invade the collateral of the lenders nor condition any postpetition refinancing arrangements on the payment of retiree benefits, because such moves would eliminate property rights and would likely frustrate the goal of public policy to rehabilitate bankrupt companies.

The court further noted that

> if retiree benefits are to be paid immediately, these payments are not in the nature of administrative expenses [which are rarely paid immediately], as their immediate payment would, in effect, grant to them a superpriority. That is, the immediate payment in full of benefits during the pendency of a Chapter 11 case would skim these claims off the top of the fund which is available to pay all such claims, perhaps requiring the reduction of others. On the other hand, if retiree benefits are to be paid according to the procedure by which all other administrative claims are paid, they will not, in a case such as the present one, be paid in a timely fashion as Congress envisioned. Hence, from a practical standpoint, it is impossible to give full effect to both subsections [of the Act], except where it is obvious that the debtor-in-possession [the bankrupt company] has adequate funds to satisfy the costs of bankruptcy administration.

The court lamented Congress's inattention to situations of bankruptcy in which the company, unlike LTV, was contemplating the formulation of a liquidating Chapter 11 plan. The court finally decided, when faced with the dilemma of reconciling the competing mandates of the Retiree Benefits Act and the underlying policy goals of Chapter 11 of the Bankruptcy Code, to order the company to make payment of retiree health benefits as soon as unencumbered assets were available. Somewhat ironically, therefore, retirees can not expect the timely payment of benefits owing to the Retiree Benefits Act, and the reorganization of the company is made somewhat more difficult.[9]

In *Chateaugay Corp.*, the Southern District Court of New York upheld the judgment of the bankruptcy court that Chateaugay, a subsidiary of LTV, was not required to make continued payments for retiree health benefits because, according to the terms of the collective bargaining agreement, there was no obligation for it to do so beyond the expiration of the wage agreement.[10] The court, however, did require the multi-employer benefit plan, in which Chateaugay participated, to make the payments to the retirees. The court imposed this requirement on the plan despite the absence of future contributions by LTV to the plan and despite a clause in the plan trust stipulating that it would pay health benefits of only those retirees who would not otherwise receive benefits, because their last signatory employers were "no longer in business." Although LTV is clearly still in business, the court determined nevertheless that it was not legally obligated to provide benefits because it was no longer a signatory to the wage agreement.

The outcome of the Chateaugay case is ironic in several ways. LTV escaped its obligation to pay at least some retiree benefits, despite the fact that the Retiree Benefits Act was passed in direct response to its attempt to stop payment of benefits. LTV escaped its obligation to pay benefits, despite its financial ability to do so, because the court determined that its obligation had ceased after the expiration of the wage agreement. Yet the court required the multiemployer plan to make payments to retirees because "the terms of the wage agreement make it clear that the retiree benefits are intended to be lifetime benefits." In its decision the court also ignored the public policy comment of the committee report accompanying the Retiree Benefits Act, which said that multiemployer plans "are generally financed solely by employer contributions, and a loss of such contributions from any one employer detracts from a plan's ability to pay benefits to the participants and beneficiaries of the plan as a whole."[11]

The ironic and ultimately disappointing results of court cases brought under the Retiree Benefits Act will no doubt cause Congress to examine more efficacious methods of satisfying retiree expectations without placing undue burdens on employers, as will be discussed further in chapter 10. Pressure on Congress to act is further augmented by the new accounting standards for retiree health benefit plans, as is discussed in chapters 5 and 9.

31

4

The Right to Terminate or Amend
—Recent Court Cases

Because no federal statute defines the precise nature of the obligation of an employer to its retirees and active workers regarding retiree health benefit plans, numerous suits and pleas for arbitration have been filed in the past decade concerning attempts by companies to terminate or amend such plans. Many of the cases involved the termination of plans by companies in reorganization, and attempts by retirees to seek reinstatement of benefits from successor companies. Some other cases, however, involved amendment or termination of plans by profitable companies. In any event, the principles invoked by the courts in all of the cases are relevant to the legal determination of whether an employer currently has the right to terminate or amend a retiree health benefit plan.

Three different views have been expressed by the federal courts.[1] One view, now dormant, maintains that retiree insurance benefits are by their nature intended to vest upon the attainment of retirement status. Hence, regardless of the terms of any plan document, retiree health benefits, as a matter of federal common law, can not be amended or terminated without at least a showing of good cause. At the other extreme, some circuits opine that the right of employers to terminate or amend retiree health benefit plans depends entirely on the language contained in plan documents. No special consideration is to be given to retirees beyond what is contained in the terms of the official plan documents.

The third view lies somewhere between the other two. It holds that primary consideration should be given to the language of the plan documents. When the language of the documents is ambiguous, however, or the documents do not exist (as apparently occurs in many instances), reference should be made to the intent of the parties as expressed in extrinsic evidence—such as statements made at exit interviews—and to the reasonable inference that retirement benefits are intended to last for the length of retirees' lives, in the form extant at the time of the former employees' retirement. This middle-of-the-road view is currently held in some circuits. In essence, it is the result of the tension between the legalistic view—that ERISA has left the subject of retiree health benefits solely to the domain of written contracts—and the common law view—that retiree benefits, by their nature, are intended to last throughout the remaining years of the retiree's life, despite the protestations of the fine print of documents.

In this chapter, some of the more important and recent court cases will be reviewed.[2] In particular, the focus will be on the decisions and dictums in these cases illustrating the three views mentioned above. The legal issues involved in a current suit brought by retirees against General Motors will also be explained. It should be noted that all of the cases reviewed concern the right of companies to change retirement benefits given to current retirees. Apparently no cases have been brought by active workers concerning unilateral changes in their future retirement benefits, perhaps owing to the advice of legal counsel that, under legal views currently being held in the courts, such cases would probably not be successful.[3]

The View of Reasonable Inference

UAW v. Yard-Man, Inc. One of the seminal cases in the area of retiree health benefits is *UAW v. Yard-Man, Inc.*[4] In this case, decided in 1983, the U.S. Court of Appeals for the Sixth Circuit upheld the decision of the lower court that Yard-Man should continue to provide retiree insurance benefits, as implicitly promised in a collective bargaining agreement. Yard-Man closed one of its plants in 1975. In 1977, upon the expiration of the collective bargaining agreement governing the payment of benefits, Yard-Man informed the retirees from the closed plant that their insurance benefits would be terminated. The United Automobile Workers (UAW) sought arbitration; when Yard-Man refused to arbitrate, the union sued for reinstatement of the benefits and for damages.

The court handed down its decision in favor of the retirees, based on the fact that although the plan documents clearly defined the contingencies (including layoffs and plant closings) of insurance coverage for active employees, no such explicit contingencies were delineated for retirees. Furthermore, the court pointed out that a provision existed in the plan document that promised early retirees (including some as young as fifty-five) that the company would pay insurance premiums when they reached the age of Medicare eligibility. In the opinion of the court, this provision clearly indicated that the company intended to promise retirement benefits beyond the three-year term of the collective bargaining agreement. Finally, the court asserted that within the context of the collective bargaining agreement, it was reasonable to infer that retirement benefits were intended to continue as long as former employees remained retired.

The Yard-Man case is extensively quoted in many later cases that were also brought in the sixth circuit (composed of the states of Ohio, Michigan, Kentucky, and Tennessee), an area of the country where many manufacturing plants were closed in the late 1970s and early 1980s. Because the appeals court set forth fairly specific guidelines on how to decide similar cases, lower courts in the sixth circuit are bound to follow the lead of the appeals court. In addition, although a decision of the U.S. Court of Appeals for the Sixth Circuit is not binding as law on federal courts in other circuits, some federal courts in other districts chose to follow the guidelines as well because the sixth circuit was the first to set out guidelines respecting retiree health benefits.

The guidelines given by the sixth circuit court to courts deciding cases involving retiree insurance benefits are as follows:

1. Look to intent of parties explicitly stated. "The court should first look to the explicit language of the collective bargaining agreement for clear manifestations of intent."[5]

2. Consider the context of the language used. "The intended meaning of even the most explicit language can, of course, only be understood in light of the context which gave rise to its inclusion."[6]

3. Ascertain intent from the plan document as a whole. "The court should also interpret each provision in question as part of the integrated whole. If possible, each provision should be construed consistently with the entire document and the relative positions and purposes of the parties. As in all contracts, the collective bargaining agreement's terms must be construed so as to render none nugatory and avoid illusory promises. Where ambiguities exist, the court may look to other words and phrases in the collective bargaining agreement for guidance. Variations in language used in other durational provisions of the agreement may, for example, provide inferences of intent useful in clarifying a provision whose intended duration is ambiguous."[7]

4. Review consistency with federal labor policy. "Finally, the court should review the interpretation ultimately derived from its examination of the language, context and other indicia of intent for consistency with federal labor policy. This is not to say that the collective bargaining agreement should be construed to affirmatively promote any particular policy but rather that the interpretation rendered not denigrate or contradict basic principles of federal labor law."[8]

The court also gave its general view of the economic transaction underlying most contracts promising retirement benefits:

34

Benefits for retirees are only permissive, not mandatory, subjects of collective bargaining. As such, it is unlikely that such benefits, which are typically understood as a form of delayed compensation or reward for past services, would be left to the contingencies of future negotiations. The employees are presumably aware that the union owes no obligation to bargain for continued benefits for retirees. If they forgo wages now in expectation of retiree benefits, they would want assurance that once they retire they will continue to receive such benefits regardless of the bargain reached in subsequent agreements.[9]

Finally, the court established a limited inference of intent that retirement benefits were "'status' benefits which, as such, carry with them an inference that they continue so long as the prerequisite status is maintained." The court explained, and limited, this inference as follows:

When the parties contract for benefits which accrue upon achievement of retiree status, there is an inference that the parties likely intended those benefits to continue as long as the beneficiary remains a retiree. This is not to say that retiree insurance benefits are necessarily interminable by their nature. Nor does any federal labor policy identified to this Court presumptively favor the finding of interminable rights to retiree insurance benefits when the collective bargaining agreement is silent. Rather, as part of the context from which the collective bargaining agreement arose, the nature of such benefits simply provides another inference of intent.[10]

UAW v. Cadillac Malleable Iron Co. Unlike *Yard-Man*, which established the proposition that there was an *inference* that retirement benefits were status benefits, the District Court for the Western District of Michigan in an earlier case, *UAW v. Cadillac Malleable Iron Co.*, opined that there was a *presumption* that such benefits were to continue for the lives of retirees.[11] The main distinction between a presumption and an inference is this: in a presumption, the burden of proof lies on the employer, to show conclusive proof that his intention was to reserve the right to terminate benefits; in an inference, the burden of proof, although lightened somewhat, remains on the retirees, to show that benefits were intended to vest upon retirement.

In *UAW v. Cadillac Malleable Iron Co.*, the district court held that the company was obligated to continue providing insurance benefits to retirees despite the expiration of the collective bargaining agreement and a subsequent strike. The court based its decision on several findings of fact and law. The court said that the plan documents did not expressly indicate the duration of benefits for retirees, while other parts of the documents indicated durational features for active employees. In exit interviews, retirees were told by a company spokeswoman that retiree benefits were ensured for life and that no distinction was made between pension and other insurance benefits. Letters written to retirees informing them of improvements in benefits did not mention that continued benefits were subject to the possibility of future cancellation. Moreover, during prior strikes, the company had always continued paying insurance premiums for retirees. Finally, the court declared that as a matter of law (citations omitted):

> In light of the inherent duration of the retirement status beyond any particular contract, the nature of retirement benefits as deferred compensation for service, and the federal policy in favor of the protection of legitimate employee expectations, it is reasonable to adopt a rule of construction which creates a presumption in favor of vested retirement benefits in the absence of clear evidence indicating a contrary intention. The cases relied on by the company for a contrary result have either involved express limiting language or have involved benefits of active workers.[12]

The employer, Cadillac Malleable Iron, appealed the lower court's ruling, which the U.S. Court of Appeals for the Sixth Circuit then affirmed, albeit with reservation.[13] The court disagreed with the lower court's finding of law that there was a presumption that retirement benefits were status benefits. In the particular case at hand, however, the court agreed that the plan documents were ambiguous, and therefore that extrinsic evidence such as statements at exit interviews was relevant in discovering intent.

The View of Federal Common Law

After the decision of the court of appeals in *Cadillac*, which occurred after *Yard-Man*, two district courts in the sixth circuit tried to extend protection of retiree insurance benefits as a matter of federal common law, even when the plan documents indicated unambiguously that the company retained the unilateral right to amend or terminate retiree benefits.

Musto v. American General Corp. In 1985, in *Musto v. American General Corp.*, the U.S. District Court for the Middle District of Tennessee decided that the company could not reduce the level of retiree health benefits, despite the express reservation of that right to the company in plan documents.[14] In its findings, the court emphasized the dissonance between the predecessor company's aggressive promotion in brochures and meetings with employees of its retirement package, including health benefits at no cost, and the existence of termination and modification clauses in master plan documents, individual certificates of insurance, and summary plan descriptions. The court held that "it would be contrary to the spirit of ERISA to hold that rights promised [in] welfare benefit plans are mere gratuities[,] terminable at the will of the employer."

Unlike active workers, retirees have no economic leverage with which to bargain with their former employer. Hence the court judged that, without a showing of good cause, it was fundamentally unfair to allow the company unilaterally to reduce retiree health benefits. The court claimed its decision was consistent with *Yard-Man*, because the conflicting provisions in plan documents (that is, the promise of retiree health benefits at no cost and the right to terminate or amend) should not be construed so as to render promises "illusory."

Hansen v. White Farm Equipment Co. In 1984, in *Hansen v. White Farm Equipment Co.*, the district court reversed the ruling of the bankruptcy court and found that the retirees were entitled to the continued provision of insurance benefits by the successor companies of White Farm Equipment.[15] The court held that although ERISA did exempt welfare benefit plans from stringent participation, vesting, and funding standards, it was "unreasonable to infer from this omission an express congressional intent to permit unregulated termination of such plans." In view of the explicit preemption of state common law by ERISA and the clear intention of Congress to prevent the "great personal tragedy" suffered by retirees whose benefits were terminated, the court fashioned a federal common law that granted to retirees a vested contractual right to continued benefits, despite the apparent existence of a termination clause in booklets given to retirees. The court molded its federal common law on the holdings of many state courts in pre-ERISA cases that common law prevented the termination of pension benefits after retirement.

Current Legal Principles in the Sixth Circuit. The U.S. Court of Appeals for the Sixth Circuit reversed or remanded the decisions of these district courts. The court of appeals thereby precluded the possibility that an inference that retirement benefits were status benefits, as allowed in *Yard-Man*, would broaden into a federal common law holding that, despite explicit contractual language to the contrary, retirement insurance benefits were to be considered vested. In reversing *Musto*, the court held quite forcefully that the existence of an explicit termination and modification clause in the master plan document overrode any promises made by the company in oral interviews that retiree health benefits would continue, at no cost, for life.[16]

The court cited the legislative history of ERISA and the conclusions of other courts to support the view that the "clear terms of a written employee benefit plan may not be modified or superseded by oral undertakings on the part of the employer." The court left open the question, however, of how it would decide a case in which no master plan document existed. The ruling of the sixth circuit was appealed by retirees to the Supreme Court, where their petition for review was denied.[17]

In remanding *Hansen,* the court of appeals held that the district court erred in adopting a federal common law regarding the vesting of retiree health benefits.[18] The court of appeals stated that it believed "the legislature, rather than the courts, should determine whether mandatory vesting of retiree welfare benefits is appropriate." The court, however, remanded the case back to the bankruptcy court, because in the absence of a master plan document, the ambiguity of language in the plan booklets did at least create a question as to the intent of the company concerning the duration of retiree health benefits.

Despite attempts to push the legal pendulum toward automatic vesting under federal common law and other, more successful attempts discussed below toward a stricter reading of contract provisions, the principles of *Yard-Man* still stand as the established law, at least in the sixth circuit. In 1988, in *United Paper Workers Local No. 1020 v. Muskegon Paper Box Co.,* the Western District Court of Michigan decided that retirees' life and health insurance benefits were vested.[19] The court found that language in the plan documents supported, or at least did not contradict, an interpretation that retirement benefits were intended to last as long as former employees remained retired, and it strengthened its interpretation by referring to the allowable inference that retirement benefits were status benefits.

Even though the union agreed to forfeit retirement benefits in a plant closing agreement, the retirees were not invited to, and did not vote at the meeting at which the union membership ratified the agreement. The court found specific language in the prior collective bargaining agreement that indicated life insurance benefits would continue as long as the former employees maintained their retirement status. The court also found that while there was a general termination clause in the collective bargaining agreement, the language of the contract did not expressly limit the duration of health benefits or state how benefits could be terminated. The court further relied on the inferences raised in *Yard-Man* that retirement benefits are vested because such benefits are a form of deferred compensation, and that retirement benefits are status benefits that continue as long as the status of retirement is maintained by former employees.[20]

The View of Strict Construction

Some courts outside the sixth circuit have been moving away from the inference that retiree health benefits are status benefits.

District 29, United Mine Workers v. Royal Coal Co. An early instance of this movement occurred in 1985, when the Court of Appeals for the Fourth Circuit in *District 29, United Mine Workers v. Royal Coal Co.* overturned a decision of the lower court and decided that the literal terms of collective bargaining agreements allowed the company to terminate its payments for health benefits to retirees.[21]

Although Royal Coal was a signatory to the National Bituminous Coal Wage Agreements of 1978 and 1981, wherein it agreed to provide health benefits to retirees, it ceased active mining operations during the term of the 1981 agreement and did not become a signatory to the 1984 agreement. When Royal Coal stopped providing health benefits in 1984, the individuals who retired prior to 1981 sued the company and the industry-sponsored multiemployer benefit trust, claiming that either the company or the trust was responsible for the health benefits. The trust declined the assumption of responsibility, on the grounds that Royal Coal had sufficient assets to pay the benefits and did not qualify under the "no longer in business" requirement for the trust to pick up responsibility for the benefits of the company's retirees. Royal Coal claimed that because it did not sign the 1984 agreement, it was no longer responsible for retiree benefits. The court agreed with Royal Coal, emphasizing the language of the 1978 and 1981 agreements: that "the benefits provided pursuant to such plans shall be guaranteed *during the term of this Agreement* by each Employer at levels set forth in such plans" (emphasis added by the court). In later cases, the court decided that the multiemployer trust indeed had responsibility for payment of the retiree benefits.

Royal Coal is notable for several reasons. Even though the court cited *Yard-Man*, a similar case involving the interpretation of language in a collective bargaining agreement, it applied none of the allowable inferences concerning status benefits. Indeed, one gets the distinct impression upon reading *Royal Coal* that the fourth circuit court did not try nearly as hard or as creatively as the sixth circuit court to find an indication of status benefits in its interpretation of the language of the relevant agreements.

It is entirely possible, given the court's later decisions regarding the trust, that the fourth circuit court knew that the retirees would get their benefits anyway, whereas in *Yard-Man* no third party was available to bail the retirees out. Burdening the trust with payment for the benefits, however, has had the ill effect of encouraging other coal companies, such as Pittston Coal, to seek to escape their responsibilities toward their retirees and toward the multiemployer trust. As will be explained in chapters 7 and 10, Pittston's action led to a bitter strike in 1989 and to the formation of the Coal Commission, appointed by Secretary of Labor Elizabeth Dole, to suggest solutions to the financial troubles of the multiemployer trust.[22]

Moore v. Metropolitan Life Insurance Co. Another more recent instance of strict construction of contractual terms occurred in 1988, in *Moore v. Metropolitan Life Insurance Co.*, where the U.S. Court of Appeals for the Second Circuit affirmed the holding of the lower court that the plan document allowed the company to modify retiree health benefits.[23] Despite presentations made by the company to employees that retiree health benefits would be provided for life and at no cost, the main plan document and summary plan descriptions expressly reserved the right of the company to modify or terminate benefits. Although the decision in this case is consistent with the principles enunciated in *Yard-Man*, the court also emphasized that Congress's intent in ERISA in excluding retiree health benefits from vesting status in ERISA was to allow companies the flexibility needed to administer health benefits in the face of "inflation, changes in medical practice and technology, and increases in the costs of treatment independent of inflation."

Other Cases. In 1989, in *Ryan v. Chromalloy American Corp.*, the U.S. Court of Appeals for the Seventh Circuit affirmed the holding of the lower court that read narrowly the relevant plan documents and collective bargaining agreement and allowed the company, Chromalloy, to terminate a retiree health plan.[24] In 1983, Chromalloy sold a division that manufactured machines and conveyers to Allied Products Corp. Chromalloy stopped providing health benefits to retired employees of that division soon afterwards, and Allied did not continue to provide the benefits. The retirees sued Chromalloy, claiming that their retirement benefits vested upon their retirement.

The welfare plan documents, however, to which the collective bargaining agreement referred, reserved the right of the sponsor to terminate or modify the health plan. No distinction between active and retired workers was made in the plan documents. In fact, the trust document stated that if the company were to sell "all or substantially all of the assets" of a division, then the trust would be terminated with respect to the employees of the division, unless "provision is made whereby the trust would be continued by the purchaser." The exact contingency of a sale of a division and a refusal by the purchaser to continue benefits occurred, and the court saw no reason to set aside the apparently clear terms of the plan documents, given ERISA's explicit exemption of employee welfare benefits from accrual, vesting, and funding requirements. While the decision in this case is again strictly consistent with *Yard-Man*, it is significant that the court here read the general termination clause to include retirees and invoked no inference of status benefits. In *United Paper Workers*, the Michigan court did not attach much weight to the general termination clause, and it invoked the *Yard-Man* inference. Furthermore, the court here emphasized the language of the trust document, which is not, strictly speaking, a controlling plan document for ERISA purposes.

In the eighth circuit, in *Anderson v. Alpha Portland Industries, Inc.*, the court expressly declared that it disagreed with the *Yard-Man* inference that retirement insurance benefits were status benefits.[25]

> We disagree with *Yard-Man* to the extent that it recognizes an inference of an intent to vest. Congress explicitly exempted welfare benefits from ERISA's vesting requirements. It, therefore, seems illogical to infer an intent to vest welfare benefits in every situation where an employee begins to receive them on the day he retires. . . . We believe that it is not at all inconsistent with labor policy to require plaintiffs to prove their case without the aid of gratuitous inferences.

Two recent arbitration cases have also upheld the right of employers to modify or deny retiree health benefits in special situations. In *Robertshaw Controls Co. and United Steelworkers of America Local 1163*, the arbitrator denied the union's grievance that the company, based on past practice, had established a binding pattern of paying a portion of the cost of medical insurance coverage for retirees.[26] The arbitrator noted that the past practice was contrary to the express language of the collective bargaining agreement entitling employees to continue medical insurance benefits after retirement only if they paid the full cost of such coverage. Furthermore, the arbitrator found that the company's practice of making partial payments for retirees' health insurance was somewhat inadvertent and, in any case, too short-lived to constitute a precedent. In *Bundy Tubing and UAW Local 1632*, the arbitrator decided that where the group medical insurance of a laid-off employee has lapsed, "so it cannot be continued without reenrolling in the group, he or she is not entitled to retiree medical coverage" under the terms of the collective bargaining agreement, even when the laid-off employee subsequently retires.[27]

41

It is clear, however, that if the plan document or collective bargaining agreement expressly promised that retirement benefits would continue for life, the courts would uphold the terms of the contract, despite the financial difficulties of the employer. In 1989, in *Keefer v. H.K. Porter Co., Inc.*, the U.S. Court of Appeals for the Fourth Circuit affirmed the judgment of the lower court that the retirees' health and life insurance benefits continued beyond the expiration of the collective bargaining agreement and that the company, as an alter ego for its subsidiary, Connors Steel, was responsible for the benefits promised to former employees of the subsidiary.[28] Between 1982 and 1983 Connors closed, sold its steelmaking plants, and advised retirees that benefits would be terminated when the last collective bargaining agreement expired in 1984. Retirees filed several suits against Connors and its parent, Porter.

The court decided that the collective bargaining agreement, interpreted under the federal common law of labor policy, indicated that Connors and the United Steelworkers Union intended that retirement benefits should extend beyond the expiration date of the agreement. In particular, a 1974 agreement distinguished between employees, who were to receive benefits for the duration of the agreement, and retirees, who were to receive benefits until they were eligible for Medicare. The court buttressed this interpretation by noting explicit language in the health benefits section of the agreement that any pensioner "shall not have such coverage terminated or reduced . . . so long as the individual remains retired from the Company . . . , *notwithstanding the expiration of this Agreement*" (emphasis added). The court further supported its interpretation by noting that company representatives had assured retirees that their benefits would continue, even after the plant closings. Finally, the court determined that Porter was an alter ego of Connors, owing, among other reasons, to Porter's close control over Connors's expenditures, its retention of the proceeds of the sale of Connors's assets, and the existence of common officers and directors.

The Case against General Motors

Perhaps because of the unsettled nature of the law and certainly because of the magnitude of the equities involved, cases continue to be brought by retirees against companies reducing retiree health benefits. *Sprague v. General Motors Corp.* is perhaps the largest case brought against a company by retirees seeking damages and the reversal of the company's unilateral actions reducing retiree health benefits.[29] The class action suit on behalf of some 84,000 retirees who were formerly salaried employees of various divisions and subsidiaries of General Motors was brought to a California district court in 1989, then transferred to a Michigan court. According to the retirees, despite repeated promises made in booklets, oral presentations, and exit interviews that basic (and sometimes enhanced) health care benefits would be provided for life at little or no cost to the retiree, General Motors increased required copayments and deductibles in 1988. Those individuals invited in the late 1970s and early 1980s to take early and special retirements, and hence not yet eligible for Medicare, have suffered the largest financial loss from the company's action. They also feel the most aggrieved because of the apparently clear impression they received from documents distributed by benefit officials at exit interviews that their health benefits would continue at no cost upon their retirement. General Motors claims that all relevant documents distributed clearly indicated that the company retained the right to amend or terminate retiree health benefits.[30]

On its face, it would seem that the retirees can not win their case because the decision of the sixth circuit in *Musto* made language in the plan documents decisive in determining the intent of parties. There are, however, three unique aspects to this case. According to the retirees, despite their repeated attempts to obtain one, General Motors has not produced an official master plan document, and therefore they doubt one is in existence. In their complaint, the retirees infer from the absence of a plan document that the entire undertaking by the company to provide retiree health benefits was not really the subject of a written instrument, contrary to the dictate of ERISA. Rather, according to the retirees, the company's welfare benefit plan is represented by the combination of booklets *and* oral presentations, and hence, presumably the court's decision in *Musto* is not applicable. The retirees demand the application of federal common law in this instance.

A second unique aspect claimed here is the great, almost jarring dissonance between the apparent promises of the company in its early retirement campaign in the early 1980s and the company's action in reducing benefits in 1988. Unlike *Musto*, where there was no early retirement campaign and the identity of the employer had changed over time, here the identity of the company, and perhaps even of certain officials, had not changed over the relevant period. GM retirees are quoted as follows: "During the conversation, I posed the question, 'Is there any likelihood that GM would ever cancel or withdraw health care coverages for retirees at some future date?' Mr. Edwards responded, 'No, that would be illegal.'" Another GM retiree said, "These assurances were constantly repeated whenever individuals questioned the fine print in the handbook, and I and others believed that we were entitled to lifetime retiree health benefits at GM's expense." Another said, "I was led to believe that the benefits were rock solid"; another, "It seemed

43

clear . . . that the only reduction that might occur would be if there was some catastrophic failing of General Motors, which everyone agreed was next to impossible. . . . During my thirty years with GM there was never any doubt implied when a presentation was made by the GM personnel department."[31]

Finally—and this is not expressed in the retirees' complaint—between the time the court decided *Musto* and 1990, Congress implicitly expressed its intention that retiree health benefits would, in essence, be vested. As will be explained more fully in chapter 10, in establishing certain provisions of the Medicare Catastrophic Care Act, Congress required companies that provide retiree health benefits to pay to retirees an amount of money equivalent to the amount the companies would have saved in 1989 and 1990 because of the act. By taking steps to prevent a windfall to companies, the maintenance-of-effort provisions demonstrated that Congress believed that retirees have some right to the value of their health benefits. Furthermore, Congress's subsequent repeal of the act primarily owed to complaints from retirees that their employer-provided coverage was being duplicated by the new catastrophic care provisions of Medicare and that maintenance-of-effort payments from their former employers (minus new additions to Medicare premiums) were insufficient recompense. In a somewhat ironic sense, therefore, the repeal also demonstrated Congress's respect for the view that retiree health benefits provided by employers were to be continued beyond the attainment of retirement status.

5

Accounting Standards

In the imaginary world of some economic theories, all information relevant to decision makers is always available in exactly the relevant form and at no cost. Hence these theories have neither paid much attention to the mechanisms whereby information is created nor to the institutions that set the reporting standards for and safeguard the integrity of this information. In the more mundane and imperfect real world, however, information is often sketchy, fragmented, and available only at significant cost. In particular, a great deal of effort is actually devoted to determining what information should be included in financial statements so as to be relevant to investors in and providers of credit to corporations; at least as much effort is spent on the setting of financial accounting standards governing the reporting of that information. In the United States, the organization responsible for determining the information reported in financial statements and setting accounting standards is the Financial Accounting Standards Board (FASB).

In the case of retiree health benefits, it is safe to say that the FASB has done more than just determine the technical aspects of the accounting standards to be used to report relevant information. In pursuit of better accounting information and internal consistency with other accounting standards, the FASB, together with the decisions in various court cases described in the prior chapter, has helped put the issue of retiree health benefits on the corporate and public policy map. Some companies, previously unaware of the extent of their obligation, are reducing benefit levels, appealing for tax relief to prefund their obligations, or negotiating with unions on ways to control health care costs. In response to the reductions in benefit levels, some retirees have filed lawsuits. Other companies, including a major auto manufacturer, have endorsed national health insurance. In response to the stress felt by companies, unions, and retiree groups on this issue, policy responses have been discussed in the Congress.

In this chapter the institution of the FASB is briefly described. The history of financial accounting standards for retiree health benefits is recounted, starting with precursors to the current standard governing disclosure of costs. Then the standard proposed by the FASB in February 1989 and adopted in December 1990 is explained in some detail, and an example illustrating the proposed standard is given. Finally, a field test that implemented the proposed standard for a few companies and the problems encountered in the test are briefly delineated.

The Financial Accounting Standards Board

Since 1973, the FASB has been the designated private-sector organization responsible for establishing the standards of financial accounting and reporting that govern the preparation of financial reports.[1] These standards are officially recognized as authoritative by the Securities and Exchange Commission (SEC) and the American Institute of Certified Public Accountants (AICPA). The SEC has statutory authority to establish financial accounting and reporting standards for publicly held companies under the Securities Exchange Act of 1934. Throughout its history, however, the SEC's policy has been to delegate to the private sector the performance of this function.[2] Prior to 1973, the Accounting Principles Board of the AICPA established accounting standards.

The Financial Accounting Foundation (FAF), a nonprofit organization, is responsible for selecting the members of the FASB and its advisory council, funding their activities, and exercising general oversight. The foundation receives more than half its funds from contributions from industry and the financial community, with the remainder coming from the public accounting profession. The board of trustees of the FAF is made up of nominees from sponsoring organizations, including associations of accountants and financial analysts. The FASB itself is composed of seven full-time members who have knowledge of accounting, finance, and business and who act in the public interest in matters of financial accounting and reporting. The board members have diverse backgrounds, including experience as corporate controllers, auditors, government chief accountants, and professors of accounting. Board members are appointed to five-year terms and are eligible for reappointment to one additional five-year term.

Because actions of the FASB have an impact on many and diverse constituents and because the FASB has quasi-governmental authority, its decision making follows an extensive "due process," modeled upon the Federal Administrative Procedures Act. Issues are suggested to the FASB by accounting organizations, the FASB professional staff, the SEC, or the FASB Emerging Issues Task Force, and they are placed on the formal agenda by vote of the board. For each major project on its agenda, the board appoints an advisory task force, studies existing literature on the subject, and conducts or commissions such additional research as may be necessary. It then publishes a discussion document setting forth the issues and possible solutions as the basis for public comment, conducts a public hearing, and distributes widely an exposure draft of the proposed accounting standard for public comment. After conducting another public hearing and further deliberations and incorporating such suggested changes as it deems appropriate, the board votes on the final standard. All board meetings are open to the public and a public record is maintained.

Until recently, a simple majority of the board was required prior to the inclusion of an issue on the agenda, the issuance of an exposure draft, or the promulgation of a final standard. In response to the perception held by some in industry that too many new and complex standards have been recently implemented or proposed, the FAF changed the voting requirement of the FASB to a five-member majority. In addition an oversight committee of trustees was formed, and in general the actions of the FASB have become subject to greater scrutiny.

Statement of Financial Accounting Standards No. 81

The FASB has been grappling with the issue of retiree health benefits since the late 1970s. The FASB stated that it was aware of the increasing cost of retiree benefits and was concerned about the lack of uniformity in accounting practices and the absence of disclosure concerning these benefits.[3] In July 1979, the FASB issued an exposure draft of a proposed accounting standard for pensions and other postretirement benefits. The standard was intended to be an interim measure, pending completion of a major project on accounting for pension and other retiree benefits. The part of the standard applying to other retiree benefits, including health benefits, would have required disclosure of the nature of the benefits offered, of the accounting policies followed with respect to these benefits, and of the pay-as-you-go costs of these benefits for the period. Statement of Financial Accounting Standards No. 35, "Accounting and Reporting by Defined Benefit Pension Plans," was promulgated in March 1980 and became effective for plan years beginning after December 15, 1980. Implementation of the proposed standard for retiree benefits other than pensions, however, did not take place at that time.[4]

Accrual Accounting for Pensions. The accounting standard for pensions reflected certain basic principles. It was agreed that pensions were a form of deferred compensation and hence that the expense to the company of providing a pension should be accrued over the working lives of plan participants. Furthermore, it was agreed that pensions represented a

47

definite obligation of the plan sponsor, particularly after the passage of the Employee Retirement Income Security Act in 1974, requiring plans to be permanent and continuing arrangements. Hence it was decided that users of financial statements should be made aware of the size of the pension obligation of the plan sponsor to retired and active workers—that is, the accrued pension liability. The definition of accrued liability was refined further in later accounting standards.

The accounting standard on pensions relied on a basic premise of generally accepted accounting principles (GAAP) that accrual accounting provides more useful information than cash-basis accounting. Although information about cash flows is not ignored, GAAP accounting goes beyond cash transactions and attempts to recognize the financial effects on an entity of transactions that have future consequences. In particular, the annual accrued pension expense for accounting purposes need not be the same as the actual cash contribution to the pension fund; the latter is influenced by tax and regulatory considerations that are often independent of the economic reality of the transaction that accrual accounting is trying to measure.

In February 1981 the FASB solicited views as to whether the accounting treatment of retiree health benefits should be similar to the treatment of pensions. Many respondents believed that postretirement benefits other than pensions should indeed be accounted for in the same manner as pensions.[5] That is, many viewed retiree health benefits as a type of deferred compensation and hence as appropriate for the application of accrual accounting. Doubts were expressed, however, about measurement problems and about the costs of the accounting outweighing the benefits. Others contended that retiree health benefits were fundamentally different from pensions. These commentators noted that retiree health benefits are not usually directly related to service, and that the legal status of these benefits as definite obligations was considerably more doubtful than implied for pensions by the legal requirements related to pensions. Some also contended that the cost of retiree health benefits was immaterial, and hence cash basis or pay-as-you-go accounting was sufficient.

In November 1982 and again in April 1983, the FASB reached the tentative conclusion that accrual accounting was appropriate for retiree health benefits. Owing to the controversy engendered by this conclusion and the energy spent in the concurrent debate about further refinements in the methods of accrual accounting for pensions, however, the FASB decided that more time and further research were required before a final standard could be implemented for retiree health benefits. A separate project was established in February 1984 to explore measurement and recognition issues. Sufficient support for some form of disclosure of retiree health benefits, however, had arisen to cause the FASB to issue Statement of Financial Accounting Standards No. 81 in November 1984 as an interim measure.

Pay-as-you-go Accounting for Retiree Health Benefits. The statement addressed only postretirement health care and life insurance benefits provided by individual employers. Health care benefits were to include dental, hearing, and vision benefits. Benefits provided by multi-employer-sponsored plans, however, were excluded from the scope of the standard.[6] It was claimed that it was not usually possible to ascertain whether or by how much the contributions of an employer to a multiemployer welfare benefit plan were being used to pay for health benefits to retirees.[7]

The statement required the disclosure of the following information:

- a description of the benefits provided and the employee groups covered
- a description of the accounting and funding policies followed for these benefits
- the cost of these benefits recognized for the period
- if the cost of any postretirement health care or life insurance benefits could not be separated from the cost of providing such benefits for active workers, the disclosure of the total cost for both active workers and retirees, as well as the number of active workers and retirees covered by the plan; active workers or retirees and members of their families covered by the plan should be counted as one unit.[8]

Implementation. The FASB required implementation of the standard for financial statements issued for periods ending after December 15, 1984. Benefits provided in the United States and foreign countries were included in the standard, but government-required employer contributions to a national health plan were excluded. The provisions of the standard were not to be applied to immaterial items—that is, costs of the plan did not have to be disclosed if, in the opinion of the accountant, they were small relative to other items disclosed in the financial statement. Voluntary disclosure of information concerning the magnitude of future retiree health benefits for active workers and retirees was encouraged.

Although Statement No. 81 was to be implemented by private companies and by state and local governments, most governments have not disclosed costs for their retiree health plans. On November 3, 1989, the Governmental Accounting Standards Board, the rule-making authority on the accounting standards followed by state and local governments, issued a special exposure draft on accounting for retiree health benefits.[9] The proposed standard, in essence, reaffirmed the requirement for disclosures like those required of private corporations under FASB Statement No. 81. The proposed standard would be effective for fiscal years ended after June 15, 1990.

Statement of Financial Accounting Standards No. 106

Accrual Accounting for Retiree Health Benefits. On February 14, 1989, the FASB released an exposure draft of a proposed accounting standard for retiree health benefits, representing the completion of a five-year project on the issue.[10] On December 19, 1990, the FASB promulgated the final version of the standard, Statement of Financial Accounting Standards No. 106.

In the exposure draft, the FASB reaffirmed quite emphatically that retiree health benefits were not gratuities but a form of deferred compensation in kind. Hence it was determined that accrual accounting was appropriate and that terminal accrual (accrual at retirement) and cash basis accounting were inappropriate and even misleading.[11] Although the FASB recognized that case law is ambiguous about the legal rights of retired and active workers to welfare benefits, as also noted in chapter 4, nevertheless "the existence of a legally enforceable claim is not a prerequisite for an obligation to qualify as a liability if for other reasons the entity has the duty or responsibility to pay cash, to transfer other assets, or to provide services to another entity." The liability could be effectively binding on the employer because of "past practices, social or moral sanctions, or customs," or because its refusal to pay benefits could risk "substantial employee-relations problems" that would effectively reduce the value of the employer's assets.[12]

The FASB concluded in the exposure draft that retiree health benefits must meet the necessary criteria for recognition in financial statements. As is discussed above, the obligation to provide benefits meets the definition of a liability. Furthermore, the FASB determined that the obligation is measurable with sufficient reliability at justifiable cost and is relevant to the users of financial statements. Because of its relevance to all users of financial statements and not just sophisticated users, the FASB required recognition of the expense for retiree health benefits in the body of the financial statements as well as disclosure in footnotes.[13]

The new standard covers all benefits, other than cash and life insurance benefits paid by pension plans, provided to employees, beneficiaries, and covered dependents during or after the retirement period. Benefits provided after employment but before retirement, such as temporary cash payments during a layoff, are not included in the scope of the standard. Benefits encompassed by the standard include all types of health care, life insurance, and other welfare benefits, such as legal services and housing subsidies.[14] Despite the inclusion of other types of benefits in the standard, it will be assumed for expositional purposes that the standard refers to retiree health benefits exclusively.[15] Also for expositional purposes, the proposed standard as it was first presented in the exposure draft will be explained. The end of this section will mention the changes made to the proposed standard by the FASB in the almost two years since the release of the exposure draft through the adoption of the final standard.

Retiree health benefits are considered a deferred compensation plan for purposes of the standard if there is an arrangement whereby an employer provides its employees with health benefits during retirement "in exchange for their services over a specified period of time, upon attaining a specified age, or both." The plan may be written or may be operated pursuant to informal guidelines. Absent evidence to the contrary, the presumption is that an employer who has provided retiree health benefits in the past and is currently promising them to future retirees will continue to provide the benefits in the future.[16]

For the most part, the method of accounting for retiree health benefits proposed in the exposure draft parallels the current method of accounting for pensions, as promulgated in Statement of Financial Accounting Standards No. 87, "Employers' Accounting for Pensions."[17] In particular, both standards use a benefits and years-of-service approach that attributes the expected benefit obligation to each year of service in the attribution period. The methods differ slightly, however, in the length of the attribution period. Retiree health benefits are assumed to be fully accrued by the date the employee is eligible to receive benefits rather than at the expected retirement date. For example, if active workers are eligible for retiree health benefits after ten years of service and attainment of the early retirement age of fifty-five, the exposure draft would require complete accrual of benefits by age fifty-five for those workers with ten or more years of service, even though they are expected to continue working until, for example, age sixty-three. In contrast, for pensions the attribution period in that accounting standard is based explicitly on the benefit formula contained in the plan contract, which generally allows continued accrual of benefits until the expected age of retirement.

The FASB made the distinction between retiree health and pension plans because in practice few retiree health plans specify a benefit formula. Rather, the exclusive requirements for eligibility to full (but not more than full) retiree health benefits are generally a minimum length of service or attainment of a specific age. In contrast, pension benefits generally increase according to formula with each year of service, including years of service beyond the early retirement age. As a result

51

FIGURE 5–1
LIABILITY CONCEPTS FOR THE ACCOUNTING STANDARD

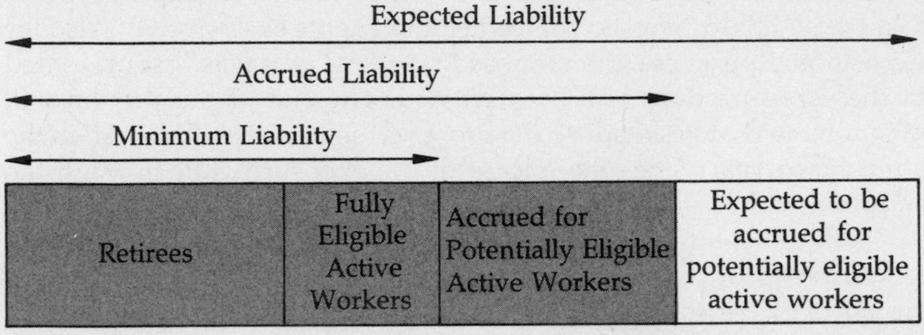

Expected Liability
◄──►

Accrued Liability
◄──────────────────────────────►

Minimum Liability
◄──────────────►

Retirees	Fully Eligible Active Workers	Accrued for Potentially Eligible Active Workers	Expected to be accrued for potentially eligible active workers

SOURCE: Author.

of the proposed standard's definition of the attribution period, the employer's obligation to provide retiree health benefits is measured for three subgroups of plan participants—namely, retirees, active workers fully eligible for benefits, and (generally younger) active workers potentially eligible for benefits.

Liability Concepts and Measurement. Three concepts of liability are relevant to the proposed accounting standard. First, the expected postretirement benefit obligation, or expected liability, is the actuarial present value of all benefits expected to be paid to active and retired workers according to the terms of the retiree health benefit plan. Second, the accumulated postretirement benefit obligation, or accrued liability, is the actuarial present value of benefits attributed to employee service rendered up to a specified date. Prior to an employee's full eligibility date, the accrued liability for an employee is the pro rata portion of the expected liability attributed to that employee's service rendered to that date. On and after the full eligibility date, the accrued and expected obligations for a plan participant are the same. Third, the minimum liability is the accrued liability for retirees and fully eligible active workers.[18] These liability concepts are shown in figure 5–1.

The liabilities are measured using explicit "actuarial assumptions and present value techniques" to calculate the actuarial present value of expected future benefits. The principal actuarial assumptions include the discount rate and the amount and timing of future benefit payments, which in turn depend on per capita claims cost by age, health care cost trend rates, and Medicare reimbursement rates. The FASB recommends that the discount rate chosen be equal to the interest rate implicit in the amount at which the postretirement benefit obligation could be settled by purchasing a contract from an insurance company.

In recognition, however, that such contracts are not yet readily available and hence may not be competitively priced, the FASB alternatively allows the discount rate to reflect rates of return on "high quality fixed-income investments currently available and expected to be available during the period that benefits will be paid."[19] The assumption about the trend rate of health care cost should represent the "expected annual change in the incurred claims cost owing to factors other than changes in the demographics of plan participants." Such factors include health care inflation, changes in health care utilization, and technological advances. The assumed rate of Medicare reimbursement should be consistent with current law; enacted changes in the law may be considered, but future changes in the law may not be anticipated.

In addition to assumptions specific to retiree health accounting, actuarial assumptions must be made about variables similar or identical to those used in pension accounting. These assumptions include employee turnover, retirement age, mortality, and the existence of covered dependents. If the retiree health plan is funded, pension-like assumptions must also be made about the expected long-term rate of return on plan assets. The assumed rate should reflect the average rate of earnings expected on the existing assets that qualify as plan assets. Plan assets need to be segregated from the general assets of the company, restricted as to use, and maintained exclusively for benefits payable or expected to be paid under the plan. The expected rate of return is used with the market-related value of plan assets to compute the expected return on plan assets. Naturally, if the plan is not funded, no such assumptions about asset returns need be made.

Accrued Expense. The accrued expense of the plan, denoted by exposure draft as the net periodic postretirement benefit cost, is the notional change in the unfunded accrued liability, ignoring any employer contributions to the plan, plan settlements, and direct payments to retirees. The following components are included in the accrued expense:

• the service cost, which is the actuarial present value of the expected liability attributed to employee service during the period
• the interest cost, which is the increase in the accrued liability owing to the passage of time, and equals the accrued liability multiplied by the discount rate
• the actual return on plan assets, if any, which is subtracted from the other components of expense because it represents a reduction in expense of the plan to its sponsor
• the amortization, which is the straight-line amortization of the unfunded accrued liability (transition obligation) in existence at the time

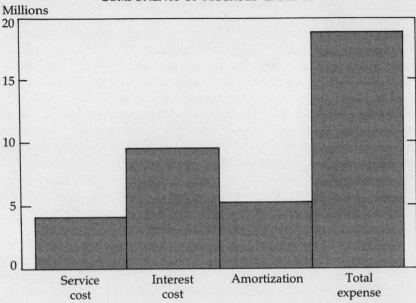

FIGURE 5–2
COMPONENTS OF ACCRUED EXPENSE

SOURCE: Author.

the proposed accounting standard is first applied (the transition date). Amortization occurs over the average remaining service period of active workers or, at the discretion of the plan sponsor, over fifteen years if greater than that period. Recognition of the transition obligation, however, should be no less rapid than recognition would have been on a pay-as-you-go basis for retirees and fully eligible active workers (the pay-as-you-go constraint). The basic expense concepts are illustrated in figure 5–2 for a hypothetical plan.

Although the accrued expense generally equals the notional and immediate change in the accrued liability over the period, as is explained above, change in the liability arising from gains and losses and the effects of a plan initiation or amendment are generally recognized on a delayed basis. Gains and losses are changes in the accrued liability or plan assets "resulting from experience different from that assumed or from changes in assumptions." At a minimum, amortization of an unrecognized net gain or loss should be included as a component of expense if "that unrecognized gain or loss exceeds 10 percent of the greater of the accrued liability or the market-related value of plan assets." If amortization is required, the minimum inclusion in expense is that excess divided by the average remaining service period of active workers. The gain or loss component of expense consists of first, the difference between the actual return on plan assets and the expected return on plan assets, and second, the amortization of the unrecognized net gain or loss from previous periods.

Another component of expense recognized on a delayed basis is the amortization of unrecognized prior service cost. Prior service cost arises from plan amendments or from initiation of a plan that attributes benefits to employee service rendered in prior periods. The prior service cost should be amortized by assigning an equal amount to each remaining year of service to the full eligibility date of potentially eligible active workers. A reduction in the sponsor's obligation owing to a plan amendment that reduces the level of retiree health benefits is first used to reduce any existing unrecognized prior service cost and then any unamortized transition obligation. Any excess would be amortized over the remaining service period to the full eligibility date of potentially eligible active workers. If, however, the retiree health plan is canceled entirely, the sponsor would report an immediate gain, computed as the reduction in the accrued liability resulting from the plan cancellation.[20]

Effective Dates. According to the exposure draft, the proposed standard is generally effective for fiscal years beginning after December 15, 1991. For non-U.S. plans and for plans sponsored by nonpublic enterprises that have fewer than 100 participants, however, the effective date of the standard is for fiscal years beginning after December 15, 1993.[21]

The proposed standard requires that a sponsor should report on his balance sheet for fiscal years beginning after December 15, 1996, a liability that is the greater of the following: the accrued postretirement benefit cost, or the unfunded minimum liability. The accrued benefit cost is the cumulative accrued expense in excess of the sponsor's cumulative contributions or, in the case of an unfunded plan, of cumulative benefits paid by the sponsor.

The rationale behind this requirement is twofold. On the one hand, the FASB is concerned that the immediate and full recognition of the accrued liability would be abrupt and would represent a jarring break from past accounting practices. Hence it requires a gradual recognition of the accrued liability, generally at the rate of the amortization—that is, over fifteen years. On the other hand, by requiring the reporting of a minimum liability, the FASB intended to limit the extent to which the delayed recognition of the transition obligation results in the omission of a liability for retiree health benefits from a sponsor's balance sheet.

Additional Disclosures. In addition to recognition on the balance sheet and in the income statement, the proposed standard requires disclosures of certain items in a separate footnote to the annual statement. Among the items to be disclosed are:

- the information required by Statement No. 81, the funding policy, and the types of assets held, if any
- the amount of accrued expense showing separately most of the component parts
- the amounts of accrued liability, remaining transition obligation, unrecognized net gain or loss, unrecognized prior service cost, and the market-related value of plan assets, if any
- the assumed discount rate, trend rate of health care cost, and expected long-term rate of return on plan assets
- the effect of a one-percentage increase in the trend rate of health care cost on accrued expense and liability

These disclosures in essence allow the sophisticated user of financial statements to "roll his own" accounting concepts, or to use his own assumptions if he is dissatisfied, for whatever reason, with the concepts chosen by the FASB, or with the assumptions chosen by the plan sponsor implicit in the amounts recognized in the body of the financial statements.

The proposed standard applies mainly to single-employer plans. Some disclosures, however, are also required of the sponsors of multiemployer plans. In particular, the contributions to and a description of the multiemployer plan—including the employee groups covered and the types of benefits provided—must be disclosed separately from any disclosure for a single-employer plan.

Adjustments to the Originally Proposed Standard. The proposed accounting standard for retiree health benefits has generated considerable interest. Nearly 500 comment letters were sent to the FASB in the months following issuance of the exposure draft. Attendance was high at the two public meetings held to discuss the proposal, and more than sixty organizations made oral presentations. Most of the comments supported the general thrust of the exposure draft, but many suggested modifications that would, in essence, reduce the reported expense and liability amounts.[22] Many articles on the standard have appeared in the daily and weekly financial press, as well as in the actuarial, benefits, and legal professional journals.

In the period since the receipt of comments and the public hearings, the FASB has met several times and reaffirmed or altered various positions it expressed in the exposure draft. In April 1990, the board deleted the pay-as-you-go constraint on the amortization of the transition obligation; it allowed sponsors to reflect future anticipated changes in cost-sharing provisions of plans if such changes have already been communicated to workers. In June 1990, the board decided to drop the proposed recognition of the minimum liability and tentatively decided to extend the minimum transition period from fifteen years to twenty years. In addition, the FASB tentatively agreed to allow firms, on a one-time basis, immediately to recognize their accrued liability for retiree health benefits. The board also postponed the effective date of the standard to calendar year 1993. Most of the board's modifications reduce somewhat the complexity and burden of the proposed standard.

Promulgation of the final standard, No. 106, occurred in December 1990 by a unanimous vote of the FASB members.[23] The board confirmed the terms of the exposure draft, combined with the changes that had been made over the period through December 1990. The board also made one substantive change in the standard, effectively reducing the amount of liability and expense that employers will be likely to recognize on their financial statements. "In some situations, an employer's cost-sharing policy, as evidenced by past practice or by communication of intended changes to a plan's cost-sharing provisions, or a past practice of regular increases in certain monetary benefits, may indicate that the substantive plan—the plan as understood by the parties to the exchange transaction—differs from the extant written plan. The substantive plan shall be the basis for the accounting."[24]

Because employers and their accountants are likely to be somewhat more liberal in their assumptions concerning future cost-sharing arrangements than in their assumptions about future benefit increases, the reported expense and liability may be somewhat lower than would be estimated by a disinterested third party. The actual extent of the underestimate will be limited, however, by the active scrutiny of financial analysts as well as by the FASB's guideline that "an employer's past practice of maintaining a consistent level of cost sharing with its retirees . . . shall not constitute provisions of the substantive plan if accompanied by identifiable offsetting changes in other benefits or compensation, or if the employer incurred significant costs, such as work stoppages, to effect that cost-sharing policy."[25]

In notes to the standard, the FASB also defended itself against accusations that the new standard would be very costly to implement and that upon implementation, benefits would be cut or federal legislation introduced. Against the first accusation the board said, "Many employers have not monitored and managed their postretirement benefit obligations and costs. Consequently, a significant portion of the incremental systems cost [required to implement the new standard] reflects costs that a prudent employer would incur in monitoring and managing the consequences of its postretirement benefit arrangement.

The board believes that those costs should be associated with the existence of those arrangements, rather than with the requirements of this statement."[26]

Against the second accusation, the board said, "Some believe that employers will change the designs of postretirement benefit plans or the way those plans are financed as a result of the new information about the financial effects of postretirement benefits. In addition, some believe that the new information may provide an additional impetus to federal legislation covering employers' obligations for those plans or the deductibility of employers' advance funding of those plans. Those actions, if taken, are not the direct result of a requirement to accrue postretirement benefits, but rather, may result from more relevant and useful information on which to base decisions."[27]

Examples

Consider this example of a company reporting its obligation for retiree health benefits under the current and new accounting standards. The example is not hypothetical, but is taken verbatim from the notes to the consolidated financial statements section of the 1988 and 1989 annual reports of a utility holding company. The company was not necessarily chosen because it is representative of other companies providing retiree health benefits, either in terms of demographics or costs. Rather it was chosen because it is one of the first companies to have implemented the new FASB standard.

Reporting under Statement No. 81. The section of the 1988 annual report describing retiree health benefits is given below:

> In addition to providing pension benefits, the Company provides certain post-retirement health care and life insurance benefits. Substantially all of the Company's employees may become eligible for such benefits if they reach normal retirement age while working for the Company. These benefits are provided through a self-insurance arrangement and through insurance companies whose premiums are based on the benefits paid during the year. The Company recognizes the cost of providing these benefits on a pay-as-you-go basis.

Years ended September 30	1988	1987	1986
Annual expense (in thousands)	$4,447	$4,021	$3,133
Employees (year-end)			
Active	1,426	1,346	1,200
Retired	380	344	336

This company apparently was unable to separate the costs of benefits between active and retired workers. Instead it reported the total cost of benefits for all plan participants and the number of active and retired workers, as allowed by Statement No. 81. If one assumed that the per capita cost of benefits for active and retired workers was identical, the pay-as-you-go cost for retired workers would have been $936,000 in 1988. The company also followed the other provisions of the current standard by indicating the covered groups, the nature of the benefits, and the funding and accounting policies used for the benefits.

Reporting under Statement No. 106. The section of the 1989 annual report describing retiree health benefits is given below:

> In addition to providing pension benefits, the Company provides certain post-employment health care and life insurance benefits. Substantially all of the Company's employees may become eligible for such benefits if they reach normal retirement age while working for the Company.
>
> During 1989, the Company changed its method for accounting for these post-employment benefits for salaried employees from the "pay-as-you-go" method to the accrual method. The change was made to accrue costs over the period of time that the employees must work to become eligible to retire. The Company believes that the new method of accounting more properly matches the costs of post-employment benefits with the service of the employee. The expense for the plan covering salaried employees for the year ended September 30, 1989, was $2,085,000, an increase of $1,468,000 over the previous method. The "projected unit credit" actuarial method was used to determine the normal cost and actuarial liability. A reconciliation of the estimated status of the obligation is as follows:
>
> (in thousands)
>
> Accumulated Benefits Exceed Assets
>
> | | |
> |---|---|
> | Vested post-employment benefit obligation | ($12,070) |
> | Nonvested benefits | ($1,082) |
> | Accumulated post-employment benefit obligation | ($13,152) |
> | Unamortized transition obligation | $11,778 |
> | Accrued post-employment benefit cost | ($1,374) |
>
> Net periodic post-employment benefit cost for the year ended September 30, 1989, included the following components:
>
> (in thousands)

Accumulated Benefits Exceed Assets

Service cost	$158
Interest cost on accumulated post-employment benefit obligation	$1,086
Amortization of transition obligation	$841
Net periodic post-employment benefit cost	$2,085

The weighted average health care cost trend rate used in determining the accumulated post-employment benefit obligation was 8.5 percent. The assumption has a significant effect on the amounts reported. To illustrate, increasing the weighted average health care cost trend rate by one percent would increase the accumulated post-employment benefit obligation by 8.6 percent and the net periodic post-employment benefit cost by 7.8 percent. The weighted average discount rate used in determining the accumulated post-employment benefit obligation was 8.5 percent.

The Company recognizes the cost of providing post-employment benefits for a limited number of employees under labor union agreements on a "pay-as-you-go" basis. These benefits are provided through a self-insurance arrangement and through insurance companies whose premiums are based on the benefits paid during the year. Expense of $695,000, $550,000, and $494,000 was charged during 1989, 1988, and 1987, respectively.

Some terms used in the above section but not defined in the FASB exposure draft should be explained. The company uses the term "post-employment" when it should use "post-retirement"; as is evident from context, only retiree benefits are intended. The term "projected unit credit" is identical to the FASB term "benefits/years-of-service"; the former term is common in the pension actuarial literature. Finally, the company uses the title "Accumulated Benefits Exceed Assets" to indicate that the plan is underfunded; indeed, it is apparently not funded at all.

The most obvious difference between reporting under the current standard and under the proposed standard is the exponential expansion of the amount of information provided and, more significantly, the expenses and liabilities revealed. Under the current standard, pay-as-you-go costs were $617,000 (not $936,000, as estimated above); under the proposed standard, the accrued expense (net periodic post-employment benefit cost) becomes $2,085,000—a tripling of the cost formerly reported. Furthermore, the pay-as-you-go cost for multiemployer plans is reported for the first time. Under the current standard, no liability is recorded; under the proposed standard, the accrued liability (the accumulated post-employment benefit obligation) of $13,152,000 is disclosed, and an accrued benefit cost of $1,374,000 is initially recognized on the 1989 balance sheet.

The accrued liability is composed of two components: the vested and the nonvested benefit obligations. The vested obligation is closely related to the minimum liability—that is, the accrued liability for retired and fully eligible active workers. The nonvested obligation is closely related to the accrued liability for potentially eligible active workers.[28] As is evident, most of the accrued obligation is owed to retired and fully eligible workers. The expected obligation is not reported, but is implicit in the calculation of service cost. The accrued liability is also broken down into two other components: the unamortized transition obligation and the amount amortized and appearing on the balance sheet; that is, the accrued post-employment benefit cost. The accrued benefit cost is the net periodic post-employment benefit cost (accrued expense) accumulated since the implementation of the new standard (in this case, over one year) minus the accumulated pay-as-you-go cost of benefits paid over the same period.

The accrued expense is composed mainly of the interest cost on, and the amortization of, the accrued liability. Although the accrued liability at the beginning of the period (the original transition obligation) is not reported, the amount of amortization charged would apparently indicate that the period of amortization chosen was fifteen years, consistent with the original version of the proposed standard. The amount of interest cost is consistent with an 8.5 percent discount rate, multiplied by an accrued liability of around $13 million.

As is stated explicitly in the section of the annual report quoted above, the calculations of expense and liability are very sensitive to the assumption about the trend rate of health care cost. Holding the discount rate constant while increasing the trend rate by one percentage point increases the expense and liability by around 8 percent. It may be further noted that by assuming the discount rate and the trend rate both equal to 8.5 percent, the company could have arrived at the same computational results by assuming a zero medical inflation rate and a discount rate of zero.

Field Test Implementation of the Proposed Standard

The Financial Executives Research Foundation sponsored a field test to study the potential impact of and implementation problems arising from the proposed accounting standard for retiree health benefits. The field test was done by the accounting firm Coopers and Lybrand, and twenty-five large and medium-sized companies participated in the study. Results were published in 1989.[29]

Coopers and Lybrand reports that four steps were taken to provide each company with a valuation as of January 1, 1988, of the obligation for retiree health benefits.[30] The steps were as follows:

- Written materials and informal guidelines were reviewed to determine the type and extent of benefits being offered.
- Information about current retirees and claims experience was examined, and average per capita costs for 1986 were identified.
- Actuarial assumptions to be used in the valuation were selected; particular care was taken with the assumption about the trend rate of health care cost.
- The framework of the FASB exposure draft was utilized to produce estimates of accrued expense and liability.

In taking these steps, Coopers and Lybrand noted many problems with the availability and quality of the necessary data.[31] Summary plan descriptions, required by the Employee Retirement Income Security Act of 1974, were often out-of-date. Sometimes guidelines relevant to cost estimates on the administration of the plans were left to "oral traditions" and had to be determined through oral interviews. Collecting information about retirees and their dependents posed numerous problems: it was difficult to determine the age of retirees and whether they had any covered dependents. The data files of insurance carriers and third-party administrators concerning claims experience were apparently not designed easily to furnish the information necessary for a valuation of the benefit obligation; the distinction between retired and active workers was not always clearly made, and eligible charges, as opposed to claims paid, were sometimes not recorded.

In chapters 8 and 9 an approach is described to implement the proposed FASB standard for a much larger set of companies and for the aggregate of companies in the private sector of the economy. Because of the large size of the sample used in this book and lack of access to some relevant materials, of necessity the methodology employed here makes more uniform assumptions than did the Coopers and Lybrand study. At the same time, however, the large size of the sample used in this book permits a more global perspective, and hence provides a firmer basis upon which to draw inferences for public policy and analytical purposes.

6

The Extent of Coverage

The extent of retiree health coverage is examined in this chapter. Based on various surveys, estimates of the number of current retirees covered by employer-provided health plans are reviewed in the first section. In the second section, some overview is given of the number of companies providing the benefits and of their industry and size characteristics. Finally, the third section provides a brief description of the extent of coverage gained through former employment with governmental entities.

A reasonable impression of the extent of coverage of retiree health benefits is that these benefits are extensively provided by large companies and governmental entities. Many of these companies are in regulated or oligopolistic industries and often face work forces represented by unions. Owing to the prevalence of small companies and the high percentage of the work force employed by these companies, however, somewhat fewer than half of all retirees—that is, about 10 to 11 million people—are currently provided health benefits by former employers. A possible explanation for the higher incidence of retiree health benefit plans among large companies and governmental entities is this: the greater financial stability and public prominence of these employers have given workers and their union representatives some assurance that the companies would remain solvent and willing to pay promised, but unfunded, retirement benefits for many years into the future.[1] (The unfunded status of these benefits may in turn owe to the somewhat poor choices available to companies for tax-favored prefunding of retiree health plans, as is explained in chapter 2.) The corporate restructuring binge of the 1980s and the financial weakness and even bankruptcies of many heretofore "rock solid" private and public employers, however, may be leading many retirees and workers to question the soundness of past confidences.

Number of Current Retirees Covered by Plans

Four major sources offer information about the number of current retirees covered by employer-sponsored health benefit plans. The General Accounting Office gathered data on company health plans for employees and retirees through a survey of firms conducted from March to August 1989.[2] The Urban Institute, under contract to the Pension and Welfare Benefits Administration of the Department of Labor, prepared tables based on data collected in a supplement to the August 1988 Current Population Survey, in which persons aged forty or older were asked about their health insurance coverage.[3] The National Center for Health Services Research estimated the number and characteristics of retirees with employment-related health insurance coverage based on data collected in the first round of the household component of the 1987 National Medical Expenditure Survey.[4] The Employee Benefits Research Institute estimated the number of people aged fifty-five or older who had health insurance coverage through an employer-sponsored plan based on tabulations of the 1984 Survey of Income and Program Participation.[5]

As might be expected, each source of information gives a somewhat different estimate of the number of covered retirees. This disparity may owe to differences in the definition of retiree, in the definition of retiree health coverage, in the statistical techniques used, as well as in the nature and date of the surveys upon which the estimates are based. Each source of information is now reviewed in turn.

The General Accounting Office Survey. To estimate the number of covered retirees, as well as to collect information about other aspects of health insurance provided to active and retired workers, the General Accounting Office (GAO) selected a stratified random sample of 5,550 companies and mailed them questionnaires. The sample was chosen from among some 7 million companies listed in the August 1988 Dun's Marketing Service database of business establishments. The strata used in the sample included four size groups, based on the number of workers employed, and six major industry groups. Hence there were twenty-four individual strata. To make estimates about the universe of companies, the data obtained were to be weighted according to the strata from which the sample companies were drawn. Because many companies in the original sample had gone out of business or did not respond to the questionnaire, however, the GAO stated that its results could be generalized to a population of only 2.5 million out of the 7 million companies in Dun's database. Smaller firms in particular were deemed to be underrepresented.

In the questionnaire, the GAO asked whether the company offered health care coverage upon retirement beyond the period required by the Consolidated Omnibus Budget Reconciliation Act (COBRA) of 1985.

COBRA requires employers who maintain health insurance plans to continue insurance to terminated workers for up to eighteen months. Workers may be charged up to 102 percent of the premium cost. (The COBRA requirements were discussed in some detail in chapter 3.) If the company indicated that it offered such extended coverage, it was asked for the number of retirees under and over the age of sixty-five covered by the plan. (Retirees in plans cosponsored by many employers [multiemployer plans] were excluded.) Based on the responses to the questionnaire and on the statistical methodology described above, the GAO estimated that in 1989 there were 5.3 million retired workers in company health plans, 2.1 million of whom were under the age of sixty-five.[6] Based on another survey and similar methodology, the GAO estimated that an additional .3 million retired workers were covered by multiemployer plans.[7] Because most companies do not keep track of the number of spouses and dependents covered by their plans, it is reasonable to infer that only workers retired from the companies providing coverage, and not spouses and dependents, are included in the estimate. It is not known, however, what percentage of these retired workers paid their former employers some or all of the insurance premium incurred for their coverage. The GAO reported a sampling error of plus or minus 2.6 million for its aggregate estimate of 5.6 million retired workers covered by all private plans.

The Current Population Survey. To collect information on the health insurance coverage of retired persons, the Pension and Welfare Benefits Administration of the Department of Labor sponsored a supplement to the August 1988 Current Population Survey (CPS), wherein all persons in the sample aged forty or older were asked questions about their health insurance. The supplemental questions focused in particular on the distribution of characteristics of the plan sponsors and on the cost to the retired worker of employment-based retiree health benefits. Tables based on the data collected were prepared by the Urban Institute.

Because the CPS is an in-person or telephone questionnaire conducted by the Bureau of the Census of a sample of households, primarily intended to calculate the unemployment rate, the supplemental survey of health insurance coverage will differ from the GAO survey of private employers in many ways. First, the information reported by household respondents is not verified for consistency with employer files. Because the household respondents may be somewhat uncertain during a short interview about the source and cost of their health insurance coverage, the information collected may be considered less accurate than information provided by employers in a mail questionnaire.

On the other hand, information collected from a random sample of households presumably does not contain the bias present in the GAO survey concerning the size of the respondents' former employers. The CPS, because of its focus on individual household units, moreover, collects information about persons employed in the public as well as private sectors of the economy, whereas the GAO survey focused exclusively on private employers.

Finally, the definition of covered retiree in the CPS is somewhat broader than that implicit in the GAO survey. Persons were counted as retired in the Urban Institute tabulation of the CPS if they reported that they were not employed but had once worked for the same employer for five or more years, that they were employed but had retired from a job, or that they were insured by a former employer. Hence the CPS count of retirees covered by insurance provided by former employers will probably include spouses to the extent that these spouses are also formally considered retirees. Spouses who had never entered the labor force and dependents, however, would presumably be excluded from the count of covered retirees. Retirees with temporary COBRA coverage will be included in the count.

According to the Urban Institute tabulations of the CPS, 10.183 million retirees reported that they were covered by employer-provided health insurance.[8] (Also see tables 2–1 and 2–2.) Of the 10.183 million retirees, 4.376 million were under the age of sixty-five. According to the CPS, 1.782 million covered retirees were formerly employed in public administration—local, state, or federal government—implying that 8.4 million covered retirees were formerly employed in the private sector.

The CPS also questioned covered retirees about the expected duration of employer-provided health insurance. As is shown in table 6–1, the vast majority of the retirees were covered until age sixty-five or for more than thirty-six months (presumably for life); relatively few came under the category of temporary COBRA coverage of one to thirty-six months.

The National Medical Expenditure Survey. The National Medical Expenditure Survey (NMES) is a massive complex of surveys conducted by the National Center for Health Services Research (NCHSR) concerning medical expenditures by a large sample of persons.[9] The main survey is composed of five rounds of interviews with households in 1987 concerning their medical expenditures, verified by checking health insurance plans and records of physicians and health facilities. Special surveys cover persons resident in nursing homes and facilities for the mentally retarded. The household sample was chosen to produce statistically unbiased estimates for the general population of health insurance coverage, use of services, expenditures, and sources of payment.

TABLE 6–1
DURATION OF EMPLOYER-PROVIDED RETIREE HEALTH INSURANCE
(millions of retirees)

Duration of Insurance Coverage	Total	Age 65+	40–64
Until age 65	1.118	.151	.967
Less than one month	.158	.076	.082
1 to 18 months	.298	.041	.257
19 to 36 months	.092	.028	.064
More than 36 months	6.920	4.785	2.135
Do not know	1.090	.583	.507
No response	.507	.144	.363
Total retirees	10.183	5.808	4.375

SOURCE: Urban Institute tabulations of the August 1988 Current Population Survey, Supplement on Retiree Health Insurance Benefits.

The NCHSR utilized data from the first round of interviews for the household survey component of the 1987 NMES to estimate the number and characteristics of retirees with employer-provided health insurance coverage. Persons aged fifty-five or older were considered to be retirees if they reported retiring from a specific job or business and had done so when they were aged fifty or older. According to this definition, some retirees can still be currently employed, although at a job other than the one from which they retired. Health insurance coverage was considered employer-provided if the respondent reported obtaining health insurance from a current or previous job or through a labor union. Hence the definition of covered retiree used in the NMES is similar to the definition used in the Urban Institute tabulation of the CPS, and it therefore has the strengths and weaknesses of that definition, as described above. The NMES may have a slight advantage over the CPS, however, because in the NMES the context of questions was clearly medical expenditures rather than labor market issues, and because answers are verified with outside sources. Therefore, perhaps, information about the source and cost of health insurance coverage to retirees may be more accurate in the NMES.[10]

According to the NMES, 10.016 million retirees obtained health insurance coverage from their former employers or the former employers of their spouses, and another .729 million retirees obtained coverage from their current employers in 1987. Of the 10 million retirees obtaining coverage from former employers, 1.651 million were identified as retired dependents of those obtaining coverage in their own right, and 2.845

TABLE 6–2

RETIREES WITH EMPLOYER-PROVIDED AND OTHER PRIVATE HEATLH INSURANCE
COVERAGE, BY SELECTED EMPLOYMENT AND DEMOGRAPHIC CHARACTERISTICS,
1987

Population Characteristic	Retirees 55 or Older (millions)	Employer-provided		Other Private[a] (percent)	None (percent)
		Worker (percent)	Dependent (percent)		
Total	22.042	38.8	9.9	32.1	19.1
Current employment status					
Employed	2.241	55.2	6.9	26.7	11.2
Not employed	19.801	37.0	10.3	32.7	20.0
Age in years					
55–59	1.723	50.1	20.6	11.2	18.1
60–64	3.818	51.9	15.0	17.5	15.6
65–69	5.230	40.3	11.1	29.7	19.0
70–74	4.848	37.1	7.6	38.7	16.6
75+	6.424	28.1	4.9	43.5	23.6
Sex					
Male	12.547	47.1	4.2	29.4	19.3
Female	9.495	27.9	17.5	35.7	18.9
U.S. Census region					
Northeast	5.258	40.7	8.8	31.8	18.7
Midwest	5.269	41.6	10.3	32.7	15.4
South	7.210	34.5	9.5	34.4	21.7
West	4.305	40.3	11.6	28.0	20.1

a. Primarily individually purchased policies, including Medicare supplement policies.
SOURCE: National Center for Health Services Research, National Medical Expenditure Survey–Household Survey, round 1.

million were under the age of sixty-five. About 1.2 million retirees obtained coverage through work in public administration.

Some demographic characteristics of retirees with employer-provided coverage, as recorded in the NMES, are shown in table 6–2. The likelihood of employer-provided coverage varies inversely with retiree age. This variation may owe to the fact that some employers cut retiree coverage at age sixty-five and, perhaps, to an increasing prevalence of retiree health coverage in recent years. Men are more likely to have retiree health benefits, probably because they are more likely to have held jobs with general access to fringe benefits. Retirees in the South are less likely to be provided coverage, probably reflecting the lower degree of unionization and the greater importance of agriculture in that part of the country. More information about the incidence of retiree health coverage by industry will be provided in the next section and in chapter 9.

The Survey of Income and Program Participation. The Survey of Income and Program Participation (SIPP), an annual survey of households, is designed to ascertain the impact of various government welfare programs. Because of its purpose, lower-income households are somewhat overrepresented in the survey sample. Based on the 1984 SIPP, the Employee Benefit Research Institute (EBRI) estimated that 11.3 million people aged fifty-five or older had health insurance coverage from an employer-sponsored plan. Of these, 7.6 million were aged sixty-five or older. About 22 percent of covered retirees paid the full cost of their health coverage, while the rest received partial or complete subsidization from employers. EBRI also estimated that about 30 percent, or 3.4 million, of these people received coverage through former employment in the public sector.

The estimate based on the SIPP of the aggregate number of people covered by employer plans is higher than the estimates of covered retirees based on the CPS and NMES, probably because the SIPP estimate incorporates all individuals above age fifty-five, including about 1.5 million spouses who never entered the work force and therefore never formally retired. The source of the larger discrepancy among the surveys concerning the number of people covered through employment in the public sector is uncertain, however, and it will be further discussed in the third section of this chapter.

The Intersection of the Surveys. Chapter 8 gives an estimate of the aggregate accrued expense and liability of private employers for retiree health benefits. To do so even somewhat accurately, an estimate is required of the number of retired workers provided lifetime health insurance at no cost or with a large subsidy owing to their former employment in the private sector. It is possible to infer such an estimate from the intersection of information contained in the surveys described above. According to the CPS and NMES, about 10 million retirees were provided health insurance, directly or indirectly, through former employers. Averaging the estimates from the CPS and NMES, about 1.5 million of these retirees obtained coverage through work for governmental entities, and according to the NMES about 1.7 million can be identified as retired spouses of retired workers.

Assuming that some government retirees are also spouses, it is estimated that about 7.2 million retired workers obtained health insurance coverage as a direct result of their own former employment in the

69

private sector. According to the CPS, about 20 percent of retirees paid the entire insurance premium for health coverage, and about 15 percent did not receive lifetime coverage. Even assuming that the full payment of premiums and lifetime coverage are independent events, one can reasonably estimate that at least 5 million retired workers obtained lifetime health insurance coverage, at no cost or with a large subsidy, as a direct consequence of their former employment with private sector sponsors of retiree health benefit plans.[11] Furthermore, this estimate is consistent with the GAO estimate that 5.6 million retired workers are covered owing directly to former employment in the private sector. The GAO estimate apparently excludes retirees and spouses with COBRA coverage, but it includes those retirees who pay the entire premium for health coverage.

Firms and Industries Offering Health Benefits to Retirees

Several sources offer information about the number and characteristics of firms offering health benefits to retirees. In addition to the one-time GAO survey described in the previous section, the Bureau of Labor Statistics of the Department of Labor conducts an annual survey of employee benefits, including retiree health benefits, offered by large- and medium-sized firms—that is, firms employing at least 100 workers.[12] These two surveys of companies give some sense of the number and type of firms offering retiree health benefits. The Current Population Survey and the National Medical Expenditure Survey also questioned retirees about the industry classification and size of their former employers offering health benefits. Although presumably less accurate because they are based on second-hand information, these surveys will also be referenced in this section.[13]

The GAO Survey. The GAO estimates that of the 2.5 million firms that the scope of its sample allows for generalization, about 4 percent, or 105,000 companies, currently extend health coverage to retirees beyond the time required by COBRA. Larger firms are more likely than smaller ones to offer coverage. About 43 percent of all companies with more than 500 employees have retiree coverage. In contrast, only 2 percent of companies with fewer than 25 employees offer health coverage to retirees. It should be noted, however, that the primary response companies give to the question why they do not offer retiree health benefits is that they currently have no retirees. Hence it is unclear whether these companies would, in the future, offer health coverage to retirees.

When comparing health coverage for retirees by type of industry, the GAO found some variation. All of the six industry groups—agriculture, mining, manufacturing, and wholesale; construction; transportation and utilities; retail trade; professional services; and consumer services—are characterized by a high percentage of small companies. Because few small companies offer retiree health benefits, as is noted above, the percentage of companies with these benefits is below 8 percent among all industry groups.

Nevertheless, despite the low incidence of the benefits among all industry groups, it can be discerned that transportation, utilities, mining, and manufacturing companies were somewhat more likely to offer retiree benefits—between 6 to 8 percent of these companies offered benefits—than were construction companies; only .6 percent of these companies offered benefits. The lower incidence of benefit coverage among construction companies may owe in part to the greater prevalence of multiemployer plans among workers in that industry and the smaller average size of companies.

The Bureau of Labor Statistics Survey. In the Bureau of Labor Statistics (BLS) survey, detailed information concerning a large array of benefit plans and schedules, including retiree health benefit plans, is gleaned from plan documents requested from a representative stratified sample of some 2,000 companies. Data are presented separately for three occupational groups: professional-administrative, technical-clerical, and production-service workers. Companies in the sample provided information on the number of full-time workers covered by specified benefit plans. Incidence tables were developed showing the percentage of employees (participants) in the survey who could receive the benefits examined. Workers were considered as covered by a benefit plan only if the employer paid all or part of the cost of the plan. Plans for which only administrative costs were paid by the employer and plans that were completely employee-financed are both excluded from the tabulations. Hence COBRA coverage is excluded from the tabulation of participants covered by retiree health plans. The 1988 BLS survey is used here.

According to the BLS, 45 percent of the health plan participants in the survey worked for employers who financed all or part of health care protection after retirement.[14] Retiree coverage was provided to 49 percent of professional and administrative participants, to 47 percent of technical and clerical participants, and to 43 percent of production and service participants. These incidence rates are largely consistent with information in the GAO survey about retiree health coverage provided by large- and medium-sized companies.

The Current Population Survey. As is mentioned above, the August 1988 CPS asked retirees for some of the characteristics of the firms from

71

TABLE 6–3

NUMBER OF RETIREES AGED FORTY AND OLDER WITH EMPLOYER-PROVIDED
HEALTH COVERAGE, BY SIZE OF FIRM FROM WHICH THEY RETIRED
(millions of persons)

Size of Firm (number of employees)	Retirees with Employer-provided Health Coverage	Total Retirees in CPS
<20	.385	3.438
20–99	.597	2.290
100–499	.962	2.749
500–999	.498	1.170
1,000+	6.398	9.773
Do not know	.614	1.807
No response	.729	2.435
Total[a]	10.183	23.662

a. Excludes 520,000 persons who did not respond to insurance questions.
SOURCE: Urban Institute tabulations based on August 1988 Current Population Survey, Supplement on Retiree Health Insurance Benefits.

which they retired. The size and industry of the firms from which almost 24 million workers retired, including about 10 million retirees who obtained health insurance from their former employers, are identified in tables 6–3 and 6–4, respectively. As is shown in table 6–3, most retirees with employer-provided health insurance retired from firms that employed more than 1,000 workers. Indeed, more than two-thirds of those workers who retired from large firms were provided with health coverage upon their retirement. Despite the significant number of retirees from small-sized firms (that is, firms with fewer than 100 workers), relatively few retirees were provided health coverage by such firms. As is shown in table 6–4, the industries most likely to provide health coverage to retirees were the manufacturing, transportation and utilities, finance, services, and public administration (government) industries. These statistics are largely consistent with the findings of the GAO survey.

The National Medical Expenditure Survey. A slightly fuller perspective on the industry of retirees with employer-provided health coverage is given in the NMES. In addition to enumerating the number and industry of retirees with employer-provided coverage as already shown in table 6–4, the NMES displays the number of retired dependents and a somewhat finer delineation of industry. As is shown in table 6–5, most

TABLE 6–4
NUMBER OF RETIREES AGED FORTY AND OLDER WITH EMPLOYER-PROVIDED
HEALTH COVERAGE, BY INDUSTRY FROM WHICH THEY RETIRED
(millions of persons)

Industry	Retirees with Employer-provided Health Coverage	Total Retirees in CPS
Agriculture	.043	.492
Mining/construction	.585	1.333
Manufacturing	2.789	5.959
Transportation/utilities	1.232	2.040
Wholesale/retail trade	.602	2.817
Finance/insurance/R.E.	.416	.871
Services	1.782	4.805
Public administration	1.788	2.440
No response	.946	2.905
Total[a]	10.183	23.662

a. Excludes 520,000 persons who did not respond to insurance questions.
SOURCE: Urban Institute tabulations based on August 1988 Current Population Survey, Supplement on Retiree Health Insurance Benefits.

of those retirees with employer-provided coverage retired from the manufacturing, transportation, communications, utilities, and professional services industries, and from public administration. These industries also had a higher incidence of employer-provided coverage than, for example, agriculture and personal services. The results of the NMES are broadly similar to those of the CPS, except that the count of retirees from public administration is higher in the CPS. As is already noted, the SIPP gave a still higher count of people covered through former public employment. More information about retiree health benefits provided to government workers and some additional statistics about the number of people covered are given in the next section.

Governmental Entities Offering Health Benefits to Retired Employees

As is noted above, local, state, and federal governments figure significantly among those employers that provide health benefits to retired workers.

Federal Government. The federal government provides nearly all retirees from civilian employment the choice of health plans offered to active civilian workers, at the same subsidized terms. Most retirees select

TABLE 6–5
RETIREES WITH EMPLOYER-PROVIDED AND OTHER PRIVATE HEALTH INSURANCE
COVERAGE, BY FORMER INDUSTRY OF EMPLOYMENT, 1987

Industry	Retirees Aged 55 or Older (millions)	Employer-provided		Other Private[a] (percent)	None (percent)
		Worker (percent)	Dependent (percent)		
Agriculture	.505	8.2	7.5	51.6	32.7
Construction	1.169	33.2	5.9	37.0	23.9
Manufacturing	5.429	47.7	7.5	27.5	17.4
Transportation/ communications/ utilities	1.922	58.9	5.2	22.7	13.2
Sales	3.297	18.9	12.7	47.2	21.3
Finance	.828	34.3	14.5	29.5	21.7
Repairs	.727	23.9	16.0	34.7	25.4
Personal services	.797	9.0	11.5	44.1	35.4
Professional services	3.686	38.3	13.1	32.1	16.5
Public administration	1.989	59.2	6.2	18.5	16.2
Total	22.042	38.8	9.9	32.1	19.1

a. Primarily individually purchased policies, including Medicare supplemental policies.
SOURCE: National Center for Health Services Research, National Medical Expenditure Survey–Household Survey, round 1.

the health plan with the most generous provision of benefits, even though that plan has a somewhat higher premium structure than other available plans. Since January 1, 1983, federal government workers, although mostly ineligible for social security, were given credit toward Medicare eligibility for federal employment prior to 1983. Hence, insurance provided by the federal government is coordinated with Medicare to provide health coverage for civilian retirees above age sixty-five. Approximately 1.6 million retired civilian (including postal) workers are holders of health benefit policies subsidized by the federal government, according to the Office of Management and Budget.

Retired military personnel below age sixty-five and their survivors and dependents are eligible for reimbursement for their health care expenditures by a program called the Civilian Health and Medical Program of the Uniformed Services (CHAMPUS). Retired military personnel and their survivors and dependents of all ages, including those eligible for Medicare, are also eligible for free treatment at military medical facilities. According to the Department of Defense, about 1.1 million retired military personnel and 1.8 million survivors and dependents are eligible for CHAMPUS, while 1.6 million retirees and 2.2 million survivors and dependents are eligible for direct military medical care. It is unknown what percentage of retirees eligible for either form of military medical benefits avail themselves of the benefits.

State and Local Governments. Many state and local governments also provide health coverage to their retired workers. In 1987, 48 percent of participants in health plans provided by state and local governments could obtain employer-financed health insurance coverage after retirement.[15] Based on a survey of a small sample of governmental entities, the National Association of State Auditors, Comptrollers and Treasurers estimated that in 1988, about 60 percent, 56 percent, 16 percent, and 60 percent of states, large cities, small cities, and public authorities, respectively, were offering or planned to offer health benefits to retirees.[16]

When the number of federal retirees is added to the unknown but surely sizable number of state and local government retirees with employer-provided health insurance, it becomes fairly clear that the estimates of public administration retirees in the NMES and even the CPS are on the low side. Indeed, the estimate of 3.4 million based on the SIPP seems much closer to the mark.

7

Underlying Trends

Chapter 6 indicates the extent of coverage; chapter 7 highlights some important continuing changes in the demographic, economic, and institutional environment relevant to retiree health benefits. All of these changes in combination have contributed to an escalation of costs for health care in general and retiree health benefits in particular, and this escalation can be expected to continue.

In response to the realization of higher costs and with no relief in prospect, many employers have sought ways to reduce the benefits given to retirees or promised to future retirees. These ways have included higher premium contributions by retirees and higher deductibles and coinsurance.[1] The outright cancellation of benefit plans is somewhat constrained by legal principles, as is explained in chapter 4. The primary constraints on cancellation, however, probably lie in the ethical and public relations concerns of employers and in the prospect of adverse reactions by currently active workers, particularly in the form of strikes and poor morale.

Demographics

Life Expectancy. Because retiree health benefits are generally lifetime benefits, a longer life expectancy for retirees and their spouses will increase the cost of benefits to employers. The life expectancy of a typical man aged fifty-five has lengthened throughout this century, and it is forecast that the improvement in life expectancy will continue into the next century.[2] As figure 7–1 shows, in 1910 a man aged fifty-five could expect to live to age seventy-two and one-fourth. By 1970, such an individual's life expectancy had increased modestly to age seventy-four and one-half. According to the Social Security Administration, life expectancy lengthened significantly and rapidly by almost three years, to age seventy-seven and one-third, over the 1970s and 1980s. It is further forecast that the life expectancy of a fifty-five-year-old man would reach age eighty and one-fourth by 2050.

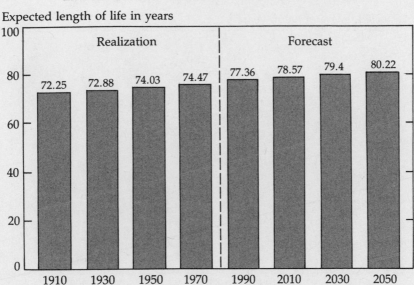

FIGURE 7–1
LIFE EXPECTANCY OF A MAN AGED 55, 1910–2050

Expected length of life in years

SOURCE: Social Security Administration, *U.S. Life Tables.*

The life expectancy of a typical woman aged fifty-five lengthened, and is forecast to lengthen, even more than that of a like-aged man over the relevant periods, as figure 7–2 shows. In 1910, a woman aged fifty-five could expect to live to age seventy-three and one-half; by 1970, such a woman could expect to live almost to age eighty, and by 2050 her life expectancy is forecast to be about age eighty-six and one-half.

Aging of Population. Another demographic factor relevant to the cost of retiree health benefits is the number of people eligible for benefits. The specific number of significance to an employer calculating the burden of retiree benefits is the ratio of retired to active workers in the employer's own work force. Some indication of general trends, however, can be derived from Census Bureau data. In particular, the percentages in recent years of the national population above ages fifty-five and sixty-five will give some feel for the increasing burden of health care costs for retired workers potentially eligible for benefits. As figure 7–3 shows, the percent of the population above age sixty-five increased from less than 10 percent in 1970 to about 12.5 percent in 1989. The percentage of the population above age fifty-five increased from about 19 percent to about 21.5 percent in the same time period. According to Census Bureau projections (middle

FIGURE 7–2
LIFE EXPECTANCY OF A WOMAN AGED 55, 1910–2050

Expected length of life in years

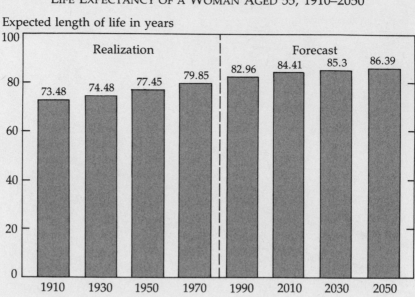

SOURCE: Social Security Administration, *U.S. Life Tables*.

series), the percentage of the U.S. population above age sixty-five is forecast to increase further to 13.5 percent in 2010 and to 22 percent in 2050.

Early Retirement

Because most retiree health benefit plans extend coverage for the entire period of retirement, the trend toward retirement at age sixty-five and even at earlier ages increases the cost of these benefits to employers. In particular, the trend toward early retirement at ages fifty-five or sixty dramatically increases the cost of benefits because there is no coverage by Medicare at these ages, leaving the employer with the entire burden of providing retiree health coverage at these ages.

Secular Trend. As figure 7–4 showns, a secular decline has occurred in the rate of labor force participation of older men since 1930. According to government statistics compiled by Professors Roger Ransom and Richard Sutch, the rate of participation in the labor force of men aged sixty and above was 64.5 percent in 1930; after the introduction of social security, the participation rate declined to about 55 percent in 1940 and

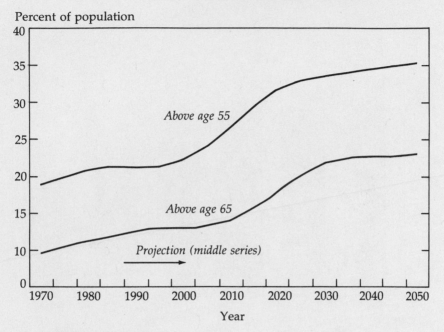

FIGURE 7–3
POPULATION ABOVE AGES 55 AND 65, 1970–2050

Percent of population

Above age 55

Above age 65

Projection (middle series)

Year

SOURCE: Bureau of the Census.

1950.[3] The participation rate of older men continued to decline until it was only 32 percent in 1980. This decline has been variously ascribed to wider coverage of the labor force by social security; to the provision of early retirement benefits in many pension plans; to attempts by many companies to pare work forces by inducing early retirement; and to the independent decision of many workers to convert increased financial security and affluence into more leisure time.

Recent Experience. More recent and detailed evidence of the trend toward early retirement among men is indicated in figure 7–5. In 1960, almost 96 percent of men aged forty-five to fifty-four, about 87 percent of men aged fifty-five to sixty-four, and more than 33 percent of men aged sixty-five and older were participants in the labor force. By 1988, the percentages for these age groups had declined significantly and continuously, to 91 percent, 67 percent, and 17 percent, respectively. By contrast, recent increases have occurred in the rates of participation in the labor force by women below age sixty-five. As figure 7–6 shows, in 1960 almost 50 percent of women aged forty-five to fifty-four and 37

FIGURE 7–4
LABOR FORCE PARTICIPATION OF MEN AGED 60 AND OLDER, 1930–1980

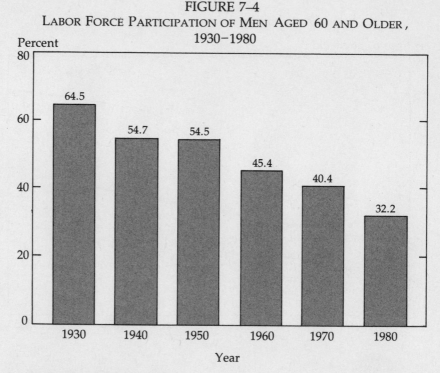

SOURCE: Ransom and Sutch (1990).

percent of women ages fifty-five to sixty-four were participants in the labor force. By 1988, the percentages had increased to 69 percent and 43.5 percent, respectively. These increases probably result from the same underlying causes of the increases in the rates of labor force participation among women in almost all age groups—namely, the feminist movement and the need to supplement family income owing to lower real wages earned by workers since the early 1970s. Among older women, however, a slight trend toward earlier retirement at age sixty-five was noticeable. In 1960, almost 11 percent of women above age sixty-five were in the labor force; by 1988, the percentage had declined to about 8 percent. The general trend toward early retirement by workers is clear.

Health Care Costs

Probably the most important factor in the cost of retiree health benefits to employers is the total cost of health care. As is well known, the cost of health care has been increasing rapidly in recent years, often at rates well in excess of the rate of general price inflation.

FIGURE 7-5
Labor Force Participation of Men Aged 45 and Older, 1960-1988

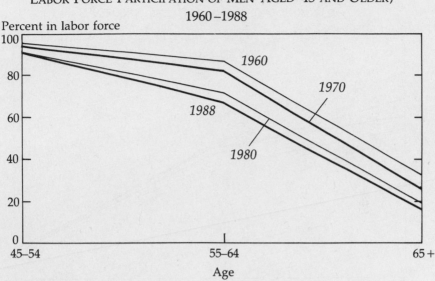

SOURCE: Bureau of Labor Statistics.

Statistical Evidence of Rapid Inflation. As figure 7-7 shows, a rate of medical inflation higher than the general inflation rate is actually a phenomenon of long standing, occurring at least since the time price indexes began to be calculated. Except in years of exceptionally large changes in the consumer price index—during and following World War II in the 1940s, for example, and during the oil price shocks in the 1970s—the changes in the consumer price index for medical care services (primarily physician and hospital care) have often been twice as large as changes in the consumer price index for all items purchased by urban workers.

A more detailed and recent look at medical inflation is given in figure 7-8. While the rate of general price inflation declined from nearly 14 percent in 1980 to less than 2 percent in 1986, the rate of inflation for medical care services and medical care commodities (primarily drugs) declined only from 11 percent and 9 percent, respectively, in 1980, to 8 percent and 7 percent, respectively, in 1986. More recently, the rate of medical inflation seems to be following the creep upward in the rate of general inflation. Prices of medical services and commodities seem to move together, with the possible exception of the years 1984 and 1985. The prices of medical services, particularly hospital services, were held

81

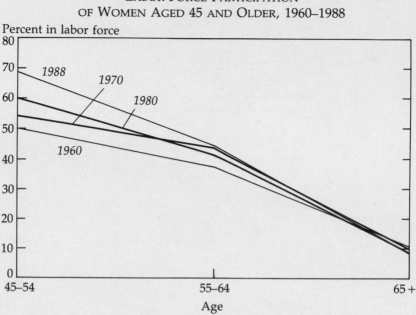

FIGURE 7–6
LABOR FORCE PARTICIPATION
OF WOMEN AGED 45 AND OLDER, 1960–1988

SOURCE: Bureau of Labor Statistics.

down in those years following the introduction of the diagnostic related group (DRG) method of Medicare reimbursement to hospitals.

Economic Studies. To some extent, the relatively more rapid pace of medical inflation reported by the Bureau of Labor Statistics results from the methods used in calculating the various components of the consumer price index. The economic theory underlying the construction of price indexes dictates that price changes owing to changes in the characteristics of the commodities and services included in the consumer market basket should be removed, so that only pure price changes are recorded. While excluding the effects of changes—mainly improvements—in technology is usually possible for many durable goods and is usually not relevant for food commodities, in practice the Bureau of Labor Statistics finds it difficult to keep track of technological changes in the provision of services to consumers. This relative weakness in excluding the price effect of technological change in the provision of services is magnified in the area of medical care because of the rapidity and significance of technological changes occurring there.

FIGURE 7-7

ANNUAL CHANGES IN PRICE INDEXES OF ALL ITEMS AND OF MEDICAL CARE SERVICES, 1939–1989

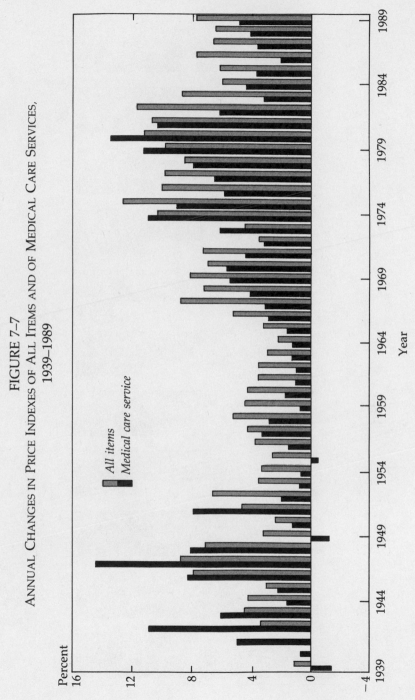

SOURCE: Bureau of Labor Statistics.

84

FIGURE 7-8

ANNUAL CHANGES IN PRICE INDEXES OF ALL ITEMS, MEDICAL CARE SERVICES, AND MEDICAL COMMODITIES, 1980–1990

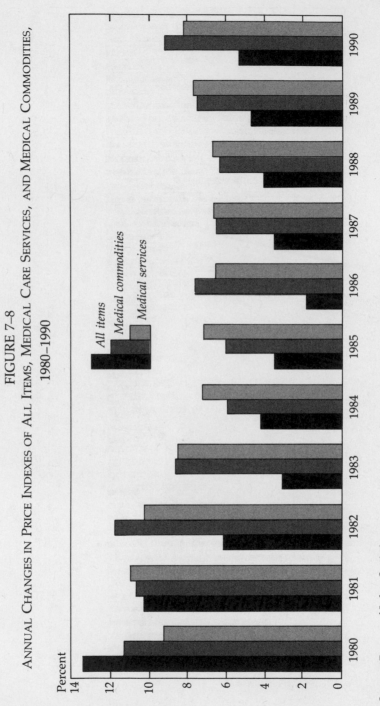

SOURCE: Bureau of Labor Statistics.

For example, while the BLS has surveyed hospitals for room charges over the years, almost no adjustment has been made for the significant changes in hospital plant, equipment, and staff sizes.[4] Among the possible reasons why the BLS has not calculated the effect of technological change in the medical care area are the lack of relevant data, the major increase in resources such a calculation would require, and the absence of a well-defined framework for judging whether and how technological changes imply improvements in the quality of medical services rendered.[5]

Despite the difficulty in disentangling the effect of technological change from pure price change, many feel that price increases for medical care have indeed exceeded price increases for other services and commodities. Several studies by Harvard economist Martin Feldstein in the early 1970s contended that one of the main causes of rapid medical inflation was the increase in insurance coverage experienced by American families in the 1950s and 1960s.[6] The increased coverage occurred owing to the increased prevalence of group health plans provided by employers and the start of the Medicare and Medicaid programs.

According to Feldstein, the demand for medical care increases as insurance against expenditure for health services becomes more widely available and as its provisions (such as deductibles and coinsurance) become more generous. In general, it is optimal for individuals to be completely insured against uncertain expenses if the insurance is actuarially fair.[7] Because the demand for health care is to some extent a discretionary decision, however, the existence of health insurance leads to a distortion in demand for care. This distortion must be weighed by public policy makers against the welfare gain of improved risk spreading inherent in any insurance scheme.

Feldstein also noted an additional distortion owing to the existence of externalities in the health care market. In particular, the price and type of health services available to an individual reflect the extent of health insurance among others in the community. Feldstein found econometric evidence that physicians and hospitals increase the prices (and sophistication) of their services when insurance becomes more extensive. Thus even the uninsured individual will find that his expenditure on health care increases as health insurance becomes more widely available in the community. Furthermore, the higher price of health care services encourages a higher demand for insurance coverage. "People spend more on health [care] because they are insured and buy more insurance because of the high cost of health care."[8] Although it is theoretically possible for the price dynamics implicit in this model of the health care market to cause the system to explode, the actual estimates of the relevant

FIGURE 7–9
DIRECT PAYMENTS BY HOUSEHOLDS FOR MEDICAL CARE,
AS A PERCENTAGE OF NATIONAL HEALTH EXPENDITURES,
1970–1987

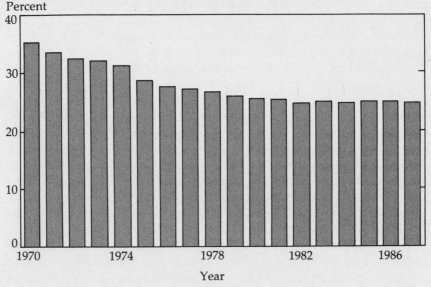

SOURCE: Health Care Financing Administration.

price elasticities obtained by Feldstein imply a stable but fairly inefficient system.

Feldstein concluded his studies of health care with the proposition that a general restructuring of health insurance, reducing its role as a method of prepaying small medical bills and increasing its role in protecting against catastrophic losses, would increase social welfare and reduce costs. It should be noted, however, that Feldstein did not take explicit account of the effect of changes in health care technology in his conclusions on the welfare implications of his model.

To the author's knowledge, no one has replicated Feldstein's model using more recent data. Nevertheless, some evidence is available that is at least consistent with his theory explaining the consistently high rate of medical inflation. As figure 7–9 shows, direct payments by households for medical care as a percentage of total national health expenditures— consisting of direct payments and payments by third-party payers, such as group health plans and Medicare—declined from about 35 percent in 1970 to less than 25 percent in 1987. Furthermore, Census Bureau data indicate a slight increase recently in the prevalence of insurance coverage. In particular, in 1983, 84.8 percent of people had some type of insurance coverage, while in 1987, 86.2 percent of people had such coverage.[9] Hence, there is some evidence that health insurance has become more generous and more prevalent in the 1970s and 1980s. This improved coverage is coincident with continued high rates of medical inflation.

Cost-shifting by Medicare and Other Government Programs

Because Medicare and other federal health programs represent very significant and growing portions of the federal budget, current and recent attempts to reduce the federal budget deficit have focused on efforts to control government expenditures on health programs. These efforts have been only partially successful. Nevertheless, owing to the coordination of benefits features of retiree health plans, any success in reducing Medicare payments will often lead directly to increased payments by employers. Among the more obvious efforts made by the federal government to pass the health care obligation for the elderly from the Medicare program to employers were provisions enacted in 1982 and expanded in 1984 and 1986, making Medicare the secondary payer to employer-provided health insurance plans. For workers above age sixty-five and for spouses above age sixty-five of workers under age sixty-five, Medicare benefits became secondary to employer-provided health insurance. Reportedly, many employers are extremely concerned that the trend to make Medicare the secondary payer might extend to retired workers.

The first budget agreement reached between Congress and the Bush administration in October 1990 (later discarded) is another example of an attempt to control the costs of the federal government for health programs. In addition to increases in the Supplementary Medical Insurance (SMI) deductible and premiums, the agreement would have held down hospital costs by not increasing payments under Medicare's DRG schedule.[10] In the absence of changes in employers' health plans and depending on the form of coordination of benefits employed, costs to employers for retiree health benefits would have increased owing to the cost control moves by the federal government in the Medicare program in the 1990 budget agreement.

Other efforts by the Medicare program to cut expenses, such as the DRG schedule explained in chapter 2 and a similar fee schedule for physicians to become effective in 1992, may lead to increased costs to employers indirectly. When Medicare reduces payments to hospitals and physicians, these health care providers may seek to push certain costs, such as the fee-for-service plans sponsored by employers, on to less resistant payers. Although this push will be felt by all employers sponsoring indemnity health insurance plans, those employers sponsoring retiree health plans will feel the push in increased measure, owing to their relatively more frequent interactions with health care providers.

Expectations of Retirees

Faced with increasing costs for retiree health benefits, a few employers have reduced or even eliminated benefits. It is possible that many more employers would do so, if not for the expectation of a very negative reaction by retirees and active workers. In the case of unionized work forces the threat of a strike looms, and in all cases litigation is almost a certainty. It is possible that the company could prevail in court in an attempt to reduce benefits, depending on the exact wording and circumstances of its contractual obligation to retirees, as is discussed in chapter 4. It is also possible that the company could "win" any strike. Aside from the difficult ethical issues involved, however, the company must also consider the possible damage its reputation would suffer from a battle with elderly retirees and surviving widows, as well as the damage to the management-labor relationship.

The Strike against the Pittston Company. The strike of the United Mine Workers against the Pittston Company, settled in February 1990, is a recent example of a long and difficult strike engendered in part by the act of a company to stop paying for retiree health benefits. In 1988, Pittston declared that it would stop making payments to the United Mine Workers 1950 Benefit Trust, a multiemployer plan that provides health benefits to the retirees of unionized coal companies. In 1989, the union struck after negotiations failed on these and other issues. Although Pittston partially restored retiree health benefits, the union held out for and eventually won the company's continued contributions to the UMW 1950 Benefit Trust and the start of contributions to another multi-employer plan, the UMW 1974 Benefit Trust. In announcing the settlement of the strike, Secretary of Labor Elizabeth Dole noted that one of the difficult issues in the dispute was the long-term security of health care benefits. She appointed a commission to review aspects of this issue and the related issue of the security of pension benefits in the coal industry and to make recommendations for a more permanent solution. The Coal Commission's report was issued in November 1990 and its conclusions (or lack of them) are discussed in chapter 10.

American Association of Retired Persons Survey. The protective attitude of retirees receiving health benefits from former employers is also evident in a 1987 survey conducted by the Policy Center on Aging at Brandeis University for the American Association of Retired Persons.[11]

The survey was sent to some 5,000 Medicare-eligible retirees from three corporations sponsoring retiree health plans. Nearly three-fourths of the respondents indicated that they were very concerned about increased out-of-pocket expenses that would result if Medicare or company plan benefits were reduced. Many of the respondents supported suggestions that their insurance coverage should be broadened to fill in gaps left by Medicare and company plans. More than half of the retirees, however, indicated that they felt they should make no personal contribution for this improved coverage. Ironically, retirees from the company with the most generous health plan felt the most strongly that they should make no personal contribution for improved coverage.[12] As is discussed in chapters 4 and 10, these attitudes are important to understanding the willingness of retirees to initiate litigation against the cancellation or reduction of benefits, and to understanding the events surrounding the passage and repeal of the Medicare Catastrophic Coverage Act of 1988.

8

Estimates of Accrued Expense
and Liability

The new FASB accounting standard for retiree health benefits is implemented in this chapter for the private sector. In particular, a simulation model is created to give estimates of the pay-as-you-go cost and of the FASB-consistent accrued expense and liability for a typical retiree health plan for several representative demographic groups. After choosing the appropriate parameter values and demographic groups, and based on the discussion in chapter 6 of the evidence on the number of covered retirees, the model is used to estimate costs, accrued expense, and liability for retiree health benefits, for all companies in the private sector of the economy (the aggregate estimate). The model is also used in the next chapter to estimate FASB-consistent accrued expense and liability for a large sample of individual companies based on the pay-as-you-go costs reported in their financial statements and on a match between the growth in companies' work forces and several of the representative demographic groups (estimates for individual companies).

The Simulation Model

The simulation model used in the estimation of the FASB-consistent accrued expense and liability for retiree health benefits at the aggregate and company levels is described in this section. The basic structure of the model entails the calculation of the expected present value of future health benefits to be received during the period of retirement for three groups of plan participants: retirees, active workers fully eligible for benefits, and active workers potentially eligible for benefits. Assumptions are made about per capita health care costs, adjusted for age, and about the portion of the tab paid by Medicare and by employer-provided health insurance. Values for relevant economic variables are inserted into the model. The model then gets a demographic overlay, which includes assumptions about age distributions and turnover rates of employees, and which can be varied to reflect the experience of various demographic groups.

The Calculation of Present Value for Retirees. For a retiree aged fifty-five, the assumed earliest retirement age, the present value calculation is relatively straightforward. The cost of health care in 1988 covered by a typical insurance plan for such an individual is the basic datum. The cost of health care increases at each age, as morbidity and mortality (and their associated expenses) increase. At age sixty-five, however, the cost incurred by the employer-provided health insurance plan is reduced by more than two-thirds, as retirees become eligible for Medicare. Per capita cost continues to rise with ages past sixty-five. The maximum length of life is assumed to be one hundred and five years. Superimposed on the cost increases owing to aging are the cost increases due to medical inflation—that is, the combined effect of general price inflation, of the introduction of more advanced (and expensive) medical technology, and of increased utilization of existing medical procedures.

The present value of benefits for the retiree is calculated by discounting by a particular interest rate the stream, at each age, of expected health care costs covered by the benefit plan. The stream of expected costs is adjusted for the probability of survival to each age; these probabilities are computed based on the 1983 Group Annuity Mortality table.[1] The probability of a fifty-five-year-old surviving to age X, where X varies between fifty-five and one hundred and five, is shown in figure 8–1. If the retired individual's spouse is also covered by employer-provided insurance, the annuity value is increased in proportion to the level of benefits provided to spouses of retired workers. The calculation of the present value of health benefits for retirees at ages older than fifty-five proceeds in a similar manner, except that the calculation begins with per capita cost at the relevant age and continues for fewer years, with the survival probabilities suitably adjusted.

Per Capita Health Care Costs. The 1988 per capita cost of health care covered by a typical health insurance plan for a retiree aged fifty-five is assumed to be $1,500. Naturally, this figure is an average for the relevant population, as most fifty-five-year-old individuals incur a smaller annual health care bill, but a few seriously ill individuals incur much higher bills.[2] The basic per capita cost of $1,500 in health expenditures covered by insurance is derived from several sources of information. The primary source, a study of retiree health benefits by Coopers and Lybrand, mentioned at the end of chapter 5, reported that eligible medical charges in 1986 for an individual aged fifty-five were approximately $1,400.[3]

91

FIGURE 8–1
PROBABILITY OF A 55-YEAR-OLD SURVIVING TO OLDER AGES, 1983

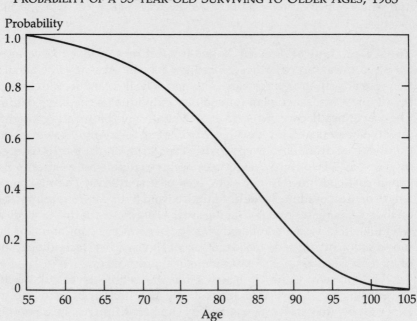

SOURCE: 1983 group annuity mortality table, Society of Actuaries.

Medical inflation would have increased these charges to about $1,625 by 1988, and assuming a reasonably generous health plan with low deductibles and copayments, would produce a per capita cost to the employer of about $1,450.

Other sources of information give lower and higher per capita costs than the Coopers and Lybrand study. A study of health expenditures by age group by the Health Care Financing Administration showed that in 1987, per capita personal health care expenditures for those nineteen to sixty-four years of age were $1,535, while per capita expenditures for those sixty-five years or older were $2,004.[4] Assuming a rate of medical inflation of 8 percent and a profile of health care expenditures by age as described below would produce health expenditures for an average fifty-five-year-old in 1988 of about $1,800. According to another study, about 25 percent of expenditures for personal medical services are paid for out-of-pocket in the 1980s, which produces a per capita cost to an employer for fifty-five-year-olds of $1,350.[5]

Finally, for those fourteen companies in my data base, described below, that reported both 1988 costs of retiree health benefits and the number of retirees, the cost per retiree averaged $2,700. If we assume that 70 percent of retirees have covered spouses and we make certain other assumptions about the demographics of these companies, the rate of Medicare reimbursement, and the profile of medical expenditures by age, the cost to these employers for a fifty-five-year-old individual would have to be $1,800.[6]

The main source of information about the profile of medical expenditures by age and rate of Medicare reimbursement used in the simulation model is a study by Blue Cross and Blue Shield of Greater New York of the claim cost experience in 1978 on small group and individual Medicare supplementary policies.[7] In particular, the study presents statistics on claim costs for hospitalization per contract year for various age and sex categories. The age profile of costs is produced by splicing together claim costs for the fifty to fifty-four, fifty-five to fifty-nine, and sixty to sixty-four-year-old categories (male and female combined) reported for group policies, with the claim costs for the sixty-five to sixty-nine, seventy to seventy-four, seventy-five to seventy-nine, eighty to eighty-four, eighty-five to eighty-nine, ninety to ninety-four, ninety-five-and-over categories (male and female combined) reported for Medicare supplementary policies. Claim costs increase by more than 5 percent per age above the ages fifty-five through seventy (excluding the obvious drop at age sixty-five because of Medicare eligibility), but the rate of increase gradually slows until costs remain essentially flat after the individual reaches age ninety-five.[8]

Statistics on claim costs for those individuals above age sixty-five but still participating in group policies indicate that hospitalization costs paid by employer-provided insurance for sixty-five-year-olds were about 25 percent of the level of costs for sixty-four-year-olds. Medicare presumably picked up much of the rest of the tab. It is assumed in the simulation model that employers pay 30 percent of eligible health care charges for those above age sixty-five. That this rate of employer plan reimbursement is slightly higher than that in the Blue Cross study owes to recognition of the secular trend of cost containment by Medicare, particularly after 1984, when the DRG method of payment was introduced. The cost per retiree (including spousal coverage at a 70 percent rate) of health benefits based on the assumptions described above is shown in figure 8–2.

The Calculation of Present Value for Active Workers. The calculation of the present value of retiree health benefits for active workers fully eligible for benefits is similar to the calculation for retirees, except that consideration must be given to the postponement of retiree benefits owing to the nonzero probability of remaining at work until retirement

93

FIGURE 8–2
Annual Employer Cost per Retiree for Health Benefits, 1988

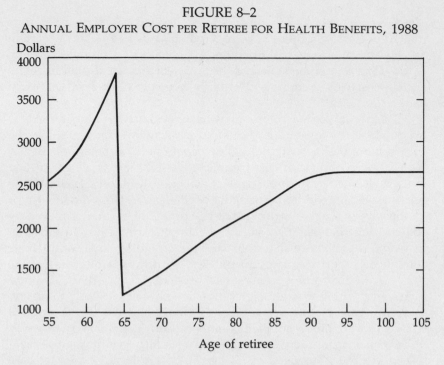

Source: Author's combination of several sources, as described in text.

at a later age. For example, the present value of benefits to an active worker aged fifty-eight, is the sum of the products of the probability of retiring at a particular age and the present value of the stream of benefits received when retirement occurs at that age. It is assumed that all workers retire by age sixty-six. Assumptions will vary about the probability of remaining at work (that is, early retirement) through ages until mandatory retirement, depending on the demographics of the employee group. The present value of retiree benefits to a fully eligible active worker is less than the value to a retired worker of the same age, because retiree benefits will likely be received by the active worker for fewer years.

The present value of accrued benefits to active workers who are potentially eligible for benefits is smaller still than the value to fully eligible workers. In the first instance, most potentially eligible workers are younger than fully eligible workers, and if the discount rate is greater than the rate of medical inflation, a stream of otherwise identical benefits farther off in the future will have lower present value. In the second instance, potentially eligible workers are still accruing benefits, while fully eligible workers have already fully accrued their benefits, according

94

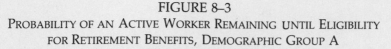

FIGURE 8–3

PROBABILITY OF AN ACTIVE WORKER REMAINING UNTIL ELIGIBILITY
FOR RETIREMENT BENEFITS, DEMOGRAPHIC GROUP A

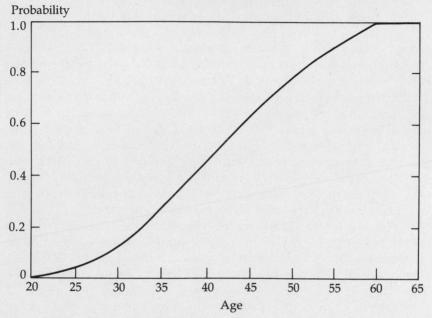

Probability

SOURCE: American Academy of Actuaries.

to the proposed FASB accounting standard. For example, a worker aged
fifty with twenty years of service has accrued 80 percent of his benefits,
assuming that the eligibility requirements of the plan are at least ten years
of service and attainment of age fifty-five. In contrast, a worker aged
fifty-five even with only ten years of service has already fully accrued
benefits under the plan.

The third and probably the most empirically significant reason why
the present value of benefits to a potentially eligible active worker is
smaller than the value of benefits to a fully eligible worker is that the
possibility of turnover (quitting) exists. A fully eligible worker is sure to
get his benefits, while a potentially eligible worker may not get his
benefits from the company, because he may leave the company (or may
be dismissed) prior to eligibility. Hence the calculation of the present
value of benefits for a potentially eligible worker is reduced by the
probability that the worker will leave the employ of the plan sponsor.

The probability of turnover depends negatively on the age and
length of service of the worker, as well as on the specific demographic
group. In any event, the probability that an active worker of age thirty
with five years of service will remain until full eligibility to receive retiree
health benefits is small. When this fact is combined with the relatively

95

small accrual of benefits, the present value of expected benefits for such a worker is very small. The probability that an active worker of age X with typical length of service will remain until eligibility, for a particular demographic group A described below, is shown in figure 8–3.

Assumptions about Relevant Economic Variables. The two main economic variables used in the simulation model are the discount rate and the expected inflation rate of future health care costs. Because a higher rate of medical inflation will increase present value and a higher discount rate will lower present value, for most calculations the significant items are not the absolute values of these rates but the difference between them. The higher the discount rate relative to the inflation rate, the lower the present value. The current yield on long-term U.S. government bonds is utilized for the discount rate, while the annual change in the medical component of the consumer price index (CPI) is utilized for the expected rate of future health care inflation.[9]

Actual rates of increase in employers' expenditures on retiree health plans have significantly exceeded the annual change in the medical component of the CPI. When consideration, as allowed by FASB, is also given to likely attempts by employers to reduce benefits and increase cost sharing, however, the rate of medical inflation is a reasonable assumption for modeling purposes. The change in the medical component of the CPI is also utilized when adjusting the per capita cost of health benefits to retirees for years other than 1988.

Calculation of Accrued Liability and Accrued Expense. The accrued liability is the sum of the present values of accrued health benefits expected in retirement for the three groups mentioned above—that is, retirees, active workers fully eligible for benefits, and active workers potentially eligible for benefits. (Recall the grey area of figure 5–1.) The accrued expense, assuming the accrued liability is unfunded, is the sum of the value of the accrual of benefits during the year for active workers potentially eligible for benefits, of the interest cost of the accrued liability, and of the amortization of the accrued liability. (Recall figure 5–2.) The interest cost is the product of the discount rate and the accrued liability; because it is assumed that the amortization of the unfunded liability occurs over twenty years, as is currently allowed by the FASB, the amortization cost is one-twentieth of the accrued liability.

Demographic Assumptions. As should be clear from the preceding discussion, assumptions about demographics are a key part of the simulation model. Demographic assumptions include the proportion of retired workers who have spouses covered by their health plans; the number, age, and length of service of retirees, fully eligible active workers, and potentially eligible active workers; the probability of retirement at certain ages; and the probability of quitting at certain ages and after certain lengths of service. In the absence of specific information about these variables for the covered population as a whole or for individual companies, one may instead rely on information for ten representative demographic groups, based on data from actual pension plans collected and refined by the American Academy of Actuaries.[10] The following is a characterization of the demographic groups.[11]

A. Normal group—This designation represents a reasonably mature and stable group that is projected to continue to grow. It is typical of many large companies.

B. Cyclical demographics—This represents a unionized group in a cyclical industry, with high turnover during the first years of employment. From cycle to cycle the group's size is approximately level. It is near the bottom of an employment cycle at the time of simulation.

C. Stable mature group—This group is a mature company with workers of relatively high age and long service and with a fairly large number of retirees. The number of employees has been the same for many years, and it is projected to continue so. Turnover is relatively low in early years of employment and very low for longer service employees.

D. Older group with long service—This represents a currently stable company that had rapid growth ten to twenty years ago that has since tapered off. The number of employees has been fairly level for several years and is projected to grow only slowly. Turnover is relatively low.

E. Volatile demographics—This represents a volatile, high-turnover company that is growing. It has very high turnover at all ages. Because of this high turnover, the average service is short and is expected to remain short. Even though the company has been in business for many years, there are no retirees.

F. Older declining group—This group represents an older, mature group that is gradually declining. Turnover is high at all ages and all durations of employment.

G. Cyclical bimodal—This is an old unionized group with a substantial number of retirees. The age distribution is bimodal. Approximately 20 percent of the employees are above age fifty-five and 25 percent are below age thirty. Employment is cyclical, but declining.

H. New group—This is a new group typical of emerging high technology companies. The company has been in business approximately five years. Most employees have been hired

TABLE 8–1

SAMPLE STATISTICS FOR TEN REPRESENTATIVE DEMOGRAPHIC GROUPS

Group	Actives Potentially Eligible	Actives Eligible	Retirees	Probability Worker Age 35 Remains	Expected Retirement Age
A	9,153	733	1,588	.28	62.56
B	8,590	1,390	7,343	.56	59.41
C	8,147	1,829	2,581	.83	63.21
D	9,060	916	1,142	.32	61.73
E	9,975	0	0	.01	61.77
F	8,522	1,422	3,033	.05	61.77
G	8,360	1,601	6,916	.52	63.69
H	9,546	45	14	.26	63.18
I	7,295	2,673	8,808	.36	63.18
J	7,281	2,697	7,618	.03	64.12

SOURCE: Author's calculations based on American Academy of Actuaries study.

since that time. It was initially formed by transferring employees from other divisions of the parent company. The average age at employment is high and is expected to remain high because of the skill and experience required in the company's business. Turnover is relatively high, particularly at younger ages and short service.

I. Old long service group—This is a unionized group with a high average age and years of service. Almost 50 percent of the employees are above age fifty, and there are almost as many retirees as active workers. Even though the group is declining, replacement of retiring employees will cause the average age and service to decline.

J. Cluster of old long service employees—This is a stable, mature company with a somewhat bimodal distribution. There are a large number of retirees. The plan covers both hourly and salaried employees.

Some sample statistics for the demographic groups are given in table 8–1. Each of the groups is normalized to 10,000 active workers. The number of active workers potentially eligible and active workers fully eligible for benefits need not total 10,000, however, because some older active workers with fewer years of service will never become eligible for benefits, on the assumption used in the simulation model that the average retiree health plan requires at least ten years of service prior to eligibility. The probability that a thirty-five-year-old with typical length of service will remain until eligibility for benefits is shown in the table to illustrate

TABLE 8–2

Costs of Retiree Health Benefits for Ten Representative Demographic
Groups, 1988
(dollars)

Group	Pay-as-you-go Cost	Average Cost per Retiree	Accrued Expense
A	3,595,176.89	2,263.97	18,703,198.50
B	17,601,986.05	2,397.14	61,083,674.37
C	6,013,990.75	2,330.55	38,872,218.19
D	2,813,014.44	2,463.73	26,022,252.10
E	0.00	0.00	1,763,347.34
F	7,270,524.79	2,397.14	26,531,612.31
G	16,578,618.34	2,397.14	51,364,711.69
H	19,535.58	1,395.40	14,334,042.99
I	19,941,006.32	2,263.97	60,796,022.13
J	17,754,149.02	2,330.55	52,805,217.01

SOURCE: Author's calculations.

the general pattern of quit probabilities for the groups. The expected retirement age varies from fifty-nine and one-half years to sixty-four years.

Simulations for the Representative Demographic Groups. The measures of costs in 1988 for retiree health benefits for the sample groups are simulated using the model and are shown in table 8–2. The pay-as-you-go cost, currently reported by companies on their financial statements, clearly increases with the number of retirees. At the extremes, Group I pays almost $20 million to provide 8,808 retirees with health benefits, while Group E pays nothing, even though it has a retiree health plan, because it currently has no retirees. The accrued expense, whose reporting will be required under the FASB standard, is generally from three to nine times larger than the pay-as-you-go cost for most of the demographic groups in the simulation model.

Instead of representing the cash outlays for benefits provided to retirees, the expense represents the accrual of benefits over the working lives of active workers, as well as the amortization and the accrual of interest on the unfunded liability for benefits already accrued by retired and active workers. Relative to the pay-as-you-go cost, the accrued expense increases most for those groups with few or no retirees. For example, while the pay-as-you-go cost for Groups E and H are zero or negligible, respectively, the accrued expense becomes material and represents the largest percentage increase among the demographic groups after implementation of the accounting standard. Even though these groups have few or no retirees now, some active workers will likely retire with benefits in the future, and the expected costs of their benefits are being accrued over their working lives. The average cost per retiree is fairly similar for the groups with significant numbers of retirees because the age distribution of retirees is identical for these groups, and only the rate of spousal coverage differs slightly from group to group.

The accrued liabilities in 1988 for the ten demographic groups are simulated and shown in table 8–3. The three components of the FASB-consistent accrued liability for the three participation subgroups— retirees, active workers fully eligible, and active workers potentially eligible—are also shown separately. The expected liability is the sum of the accrued liability for the three subgroups plus the present value of benefits expected to be earned, but not yet accrued, by active workers potentially eligible for benefits. The liability (accrued or expected) increases with the number of retirees; the accrued liability ranges from $4.7 million for Group E, which has no retirees and high turnover, to $406.5 million for Group I, which has a large number of retirees and active workers fully eligible for benefits, and modest turnover.

The ratio of accrued liability to pay-as-you-go cost (not shown) generally ranges from twenty to one to fifty to one for most of the demographic groups. These ratios are similar to those reported in the Coopers and Lybrand study. Depending on the value of other corporate assets and liabilities per active worker, the introduction of accrual accounting for retiree health benefits could have a large impact on the reported earnings of many companies, particularly those in declining industries, as is discussed further in chapter 9.

The values reported in tables 8–2 and 8–3 were calculated using a discount rate of 9 percent and a rate of medical inflation of 8 percent. Varying the discount and medical inflation rates can have a significant impact on calculations of accrued expense and liability. For example, as is shown in figure 8–4, the 1988 accrued liability for Group A varies from $151.4 million where the discount rate is 7 percent and the rate of medical inflation is 8 percent, to $78.2 million where the discount rate is 10 percent and the rate of medical inflation is 7 percent. As was explained earlier, the significant factor for the calculation is not the absolute value of the rates, but the difference between them.

Estimate of Accrued Expense and Liability in the Aggregate

Each of the ten demographic groups are presumably representative of at least some of the companies that provide retiree health benefits to their

TABLE 8-3

Liability for Retiree Health Benefits for Ten Representative Demographic Groups, 1988

(dollars)

Group	Actives Potentially Eligible	Accrued Liability Actives Eligible	Retirees	Total	Expected Liability
A	37,337,400	22,094,500	46,050,600	105,482,500	143,360,900
B	111,756,500	51,048,100	225,463,700	388,268,200	471,556,400
C	96,842,400	56,309,300	77,033,100	230,184,900	321,882,800
D	80,474,200	31,945,100	36,031,900	148,451,200	203,003,800
E	4,680,300	0	0	4,680,300	10,811,400
F	32,294,200	47,966,400	93,128,100	173,388,700	188,460,400
G	67,840,400	49,844,500	212,355,400	330,040,300	389,266,200
H	42,360,900	1,321,700	362,600	44,045,100	102,562,500
I	73,909,600	77,199,300	255,424,100	406,533,100	447,019,400
J	55,434,200	77,366,800	227,412,700	360,213,700	381,062,600

Source: Author's calculations.

101

FIGURE 8–4
ACCRUED LIABILITY FOR DEMOGRAPHIC GROUP A, USING
VARYING RATES OF DISCOUNT AND MEDICAL INFLATION
(millions of dollars)

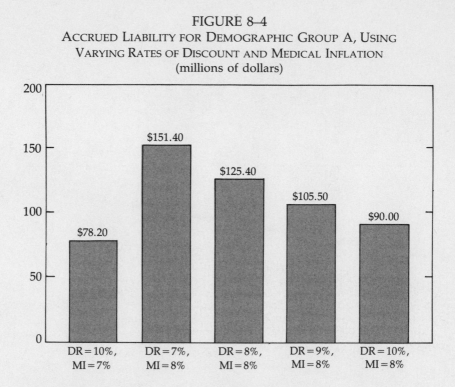

NOTE: DR denotes discount rate and MI denotes medical inflation rate.
SOURCE: Author.

workers. When the accrued expense and liability are estimated for individual companies, five of the ten demographic groups are utilized and matched with companies, as is explained in chapter 9. For the aggregate estimate, however, Group A seems most appropriate because it represents a "normal" company similar to many large companies that sponsor defined benefit pension plans and also, presumably, retiree health benefit plans. Furthermore, Group A has the desirable properties of modest turnover rates and subgroup populations representing a growing company. If another group, such as C, were used, the aggregate estimates of accrued expense and liability would be higher.

An Aggregate Estimate. The calculation of an estimate of the FASB-consistent accrued expense and liability or pay-as-you-go cost at the aggregate level uses the following simple methodology. Group A has 1,588 retirees. An aggregate estimate expands upon the simulation model by multiplying the model's estimate of per retiree accrued expense, liability, or cost for Group A and the estimated number of retired workers covered by health benefit plans offered by all private employers in the

TABLE 8–4

ESTIMATES OF PAY-AS-YOU-GO COSTS, ACCRUED EXPENSE, AND LIABILITY FOR
HEALTH BENEFITS PROVIDED TO RETIREES FOR ALL PRIVATE CORPORATIONS,
1986–1989

	Pay-as-you-go Costs	Accrued Expense	Accrued Liability	Discount Rate	Medical Inflation Rate
		(billions of dollars)		(percentage points)	
1989	12.225	73.096	426.462	8	8
1988	11.320	58.889	332.124	9	8
1987	10.580	52.388	312.841	8	7
1986	9.886	48.950	292.125	8	7

SOURCE: Author's calculations.

domestic economy. For example, assuming that 4 million retired workers
(not including spouses) were covered by retiree health plans, the
simulation model would produce an estimate of aggregate accrued
expense in 1988 of $47.111 billion and pay-as-you-go costs of $9.056
billion. In other words, the simulation model produces per retiree
estimates for accrued expense and pay-as-you-go costs of $11,777.83 (that
is, $18,703,198.50 ÷ 1,588) and $2,263.97 (that is, $3,595,176.89 ÷ 1,588),
respectively and these estimates are multiplied by 4 million.

Table 8–4 shows estimates of the aggregate pay-as-you-go costs,
accrued expense, and liability for the years 1986 through 1989, in current
dollars. The estimates are based on the simulation model using the
demographic Group A, an estimate of 5 million covered retired workers
(an inference based on several surveys described in chapter 6), and
discount and medical inflation rates as indicated in the table.

It is estimated that pay-as-you-go costs of retiree health benefit plans
reached $11.3 billion in 1988. Under the proposed FASB accounting
standard, it is estimated that the accrued liability would have been $332.1
billion in 1988 (approximately 10 percent of the market value of equity
of U.S. corporations) and that expenses for these plans, calculated on an
accrual basis, would have been $58.9 billion in 1988.[12] The increase in
expense under the proposed standard ($58.9 billion less $11.3 billion, or
$47.6 billion) represents about 20 percent of profits in 1988. Accrued
expense and liability rose rapidly in 1989 because of the drop in the
discount rate and a continued high rate of medical inflation.

Aggregate Estimates of Other Analysts. Other analysts have estimated
the accrued liability of the corporate sector for retiree health benefits.

TABLE 8–5

ESTIMATES BY VARIOUS ANALYSTS OF ACCRUED LIABILITY FOR RETIREE HEALTH
BENEFITS FOR ALL PRIVATE CORPORATIONS
(billions of dollars)

Analyst (estimate for year)	Retirees	Actives	Total
Labor, 1983	40.7	57.4	98.1
GAO, 1988	93.0	128.0	221.0
EBRI, 1988	98.0	149.0	247.0
Warshawsky, 1988	145.0	187.1	332.1

SOURCES: Various papers and table 8–4. See citations in endnotes to text.

The first estimate was made by researchers at the Department of Labor.[13] Several assumptions are key to their estimate for 1983. For example, no employees under the age of forty have accrued benefits. The average employer's contribution to retiree health insurance in 1983 was $1,378 per retired worker under the age of sixty-five, and $533 per retired worker over the age of sixty-five. These cost estimates include an amount for spousal coverage: approximately half of the retired workers had spouses covered by their plans. It was estimated that 4.6 million retired workers and 2.3 million spouses were covered by employer-provided plans; of the total 6.9 million plan participants, 4.3 million were above the age of sixty-five and 2.6 million were below the age of sixty-five. The discount rate is assumed to be 8 percent and the rate of health care cost inflation to be 8.5 percent. As shown is in table 8–5, the aggregate liability was estimated to be $98.1 billion in 1983.

The General Accounting Office prepared an estimate of the accrued liability in 1988 by updating and expanding the model used by the Department of Labor.[14] The GAO assumed that 6.6 million retired workers were receiving benefits, while 13.4 million active workers aged forty through sixty-four had retiree health coverage. Retiree health costs for 1988 were assumed to be $2,602 per retired worker under sixty-five and $777 per retired worker above sixty-five. These costs include spousal coverage. The discount rate was assumed to be 7 percent and the rate of medical inflation was assumed to decline from 8.5 percent for 1988 through 2001, to 7.75 percent through 2015, and to 7 percent thereafter. The GAO estimate of accrued liability in 1988 was $221.0 billion.

The Employee Benefits Research Institute (EBRI) also estimated the 1988 accrued liability.[15] EBRI's approach was apparently similar to Labor's and GAO's approaches, and its estimate of $247 billion is largely in line with the other estimates.

Many reasons might explain why the estimate of accrued liability in 1988 produced by the author is significantly larger than the estimates of other analysts. First, a framework explicitly consistent with the FASB standard is used. In particular, all potentially eligible active workers (including those younger than forty) are included in this estimate, although their present values are discounted by the probability of quitting prior to eligibility. Furthermore, all fully eligible active workers (generally those above age fifty-five) are considered as having fully accrued their benefits. Second, a much richer and more accurate set of assumptions about demographic variables is used, including recent estimates of mortality probabilities for group annuitants, probabilities of early retirement, age distributions of active and retired workers, and spousal coverage.

Finally, the per capita costs of retiree health benefits assumed by other analysts seem to be underestimates. As is indicated in the prior section, it is assumed that for an individual aged fifty-five, costs to the employer providing health insurance were $1,500 in 1988; assuming 70 percent spousal coverage produces a cost for fifty-five-year-olds of $2,550. Furthermore, in the simulation model here, costs increase significantly (excluding the downward shift for Medicare) as retirees age. As is noted above, the simulation model produces an average per retiree cost of $2,263.97 in 1988 for Group A. In addition to relying on the sources of information previously cited for the estimate in this book, some data reported by a benefits consultant at least support an estimate of per retiree cost higher than the GAO's estimate. The consultant reported that, based on a sample of about 200 companies, a typical employer's 1988 cost per retiree under sixty-five was $2,400 (close to GAO's assumption of $2,600), while the cost for a retiree over sixty-five was $1,400, significantly higher than the $777 value used by the GAO.[16] Furthermore, the consultant noted that companies with large numbers of employees had higher than average costs.[17]

9

The Economic Burden and
Market Recognition

In this chapter, measures of the accrued expense and liability are estimated for those corporations in a constructed sample indicating that they offer retiree health benefits. The burden for, as well as the characteristics of, the sponsoring corporations in the sample are reported. The chapter then discusses the likely future impact of FASB-imposed disclosure standards on the stock and bond markets, an impact that depends in part on the extent to which the markets have already recognized the retiree health burden.

Estimates of Accrued Expense and Liability for Individual Corporations

Selection of Corporations for the Sample. The process of estimating the accrued expense and liability for retiree health benefits for individual companies began with the construction of a data base of a set of companies selected for analysis. Corporate Text, a McGraw-Hill Compact Disc–Read-only Memory (CD-ROM) product, contains the complete texts of annual reports, 10-Ks, 10-Qs, and proxy statements of more than 2,800 companies—mainly those whose shares are traded on the New York and American Stock Exchanges.[1] From the CD dated November 12, 1990, containing companies currently filing with the SEC, only domestic companies whose shares are (or were) traded on the NYSE or Amex, that are not subsidiaries of other companies, and that filed either an annual report or a 10-K in 1988 or 1989 with the SEC were selected for inclusion in the sample.[2] From the original 2,800 companies on the Corporate Text CD, 2,215 companies remained, satisfying the selection criteria. The companies selected were mainly large and medium-sized firms from a wide variety of industries, but excluding all NASDAQ-listed companies and mutual organizations. A few privately held or reorganizing firms were included in the sample because they still filed statements with the SEC. No liquidated or acquired companies, however, were included in the sample.

The next step in the construction of the sample was the selection of companies whose financial statements would be more closely scrutinized for information about health benefits provided to retirees. This selection entailed viewing the 1987, 1988, or 1989 annual reports or 10-Ks of companies revealed by computerized word searches to contain, in some form, the words retire, health, and benefit or retire, medical, and benefit. Approximately 1,500 companies had statements that contained these words. The notes-to-financial-statement sections of the statements of the designated companies were then examined closely for information relevant to retiree health benefits. Many statements did not have any such information, because the searched-for words appeared in some other context. In the end, only 676 companies could be identified as indicating in their financial statements that they provided health benefits to retired workers.[3]

There was some variability in the way companies reported information about retiree health benefits while remaining within the guidelines of Statement No. 81 of the FASB. Most companies (in the group that indicated they provided such benefits) appended a few lines to the end of the section on pension benefits in the notes to the financial statement, indicating that they did in fact also provide health benefits to retirees. A few companies, however, devoted an entire section to retiree health benefits. Most companies reported the pay-as-you-go costs of benefits to retirees for the current and past two years. Significant minorities, however, either reported total costs of health benefits to retired and active workers (usually combined with information about the numbers of retirees and active workers) or did not report any information about costs. The latter subgroup often justified the lack of information about costs as immaterial, as allowed explicitly in Statement No. 81. The former subgroup often justified the reporting of total costs by citing the lack of a data base distinguishing between active and retired workers.

Some companies also made reference to retiree health benefits in the section of the financial statement outlining significant accounting principles. There they often noted that accounting for retiree health benefits was currently done on a pay-as-you-go (cash) basis, but that the FASB had proposed full accrual accounting as the future standard. In this regard, some companies, the prices of whose products are apparently set by regulatory authorities, noted that even though reported profits would be reduced by the proposed accounting standard, they could expect to recoup the losses by obtaining regulatory approval for increases in prices. A very few companies, in fact, already reported information about retiree health benefits on an accrual basis explicitly consistent with the proposed FASB standard.[4] A few companies also noted retiree health benefits in the section of the statement describing litigation when the company has canceled or significantly reduced benefits and retirees or unions have filed lawsuits seeking reversal of the company action. Many companies, whether in the legal or pension benefits sections of the statement, maintained their right to unilaterally reduce or eliminate retiree health benefits.

Companies are identified on the data base in several ways. The company name, as given on the Corporate Text file, is the primary means of identification. The ticker symbol enables the matching of companies on the data base with information on the Compustat file.[5] Such information includes the companies' standard industrial classification (SIC), profitability, reported net worth, market value, pension expenses, assets, and liabilities. Finally, companies are identified by their Committee on Uniform Security Identification Procedure (CUSIP) code, assigned to any company that has ever issued public securities. Using the CUSIP, the data base can be matched with the Center for Research in Security Prices (CRSP) file, containing histories of daily share prices. Nearly all of the companies can be identified by any of the classification methods.

Variables Included in the Data Base. Based upon perusal of the texts of statements, the following variables were created in the data base. A zero-one variable was established to flag whether the company has indicated in its financial statement that it provides health benefits to retirees. The cost variables are the pay-as-you-go costs (in millions of dollars) for the years 1985 through 1989, if such information was reported, as required by FASB Statement No. 81. For those companies that reported costs for health benefits for all plan participants, active and retired, costs for retiree benefits were estimated by assuming that costs were proportional to the ratio of retiree to active workers in 1988, which was reported for most of the relevant companies. The number of active workers reported by companies as potentially or actually eligible for retiree health benefits will often differ from the number of workers employed by the company, as reported on the Compustat file. The difference arises because foreign workers are almost never covered by company-provided retiree health plans, owing to mandatory participation by many foreign nationals in their government-sponsored national health plans.

There are also zero-one variables for the reporting of relevant legal issues or litigation; for the mention of the proposed FASB standard; for the utilization of some form of accrual, as opposed to cash basis, accounting; for the cancellation or severe reduction of retiree health benefits; and for prefunding.

Accrual accounting by companies in the data base can, and in most cases does take the form of terminal benefit accrual, whereby retiree benefits are recognized as an expense, at their annuity value, when a worker retires. In contrast, the FASB standard requires accrual of expense throughout the working lives of plan participants until they are fully eligible for benefits. Prefunding—done by very few companies—although it entails an implicit recognition of a company's long-term obligation to its retiree health plan, is not necessarily accompanied by any form of accrual accounting, despite the logical connection between the two subjects. Similarly, accrual accounting of any sort is not necessarily (and often is not) accompanied by prefunding. Summary statistics of the variables culled from financial statements of the corporations in the sample and included in the data base are shown in table 9–1.

An indication of the accuracy of the simulation model for aggregate estimates can be inferred from the above statistics. The simulation model estimates that pay-as-you-go costs were $11.3 billion in 1988 for all companies in the private sector (recall table 8–4). According to the statistics reported above, pay-as-you-go costs were $7.7 billion in 1988 for 548 companies. It is not hard to imagine that costs could total another $3.6 billion among the rest of the 105,000 companies in the private sector providing retiree health benefits (according to the GAO survey estimate), particularly when costs for multiemployer plans (not currently reported by companies) are included. It should also be noted that the reported pay-as-you-go costs for only 170 companies in 1985, $3.6 billion, are not much below the cost for *all* private companies estimated by the simulation model of the Department of Labor for 1985—$4.6 billion.[6] This would seem to indicate that the estimates of aggregate costs made by Labor, and hence the estimates of aggregate liability and expense made by Labor and the GAO, are low.

Estimates for Individual Corporations. The next step was the creation of variables representing FASB-consistent estimates of accrued expense and liability for those companies that reported having retiree health benefit plans. To create these variables, companies were first classified into five demographic groups, corresponding to five of the ten representative demographic groups defined by the American Academy of Actuaries (AAA), as described in chapter 8.

More specifically, if the number of active employees over the period 1986 through 1989, as reported on the Compustat file, grew by 10 percent or more, a company was classified as a Normal Group (AAA Group A). If the number of employees grew by more than 2 percent but less than 10 percent, a company was classified as an Older Group with Long

TABLE 9–1
SUMMARY STATISTICS FOR CORPORATIONS IN A CONSTRUCTED SAMPLE, 1985–1989

Number of companies in data base	2,215
Number of companies reporting existence of retiree health benefits plan	676
Pay-as-you-go cost—1989 (499 companies reported cost)	$8.078 billion
Pay-as-you-go cost—1988 (548 companies reported cost)	$7.745 billion
Pay-as-you-go cost—1987 (545 companies reported cost	$6.750 billion
Pay-as-you-go cost—1986 (471 companies reported cost)	$5.686 billion
Pay-as-you-go cost—1985 (170 companies reported cost)	$3.641 billion
Number of companies for whom retiree cost was estimated from total cost for retirees and active workers	66
Number of retirees (81 companies reported retirees)	526,900
Number of active workers (72 companies reported active workers)	1,361,400
Ratio of active workers to retirees (70 companies reported both retirees and active workers)	3⅓ to 1
Per retiree cost of health benefits in 1988 (14 companies reported 1988 retiree costs and number of retirees)	$2,712.39
Number of companies noting legal issues	12
Number of companies noting proposed FASB standard	34
Number of companies using some form of accrual accounting	49
Number of companies eliminating or curtailing severely retiree health benefits	18
Number of companies prefunding benefits	19

SOURCE: Author's calculations.

Service (Group D). If the number of employees declined by less than 2 percent but did not grow by more than 2 percent, the company was classified as a Stable Mature group (Group C). If the number of employees declined by less than 10 percent but not by less than 2 percent, or if the decline was more than 10 percent, the company was classified as a Cyclical Bimodal (Group G) or Old Long Service (Group I) group, respectively. If it was impossible to determine the rate of growth of the number of employees, a company was assigned to Group D.

Although these classification criteria are rather simplistic, it was thought that the rate of growth of the number of employees is correlated in a negative way with the relative proportion of older long-service active workers and retirees among plan participants, and is correlated, although weakly, in a negative way with the probabilities of active workers remaining with the company until eligible for retiree health benefits. Of course, a complete and exact FASB-consistent evaluation, as opposed to an estimate, would require specific information about company demographics and turnover rates.[7]

After companies were classified into demographic groups, accrued expense and liability were estimated, based on the pay-as-you-go cost reported by companies or on the number of employees reported on the Compustat file. More specifically, for the 1988 estimates, the ratios of accrued expense to pay-as-you-go cost simulated using the model were calculated for the five demographic groups and parameters reflecting 1988 economic experience. For companies that reported pay-as-you-go cost in 1988, the reported cost was multiplied by the aforementioned ratio specific to the relevant demographic group, to give an estimate of the FASB-consistent accrued expense for these companies.

A similar exercise using the relevant ratio was done to estimate accrued liabilities. This method of calculating accrued expense and liability is denoted as Method A. For companies that did not report pay-as-you-go cost in 1988, accrued expense (liability) was estimated by multiplying the simulated accrued expense (liability) per active worker in 1988 for the relevant demographic group by the number of employees reported on the Compustat file. This method of calculation is denoted as Method B; it is very similar to the method used to calculate aggregate estimates.

For many reasons, Method A is more likely than Method B to give a more accurate estimate. Because it uses the reported cost, Method A utilizes implicit information specific to the company about per capita health cost and the number of retirees. In contrast, for Method B it is necessary to have a uniform assumption about per capita cost and to use data about the number of active employees that may be biased upwards because of the inclusion of foreign workers.

The estimates of accrued expense and liability for the years 1986, 1987, and 1989 were calculated using Method A if pay-as-you-go costs were reported in those years. If pay-as-you-go costs were not reported by the company in those years, however, as occurred for many more companies than occurred in 1988, then Method B was *not* used. Rather, to ensure consistency with the estimates for 1988, the estimate of the 1986 accrued expense, for example, was calculated by taking the ratio of accrued expense simulated using 1986 economic experience to accrued expense simulated using 1988 economic experience and multiplying this

TABLE 9–2
ESTIMATES OF ACCRUED EXPENSE AND LIABILITY FOR RETIREE HEALTH BENEFITS
FOR CORPORATIONS IN THE SAMPLE, 1986–1989
(billions of dollars)

Year	Sum of Expense	Highest Expense	Sum of Liability	Highest Liability
1989	54.8	4.1	344.5	28.8
1988	42.2	3.4	255.5	23.0
1987	36.1	2.8	231.5	19.9
1986	32.1	2.5	205.9	17.8

SOURCE: Author's calculations.

ratio by the 1988 estimate of accrued expense. Estimates of accrued expense and liability in other years were calculated in a similar fashion.

Summary statistics of the estimates of accrued expense and liability for the 676 companies providing retiree health benefits and hence having nonzero values are shown in table 9–2.

The estimates for individual companies seem consistent with the estimates for the aggregate private sector. For example, in 1988 the sums of accrued expense and liability for companies in the data base were $42 billion and $256 billion, respectively. The comparable estimates for the aggregate private sector were $59 billion and $332 billion. This consistency is especially encouraging because the estimates for the individual companies utilize available information about reported pay-as-you-go cost and the growth (or decline) in the number of employees. It is also worth noting that the sum of estimated 1988 accrued liabilities for only 676 (albeit large) companies exceeds the aggregate liability estimates of the GAO and EBRI for the aggregate private sector.

As is clear from table 9–2, the burden of retiree health benefits varies greatly from company to company. At one extreme are companies that do not provide these benefits; at the other extreme is a company that would have accrued $4.1 billion in expenses in 1989 if the FASB standard had been in place. Naturally the relative burden is attenuated somewhat by consideration of the size and profitability of companies. The relative burden of liabilties for retiree health benefits on reported profits and net worth, their incidence by industry and size of company, and the impact on share prices are discussed further in the next sections.

Characteristics of Firms and Measures of Burden

Some simple sample statistics characterizing corporations in the con-

TABLE 9–3

CHARACTERISTICS OF CORPORATIONS IN THE SAMPLE OFFERING RETIREE HEALTH
BENEFITS, USING YEAR-END 1989 DATA

Characteristic	Offering Retiree Health	Not Offering Retiree Health
Average net worth	$1,675.04 million	$233.71 million
Average market value of equity	$2,951.98 million	$494.38 million
Average number of employees	23,565	4,640
Weighted average price/earnings ratio	14.54	21.37
Average S & P bond rating	A-/BBB+	BB+/BB
Number of corporations in sample	676	1539

SOURCE: Author's calculations, based on constructed sample and Compustat.

structed sample offering retiree health benefits and not offering retiree health benefits are shown in table 9–3. Whether measured by reported net worth, the market value of equity, or the number of employees, corporations offering retiree health benefits are on average significantly larger than corporations not offering the benefits. For example, the market value of equity of a firm offering benefits at year-end 1989 averaged nearly $3 billion, while the value of a firm not offering the benefits averaged about $500 million. In fact, by all measures, firms offering benefits are about five to six times larger than firms not offering benefits. Consistent with their larger size and hence greater stability and perhaps profitability, the lower price/earnings ratio and higher average Standard and Poor's bond rating indicate that the firms offering retiree health benefits are those firms for which the stock market demands a lower rate of return, and which are more sound financially than firms not offering benefits.[8]

The industrial classification, based on one and two digit standard industrial classification codes, of corporations in the constructed sample offering retiree health benefits are shown in table 9–4. While the provision of these benefits is widespread among all industries, certain concentrations are noticeable. In particular, more than half of the companies in the utilities, petroleum refining, primary metal, transportation equipment, and airlines and pipelines industries offer retiree health benefits. By contrast, relatively few companies in the services, retail, wholesale, textiles and apparel, and agriculture and forestry

113

TABLE 9–4
INDUSTRIAL CLASSIFICATION OF CORPORATIONS IN THE SAMPLE OFFERING RETIREE HEALTH BENEFITS

Industry	Corporations Offering Retiree Health	Total in Sample
Agriculture and forestry	1	5
Mining and oil extraction	23	106
Construction	4	24
Food and tobacco	28	62
Textiles and apparel	10	55
Lumber, furniture, and paper	21	64
Publishing	10	38
Chemicals	54	114
Petroleum refining	24	31
Rubber, leather, and stone	24	66
Primary metal	27	45
Fabricated metal	15	48
Industrial machinery (including computers)	51	138
Other electronic equipment	19	121
Transportation equipment	40	71
Instruments	19	71
Miscellaneous	5	35
Transportation (except airlines)	11	25
Airlines and pipelines	15	27
Communications	18	41
Utilities	134	175
Wholesale—durables	6	61
Wholesale—nondurables	7	36
Retail	17	142
Depository institutions	44	123
Other financial (including REITs)	38	308
Services	11	183
Total	676	2,215

SOURCE: Author's calculations.

industries offer the benefits. While it is difficult to ascertain with certainty, it does seem that companies in regulated (either currently or in the past), concentrated, or unionized industries are more likely to offer retiree benefits than companies in highly competitive and unprotected industries. The size and industry characteristics of companies offering retiree benefits reported here are consistent with the characteristics reported in chapter 6 based on other surveys and samples.

TABLE 9–5
RATIOS OF LIABILITY FOR RETIREE HEALTH BENEFITS TO NET WORTH AND MARKET VALUE OF EQUITY FOR CORPORATIONS IN THE SAMPLE OFFERING RETIREE HEALTH BENEFITS, YEAR-END 1989 DATA

	Ratio of Liability	
	To net worth	To market value of equity
Weighted average	.307	.174
Simple average	.382	.488
Maximum	16.504	38.457
Standard deviation	1.175	2.146

SOURCE: Author's calculations and Compustat.

Some sense of the economic burden of offering retiree health benefits can be gained by examining the expense of the benefits relative to reported earnings and the accrued liability relative to the reported net worth or market value of equity. In particular, using year-end 1989 data and the proposed FASB standard for the 676 corporations in the constructed sample offering benefits, the accrued expense for retiree health benefits was calculated and represents nearly 40 percent of reported earnings. The actual reduction in reported earnings of these corporations, owing to the implementation of the FASB standard, will be smaller than 40 percent (in fact, about 30 percent), however, because the current pay-as-you-go cost of the retiree plans will no longer be deducted from earnings.

Other measures of burden are the ratios of the FASB-consistent accrued liability to reported net worth and the market value of equity. As is shown in table 9–5, the weighted average of the ratio of liability to net worth, using year-end 1989 data, is over 30 percent, while the ratio of liability to market value of equity is about 17.5 percent. As is indicated by the simple average and by maximum measures calculated using the distributions of these ratios, the burdens for some companies exceed significantly the typical burden represented by the weighted average.

As is explained in chapter 5, reported net worth will not necessarily be reduced immediately by the entire accrued liability disclosed under the proposed FASB standard. The liability can be amortized over a twenty-year period, and hence net worth will become gradually smaller than it would otherwise have been without the FASB standard, because of the steady reduction in earnings caused by increased accrued expense. Those companies opting for an immediate recognition of the liability, however, will experience a more sizable and noticeable reduction in reported net worth. Whether share prices or bond ratings will be depressed upon the realization of the burden of retiree health benefits in financial statements is examined in the next two sections.

The Impact on Stock Market Valuation

While only one other academician, Julia Grant, has begun to study the impact of the provision of retiree health benefits on stock market valuation, professors of economics, finance, and accounting have already studied rather extensively the impact of unfunded pension liabilities.[9] These pension studies give considerable guidance to the approach taken here for examining the impact of retiree health benefits because of the strong similarities between the two subjects. In particular, pensions and retiree health benefits both have been subject to years of evolution in accounting standards and practices and hence in the extent of investor knowledge and awareness. Both pensions and retiree health benefits also represent types of deferred compensation, albeit with differing levels of legal obligation of the firm to pay benefits. More generally, the pension studies represent intelligent and careful attempts at understanding the way in which the values of firms are determined in the stock market.

Pension Studies. One of the first studies to examine the impact of unfunded pension obligations on share prices was done by Martin Feldstein and Stephanie Seligman.[10] They analyzed data for some 200 large manufacturing firms for 1976 and 1977. Feldstein and Seligman posited a valuation model where the market value of equity for a firm depended as follows: positively on the growth rate of earnings; positively on expenditures on research and development; positively on the riskiness of the firm's stream of earnings; in an indeterminate way on the riskiness of its capital structure; and negatively on unfunded vested pension obligations.

All variables were divided by the value of the firm's tangible assets, minus debt and preferred stock, so as to standardize the variables for the size of the firm and to reduce certain econometric problems. Feldstein and Seligman found that the coefficient on the pension variable was generally larger in absolute value than negative one—indicating that the market reduced, by some multiple greater than one, the value of a firm's equity by the amount of the reported unfunded vested pension obligation. Feldstein and Seligman attributed the fact that the estimated coefficient was larger in absolute value than the expected negative one to the market's apparent belief that the accounting data for pension obligations then available (prior to further significant refinements by the

FASB) understated the true extent of a firm's obligation to provide pension benefits.

A later study by Wayne Landsman differed from the approach taken by Feldstein and Seligman in four ways.[11] First, the Landsman study focused on the separate effects that pension assets and pension liabilities have upon the market value of equity. Second, Landsman employed a simpler valuation model; in particular, the value of equity was based simply on the residual of the reported value of corporate assets minus corporate liabilities. Third, certain econometric problems were more carefully treated, and an alternate measure of pension liability was investigated. Fourth, the size of the sample of companies examined was increased to some 600 firms, and more recent data, for the years 1979, 1980, and 1981, were used. Landsman concluded that the stock market prices pension fund assets and liabilities in the same way and with the same emphasis as corporate assets and liabilities. Landsman found that generally the coefficients on the pension asset and liability variables were around one and negative one, respectively, as expected. Landsman indicated some doubt, however, about his excessively simple specification of a valuation model.

The Valuation Model. Following Feldstein and Seligman, Grant uses a valuation model in which the market value of the firm is equal to the replacement cost of the assets multiplied by a factor, q, to study the impact of the existence of retiree health benefits on the valuation of the firm's equity. She uses a rather small sample of about sixty companies reporting the cost of providing retiree health benefits. Professor Fred Mittelstaedt and the author, in turn, follow Feldstein and Seligman and Grant. We employ, however, alternate measures of the firm's obligation for retiree health benefits and a much larger and more recent sample of companies offering and not offering retiree health benefits, as is explained below.

Following Feldstein and Seligman, the market value of the firm's total assets is represented by MVA, and the replacement cost of the physical (tangible) assets is MVT. Then

$$MVA = q(MVT)$$

and

$$q = MVA/MVT$$

In general it is thought that for most firms q will exceed one, because of the existence of some intangible assets, such as market power, owing to patents, market concentration, unique factors of production, advertising, and other factors.

The market value of the firm's equity, represented by MVE, equals MVA minus its liabilities, denoted by MVL. Hence

$$MVE = q(MVT) - MVL$$

Again following Feldstein and Seligman and Grant, in the empirical estimation of the model, q is a function of growth, research and development, advertising, and risk.

Following Landsman, the market value of equity is the simple subtraction of the market value of liabilities from the market value of assets. Hence

$$MVE = MVA - MVL$$

Because the focus of Landsman's study is the valuation of pension assets and liabilities, he includes these assets and liabilities as separate variables in the estimated equation.

The market value of the firm's liabilities following both the Feldstein and Seligman and the Landsman approaches includes short-term and long-term debt liabilities, taxes and accounts payable, pension liabilities, and measures of the firm's obligation for retiree health benefits. Like Grant, we use the reported pay-as-you-go cost for retiree benefits as a proxy of the firm's obligation. If the market were fully aware of the extent of the firm's obligation for retiree benefits, the coefficient on the cost variable would indicate the multiple used to calculate the relevant liability of the firm. If the simulation model for estimating the liability explained in chapter 8 is correct, the coefficient will be around negative thirty, plus or minus ten.

We also use the measures of FASB-consistent accrued expense and liability, constructed for this book and explained earlier in this chapter, as more direct proxies of the firm's obligation. If the accrued liability measure is accurate and the market is fully aware of the extent of the firm's obligation for retiree health benefits, the coefficient on the health liability in the equation will be negative one. If, however, the market is not fully aware of firms' obligations, or if it believes that companies can reduce or cancel their retiree health plans at will, then the coefficient will be closer to zero. Finally, the market may believe that government action of some sort will be taken or wages of current workers can be decreased to reduce the size of companies' net obligations for current and deferred compensation.

Empirical Evidence. The dependent variable in the equations is the market value of equity as of the general date of issuance of annual statements for the proceeding year. In particular, market values were measured on April 15, 1987, on April 14, 1988, and on April 13, 1989.

TABLE 9–6
The Estimated Impact on the Market Value of Equity of Corporations with and without Retiree Health Benefits, 1986–1988

	Estimated Coefficient (t value in parentheses)					
	Reported cost			Accrued liability		
Variable	1986	1987	1988	1986	1987	1988
Intercept	1.58	1.09	1.19	1.58	1.09	1.18
	(11.76)	(11.54)	(9.36)	(11.78)	(11.51)	(9.35)
Research &	3.82	4.46	1.34	3.78	4.42	1.30
development	(1.70)	(4.07)	(1.25)	(1.69)	(4.05)	(1.23)
Advertising	3.60	3.63	3.40	3.63	3.64	3.42
	(1.80)	(2.19)	(2.08)	(1.81)	(2.21)	(2.11)
Growth	1.28	0.89	0.33	1.29	0.90	0.34
	(3.77)	(5.00)	(2.12)	(3.78)	(5.03)	(2.16)
Risk	.04	.01	.08	.05	.01	.08
	(0.46)	(0.19)	(2.37)	(0.63)	(0.18)	(2.37)
Book value	–1.58	–1.08	–0.84	–1.59	–1.08	–0.84
liabilities	(8.60)	(11.19)	(6.99)	(8.56)	(11.14)	(6.99)
Net pension	1.13	0.71	0.58	1.13	0.71	0.61
assets	(1.86)	(1.91)	(1.34)	(1.90)	(1.93)	(1.40)
Reported cost	–22.80	–13.90	–14.32	—	—	—
	(3.66)	(3.16)	(4.32)			
Accrued liability	—	—	—	–0.76	–0.39	–0.46
				(3.53)	(3.18)	(4.31)
Number of observations	440	461	484	440	461	484
Adjusted R^2	.45	.48	.41	.45	.48	.41

Note: Coefficients on industry dummy variables are not shown.
Source: H. F. Mittelstaedt and M. Warshawsky, working paper, table VI.

Because pension variables are not found in the Compustat file for most companies in the utilities and banking industries, empirical estimation is done using only those companies in the manufacturing industries. In addition, many companies are dropped because necessary information about variables, such as advertising and research and development, is not reported. Most of the variables in the equations are standardized by sales or by the book value of tangible assets, so as to reduce the influence of certain statistical problems.

Table 9–6 shows the results for the Feldstein and Seligman and Grant approach. (The Landsman approach is not shown, as the results are largely the same.) Separate equations are estimated for the two measures of obligation for retiree health benefits, reported pay-as-you-go cost, and estimated accrued liability. As is shown in the first three columns of table 9–6, the coefficients on the cost variable are significant but are somewhat below the expected order of magnitude; that is, instead of being approximately negative thirty, the coefficients hover around negative sixteen. The size of these coefficients is broadly similar to the coefficients estimated by Grant. The coefficients on the accrued liability variable, shown in the last three columns of table 9–6, are also significant; but at values of approximately negative one-half, they are somewhat larger (smaller in absolute value) than the expected value of negative one. The coefficients on the other variables are largely in line with expectations.

Perhaps the most surprising result of the estimation is the uniform fact that the coefficients moved away from expected values over the period from April 1987 through April 1989. This movement is somewhat surprising in light of the increased attention in the general and financial press to the subject of retiree health benefits, in general, and to the release of the FASB proposed accounting standard in February 1989, in particular.[12] The movement away from expected values may owe to the passage of the Medicare Catastrophic Care Act in 1988 and the concomitant reduction in the size of corporate obligations for retiree health benefits. Medicare Catastrophic was repealed in October 1989. Because the repeal was viewed as somewhat surprising, however, the stock market from 1987 through summer 1989 had probably grown increasingly sure that the legislated Medicare benefits would indeed be implemented. Estimation of the equations using 1990 stock market values awaits the completion of the data base using 1989 financial statements.[13]

A summary statement of the empirical results obtained so far is that although the stock market is certainly aware of the existence of the corporate obligation for retiree health benefits, some partial and preliminary evidence suggests that the recognition is not entirely complete. The lack of full recognition may owe to the market's anticipation of lower medical costs, to curtailment of benefits by corporate sponsors, to government intervention, to reduction of wages and benefits of current workers, to a lack of full knowledge, or to some combination of these five reasons.

The Impact on the Credit Market

The main reason for interest in the reaction of the market to the reporting of liabilities for retiree health benefits is that the cost of capital might increase for those companies with significant obligations. This increase in the cost of capital would be a good thing in the long run, because the allocation of scarce investment resources would be improved as a result of more accurate information about companies' true profitability and level of liabilities. In the short run, however, some companies might experience considerable difficulties in obtaining capital, and problems of transition to a new equilibrium would arise. The concern about an increase in the cost of capital is appropriate in the case of the stock market, to the extent that the market has not yet fully recognized the magnitude of firms' obligations, and that companies rely on the stock market as a significant source of financing operations. The concern may be even more appropriate in the case of the credit (bond and loan) market, because the credit market certainly is the prime if not the only source of external financing for many companies. Furthermore, it may be that the credit market has not yet and may not in the future fully adjust to the magnitude of the companies' obligations for retiree health benefits.

On September 11, 1989, Standard and Poor's (S & P), a major credit-rating agency, took the highly unusual step of publicly announcing its fundamental disagreement with the FASB on the subject of retiree medical liabilities. In particular, S & P announced that it would effectively ignore the proposed disclosures under the proposed FASB standard.[14] S & P supported its decision as follows:

> . . . S & P believes that the proposed disclosures, despite the conceptual appeal, would be of limited value in assessing the impact on credit quality. First, quantifying the obligation and related expense would require the same types of highly uncertain assumptions about employee turnover, retirement age, mortality, dependency status, and appropriate discount rate that are used in pension accounting. Second, the proposed method would require additional, speculative assumptions about anticipated changes in health-care costs, taking into account health-care inflation, changes in health-care utilization or delivery patterns, technological advances, and changes in the health status of plan participants.
>
> In addition, FASB excludes from consideration a company's potential cost-cutting efforts and changes in government funding of health care, both of which could have an important effect on future cash requirements. In the most extreme cases, the FASB approach could result in material changes to financial statements, reducing reported and operating earnings and giving rise to liabilities that could dwarf other financial liabilities on the balance sheet. Moreover, reported liability and expense amounts would be very sensitive to the underlying assumptions, and credit comparisons between companies would be extremely difficult.
>
> Accordingly, if the proposed exposure draft is adopted, S & P may make analytical adjustments to reported financial statements.

S & P's approach for debt rating purposes will be to focus on current cash outlays and view them as a component of cost position.

S & P seems to be taking the position that retiree health benefits are not deferred compensation but a gratuity that can be amended or canceled at will by the sponsoring company. To the extent that this position is incorrect and the position of the FASB is correct, the credit ratings of companies with significant retiree health obligations are (and will be) too high; to the extent that creditors (particularly bond investors) are influenced only by credit ratings, the cost of capital to these companies is (and will be) too low. Those creditors who place a heavy weight on companies' credit ratings will therefore continue to be uninformed and will be unpleasantly surprised about the extent of obligations for retiree health benefits should companies begin to get into trouble. Evidence suggests, however, that at least some creditors look beyond credit ratings to stock market prices, accounting, and other information. To the extent that these creditors are not currently aware of the magnitude of firms' obligations for retiree health benefits, the new disclosure required by the FASB might lead to a higher cost of capital through credit for some companies.

10
Policies and Politics

The most recent major attempt by Congress to deal with the general issue of retiree health benefits, the Medicare Catastrophic Care Act of 1988, is described at the beginning of this chapter. It emphasizes some of the difficult political problems that Congress faced, explaining why Congress was forced to repeal the program, and outlining some of the political constraints that policy makers in the area of retiree health benefits must consider. The inability of the recently impaneled Coal Commission to reach a consensus on solving the financial problems of the multiemployer health plans in the coal industry offers another example of the difficulties faced when dealing with the issue of retiree health benefits in the context of a specific industry. The chapter then continues with a focus on desirable policy goals and possible policy options—the status quo and "ERISA-fication"—for solving some of the problems arising from employers' provision of retiree health benefits.

The Medicare Catastrophic Coverage Act of 1988

Congress designed and passed the Medicare Catastrophic Coverage Act of 1988 (MCCA), reversing a trend of effectively reducing Medicare benefits. The action was taken with great fanfare, and in close cooperation with the Reagan administration and the American Association of Retired Persons. And with a sense of political panic, against a background of unprecedented opposition by the elderly and of only weak support from the Bush administration, Congress repealed the MCCA in 1989. The MCCA would have filled in some, but not all of the major gaps existing in Medicare coverage. Senior citizens, particularly those with high levels of income, would have picked up the entire bill in the form of higher Medicare premiums.[1]

Provisions of the MCCA. Beginning in 1989, the MCCA would have provided full coverage of hospitalization by Medicare instead of the current schedule of coverage with increasing copayments based on the patient's length of stay. There would have been only one deductible per hospitalization annually, instead of a deductible for each spell of illness. In some sense these changes passed along to the patient the cost savings received by Medicare when it introduced the Diagnostic Related Group method of payment to hospitals in 1983. Incentives for cost control presumably were no longer needed at the patient level because they were being applied at the hospital level. Coverage of various types of care, such as home health and skilled nursing facilities, would also have been expanded.

Beginning in 1990, MCCA would have given full coverage, instead of 80 percent coverage, to SMI expenditures when copayments reached $1,370 per year. Coverage for respite care, home intravenous therapy, and biannual mammography screening would also have been provided. Finally, beginning in 1991 outpatient prescription drugs would have been partially covered by Medicare after payment of an indexed deductible starting at $550 in 1991, separate from the HI and SMI deductibles. After the deductible had been met, coinsurance of 50 percent in 1991, 40 percent in 1992, and 20 percent thereafter would have been required.

In a unique and ultimately unsuccessful departure from past congressional practice for financing new or expanded government programs, the improved Medicare benefits would have been financed entirely by the class of recipients of the benefits. Moreover, the schedule of financing was as progressive as the income tax schedule, hitting high-income retirees with premiums significantly higher than those to be incurred by low-income retirees. In particular, the SMI premium was to be increased somewhat for all Medicare beneficiaries. In addition, a premium was to be assessed based on the federal tax liability of Medicare-eligible individuals with a tax liability in excess of $150. The additional premium would have been "approximately" 15 percent of the individual's federal tax liability, up to a maximum of $800 per individual. The Health Care Financing Administration (HCFA) indicated an approximate tax rate because, according to the MCCA, the costs of the catastrophic care and drug program, which were subject to some considerable uncertainty of estimation, had to be financed entirely from increased premium payments. Unlike earlier expansions of the Medicare program, in the MCCA there was to be no call, even indirect and after-the-fact, on general federal revenues.

Maintenance-of-Effort Payments by Employers. Congress recognized that the MCCA would duplicate coverage already provided by employers to millions of retirees in the form of retiree health benefit plans. In order to prevent a complete windfall to employers and to ameliorate somewhat the higher Medicare premiums required of retirees, a maintenance-of-effort (MOE) amendment was added to the MCCA. Under MOE every employer, except the federal government and multiemployer plans, providing retiree health benefits was to be required to provide additional benefits equal to the value of the duplicative benefits, or to refund the actuarial value of the duplicative benefits. MOE required this refund, however, only in 1989 and 1990, and only for the value of duplicative benefits in those years as determined by HCFA. In other words, no refund of the actuarial present value of future duplicative benefits was required, and no refund for the value of drug benefits, the most significant value in the MCCA, was required. HCFA announced that the MOE payment in 1989 was to be only $65. Hence, while reasonable in concept, MOE was not particularly significant in practice for retirees. For employers, on the other hand, MOE in combination with the MCCA more generally promised a significant reduction in costs for retiree health benefit plans.

Opposition by the Elderly. Owing to its reliance on the tax schedule as the method of calculating the increase in premiums and its replication of benefits provided by many employers, the MCCA caused a severe skewedness in expected benefits and costs. While every Medicare enrollee could expect the same actuarial value of benefits, those with higher incomes would with certainty pay significantly higher premiums than those with lower incomes. In addition, because these same high income individuals are more likely to have free or subsidized retiree health plans from their former employers, many individuals did not feel that the improvements in Medicare coverage owing to the MCCA offered them much beyond what they already had from retiree health benefit plans. And while satisfactory in concept, the maintenance-of-effort payments required of employers were quite small and short-lived. Hence these individuals, joined by other senior citizens who were confused about the extent of the increased premiums they would have to pay, were quite vociferous in their protests to Congress, opposing the MCCA.

While it is easy to understand why many retirees would be opposed to the MCCA, it is more difficult to understand why employers were not more outspoken in favor of the MCCA. It is likely that concerns about public relations played a part; it is hard to support something, even if it benefits you, if influential others are strongly opposed to it. Another cause for the stance of employers was probably the concern that MOE represented a Trojan horse. It is true that MOE in practice would not cost employers very much and the MCCA would have saved significant amounts. Establishment of the principle in law that retiree health plans were in essence obligations of employers, however, was no doubt unpopular with many employers—particularly in light of some court decisions in 1988 allowing employers to amend or cancel plans precisely because the judges could find no instance of an expression by Congress that retiree health benefits were status benefits (see chapter 4). Furthermore, although MOE would not cost employers much in 1988 and 1989 and did not require payments beyond 1990, a prudent employer could not be assured that Congress would not eventually require future, more significant payments.

Hence, in the face of strong opposition and with no significant support, Congress repealed the MCCA in 1989. Although as a complex piece of legislation drawn up over a period of nearly three years, the act no doubt represented tens of thousands of man-days of drafting effort, administrative preparation, and political negotiations, and although the repeal came at a cost to some political reputations, Congress decided to scrap the entire project. It is reported that some damage to Congress' future willingness to tackle difficult questions related to retirees and health benefits has occurred owing to the entire MCCA episode. In this regard, it appears that the rejection by the House of Representatives of the October 1990 budget agreement between President Bush and the congressional leadership was motivated, in part, by objections from retirees to cuts in the Medicare program and increases in deductibles and premiums, similar to the objections raised in the MCCA catastrophe.

The Coal Commission Report

As is mentioned at the end of chapter 7, one of the conditions for the resolution of the bitter strike by the United Mine Workers against the Pittston Coal Company was the establishment of a national Coal Commission to suggest a solution to the deteriorating financial condition of the industry's multiemployer health plans. Headed by W. J. Usery, Jr., the commission issued its report on November 5, 1990.[2] Although there was agreement on the causes of the problems of the plans and on the fact that miners are entitled to lifetime health benefits, there was strong disagreement among the members of the commission on the methods to be used to solve those problems.

All the members of the commission agreed that the growing deficit of the multiemployer health plans could be attributed to a combination of three factors. First, health care costs have increased rapidly in recent years. Because these costs are overlaid on plans generous in terms of benefit provisions and coverage, the cost per retiree in 1989, $5,714, is higher than in most industries. (Recall the discussion in chapter 8, where the average cost per retiree in 1988 is assumed to be $2,264.) Second, much of the aggregate cost is attributable to "orphaned" retirees whose companies have gone out of business or ceased paying for benefits. In fact, more than half of the plans' population are such orphans. The benefit plans have been extremely unlucky in the outcomes of court cases, such as *Royal Coal*, cited in chapter 4, where still-operating companies not signatory to current Wage Agreements were allowed to escape their obligations to contribute to the plans. Third, the shrinking percentage of industry still signatory to the Wage Agreements is increasingly unwilling to increase their plan contributions to make up for what they view as an industry-wide problem.

Most of the members of the Coal Commission were able to agree on some steps to take to temporarily fix, or at least prevent the worsening of the problems of the health plans. It was agreed that mechanisms should be enacted to prevent future dumping of obligations on the plans. The commission supported statutory authority for the parties to use excess pension assets to reduce existing deficits of the health plans. The implementation of managed care and cost containment activities was also supported.

Strong disagreement among commission members existed, however, about the extent of the financial responsibility of past signatories and other coal producers to pay for health benefits of retirees who have no company to provide such benefits. The majority of the commission supported the statutory imposition of a contribution obligation on past signatories, reaching back to the signatory class of 1978. There was also support for an industry-wide fee that "applies to all employers in the coal business, including a fee on imported coal." A minority of the commission, however, believed that only current signatories should be required to pay for retiree benefits.

In essence, the disagreement among commission members was a philosophical one. Everyone agreed that "reprehensible practices as regards successorship exist in this industry. Thinly capitalized operators, often the sham invention of larger firms, come and go in a fashion that appears to exist only to avoid the risk of being held as a party to the collectively bargained agreement regarding pension and welfare benefits."[3] The majority apparently believed that these practices implied moral as well as practical reasons to hold past signatories in particular and the entire industry more generally responsible for orphan retirees. The minority, however, held the legalistic view that "operators who made decisions in the past to move to different locales, invest in different technology, or pursue their business with or without respect to union presence must be recognized," and " . . . there are many companies who, for very valid strategic or economic reasons and using entirely legitimate means, have withdrawn from the Union and, at least according to the courts today, from their obligations" to the plans.

It is unclear what the next step will be in this area. In the minority view, the dynamic of the collective bargaining process should operate undisturbed by the intervention of the federal government. When negotiations on the 1993 Wage Agreements begin, the parties will have to deal with the bankrupt multiemployer health plans. If the signatory employers do not agree to increased contributions or the union does not agree to a cut in benefits, a strike will almost certainly result. In the majority view, the intervention of the federal government is required, particularly to impose the cost of promised benefits on past signatories.

Policy Goals for Market Failures and Welfare Concerns

Five major policy goals should be considered in any discussion of appropriate policy responses to the problems of health care generally and employer-sponsored retiree health care more particularly.

No Illusory Promises. First, in line with the major goal embodied in ERISA for pension plans, promises of retiree health benefits should not be "illusory and nugatory." That is, a retiree should be able to count on an employer's promise to provide health benefits, even in the event the former employer later becomes bankrupt or sells his business to another company. At the same time, the employer's promise should be realistic and well within his means to fulfill. More specifically, a requirement to prefund benefit promises would force employers and employees to focus on the nature and value of benefits being given, leading to greater realism in the negotiation and contracting process.

Balance between Access and Containment of Cost. The second major policy goal should be an appropriate balance between access to adequate and fairly priced health care and the containment of health care costs. In the case of health benefits provided to retirees below age sixty-five, the appropriate balance would probably dictate the encouragement of employer-provided plans. Because early retirees are not eligible for Medicare, in the absence of employer-provided coverage they must purchase coverage in the private market. Most major insurance companies have left the market for individual health insurance policies over the years because of the difficulties they faced in earning adequate profits. Often those companies and Blue Cross–Blue Shield organizations remaining in the market offer policies with very large deductibles and very high premiums only after a physical examination or questionnaire assures the insurance company that the applicant has no preexisting medical conditions. In addition, it is reasonable to strongly encourage the employer to provide the early retiree with health insurance as a way of making the employer incur the costs of early retirement more generally at a time when the population is aging.

The balance of considerations in the case of retirees eligible for Medicare is less clear. On the one hand, it is certain that Medicare coverage is incomplete, creating a demand for private Medigap policies and employer-provided plans and eventually leading to the short-lived Medicare Catastrophic Coverage Act. On the other hand, it is also fairly certain that health care costs rise in the presence of overinsurance. It is possible that the existence of policies and plans supplementing Medicare vitiates any cost containment features enacted by Medicare to the detriment of all health care consumers, particularly the elderly. Hence if the provision of employer-sponsored health plans to retirees above age sixty-five is to be encouraged, careful consideration must be paid to the cost containment features of plans and their interaction with Medicare. It should be stated, however, that as the federal government continues to try to control the growth of Medicare expenditures and coverage, the case for encouraging health plans provided by employers to retirees above age sixty-five is somewhat strengthened.

Internal Consistency and Equity in the Tax Code. The third major policy goal may be called "tax equity and consistency." Although, willy-nilly, the tax code is an expression of political preferences and broad national goals, the code must also reflect concerns for equity among people and industries and must be internally consistent. In the case of health benefits provided by employers, the political preference is currently too clear in the fact that the receipt of health benefits from a current or former employer is not considered taxable income to a household and is a deductible expense to an employer. Even other "favored" items in the tax code, such as pension and some social security benefits, are eventually partially taxed as income to the recipient household.

Furthermore, individuals who do not receive health benefits from current or former employers and who must purchase private individual policies receive little tax credit or preference for their purchase of insurance. Hence these individuals implicitly subsidize individuals receiving health insurance through their employers. Because the provision of health benefits through employers is favored, the health care industry, including physicians and hospitals, also becomes generally favored. Especially in light of the concern that overinsurance might lead to rising health care costs, the extremely favorable tax treatment to households receiving health benefits from employers might be questioned. This concern for equity and consistency in the tax code would be magnified if companies were given tax incentives to prefund retiree health benefits similar to pension benefits so as to strengthen the security

129

of retiree health plans, but the exclusion of the value of health benefits from taxable income for those receiving retiree health benefits remained.

Do Not Worsen Federal Budget Deficit. The fourth policy goal would be that any policy response should not worsen the already sizable budget deficit of the federal government.

Minimize Government Regulation and Intervention. The final policy goal is to ensure that the retiree health benefits be free of government regulation and intervention to the maximum extent possible. For example, any policy response should endeavor to avoid a major criticism of ERISA, particularly in the case of defined benefit pension plans—namely, that it introduced extensive and expensive regulation by several government agencies. In particular, some flexibility should be allowed for the design of new types of coverage to respond to changes in the health care market. It should be mentioned, however, that the complete absence of government regulation can also lead to sometimes erratic and inefficient intervention in the form of appeals to the court system for the adjudication of grievances and disputes. Moreover, current inefficiencies in the delivery of health care, especially in the face of an aging population, will eventually have to be addressed.

It is my belief that any proposals for legislation or regulation in the area of retiree health benefits must be assessed in the light of their effectiveness in achieving the five policy goals listed here.

Policy Options

Two major categories of policy options are available concerning the issue of retiree health benefits: the status quo and "ERISA-fication."[4] The options are listed in the order of increasing degree of governmental intervention. Each option has strengths and weaknesses vis-à-vis the policy goals enumerated in the previous section and also in terms of political viability.

The Status Quo. Under the status quo option, no changes would be made either in the laws or regulations pertaining directly to retiree health benefits. The current framework would be kept for the foreseeable future exactly as it exists today.

Although no changes would be made in the legal framework, changes by employers in the provision of retiree health benefits would nevertheless be likely. As a result of the implementation of the FASB accounting standard, the significance of employers' obligations for retiree health benefits will be highlighted, and the underestimate of the costs entailed by employers will be manifest to managers, investors, and workers. Even without the not-so-unlikely bankruptcy in a severe recession of any of the major providers of retiree health benefits, the resulting publicity engendered by the accounting standard will likely lead to increasing concern about the security and permanence of these benefits. This concern will in turn probably cause employees, particularly those represented by unions, to demand prefunding of the benefit obligation.

Pressures for change will also arise from creditors and shareholders. In addition to the accounting standard and despite the stance of the credit rating agencies, the creation of a priority to retiree health benefits resulting from the Retiree Benefits Bankruptcy Protection Act of 1988 causes creditors to be concerned about their exposure to the obligation for retiree health benefits. Pressures will therefore arise from creditors on companies either to reduce or to cancel retiree health benefits, or to prefund the obligation fully. Shareholders will also react to the extent that share prices do not currently fully reflect companies' obligations for retiree health benefits. Shareholders might demand the cancellation or severe reduction of retiree health plans.[5]

Companies' responses to the pressures described above will differ depending on their profitability, the degree of unionization of the work force, the funding status of the defined benefit pension plan, and the firmness of the companies' commitment to provide retiree health benefits as reflected in plan documents and past practices. If the company is in difficult financial straits and its work force is not unionized, it might try to cancel its retiree health plan. In the event that the relevant plan documents do not allow the complete cancellation of the plan, however, some attempt at a reduction in benefits will be made. Even this step might risk a lawsuit, but the company should be able to prevail in the current legal environment, particularly if it can show need. In addition to increased cost sharing, companies seeking to reduce benefits might make eligibility criteria stricter or replace high-cost defined benefit health plans with lower-cost defined contribution plans.

If the company is profitable and its work force is unionized or is highly sensitive to unilateral changes made by the employer, it will begin prefunding the currently constituted retiree health plan. In general, a VEBA account is inferior, in terms of tax benefits, to a 401(h) account. If, however, the company's pension plan is overfunded and it chooses not to avail itself of the option to transfer excess pension assets, a VEBA account is the only tax-favored method of prefunding currently available.[6] If the company is only modestly profitable, its work force is not unionized, and the plan documents seem to give some latitude for cancelling benefits, then the preponderance of pressures might lead

131

either to cancellation or to reduction of retiree health benefits. If plan documents do not leave room for change, however, the company has no choice but to muddle through with a pay-as-you-go approach to funding.

In summary, there will be a trifurcation of companies offering retiree health benefits. Some companies will cancel or severely reduce the benefits outright. Profitable companies will begin prefunding the benefits. A relatively less profitable company with a unionized work force or an unfortunately worded plan document will continue to muddle through with a pay-as-you-go approach, either until the company's fortunes improve enough to begin prefunding or the company enters tough times and eventual bankruptcy.

The likely scenario described above resulting from the status quo option scores only moderately well in terms of the policy goals enumerated in the previous section. Clearly the security of the benefit obligation is not affirmed for many workers under this option. Although costly and uncertain litigation is likely to continue, some retirees, including those below age sixty-five who most clearly need employer-provided health coverage, will lose benefits entirely. Employees of highly profitable companies will gain security of benefits. This security, however, comes at the expense of other taxpayers because of the significant subsidization implicit in any scheme of prefunding combined with no taxation of benefits received. Moreover, utilization of 401(h) accounts and, to a lesser extent, of VEBA accounts means the eventual loss of revenues to the federal government. The clearness and permanence of employers' promises for retiree health benefits will continue to be compromised. The status quo option, however, does score high in inducing economies in the purchase of health care, as benefits and coverage are reduced or eliminated, and in terms of the minimization of governmental interference.

The political feasibility of the status quo option is questionable. Although it has the considerable advantage of "do nothing" inertia, this option is actually highly unstable. In the not unlikely event of the bankruptcy of a major corporation offering retiree health benefits or the cancellation of an important plan, the political pressures on Congress to preserve retiree benefits would be significant, particularly in light of the political pressures felt by Congress in the MCCA and in the October 1990 budget agreement incidents. Because a "catastrophic" event is not out of the realm of possibility, more enlightened interests will likely seek an early and more considered response to the issue of retiree health benefits than would be possible after such an event.

ERISA-fication. ERISA-fication of retiree health benefit plans entails the construction of a legislative and regulatory edifice similar to the laws and regulations that surround the private pension system as a result of the Employee Retirement Income Security Act of 1974 (ERISA).[7] The unique character of health benefits, however, will need to be taken into account in any ERISA-fication, as well as the experience gained, and lessons learned, from the history of the application of ERISA.

In brief, ERISA imposes many fairly stringent and complex standards on private pension plans by invoking a threat that the deductibility from taxes of employer contributions for the pension plan could be removed. In this way, it imposes a minimum level of fairness within a company in the crediting of pension benefits through the mandate of minimum participation, coverage, and vesting standards. Discrimination in favor of highly compensated employees is limited, as are the maximum benefits payable. ERISA mandates minimum funding requirements, establishes the Pension Benefit Guaranty Corporation (PBGC) program insuring vested pension benefits, and requires trustees of pension funds to manage assets solely in the interest of participants and beneficiaries. As part of the determination of minimum (and maximum) funding requirements, several definitions of the pension liability have been given in the ERISA code and attendant regulations.

Many of ERISA's requirements translate very naturally to retiree health plans. In particular, in light of the FASB's definition of the employer's liability for retiree health benefits, a natural goal for mandatory full funding is established. Annual deductible contributions to the retiree health fund could equal the expense of the plan, as is established by the FASB. Using the FASB definition of liability would also have several considerable administrative advantages over past and current pension practices. Under ERISA, several definitions of pension liability are allowed, independent of the definition used in annual statements reported to shareholders.[8]

By establishing a single definition for retiree health liability, the sponsors' administrative costs would be reduced. Sponsors would also be prevented from gaming the tax system by clever choices of actuarial methods and assumptions to minimize or maximize contributions to the health fund. By using the FASB definition of liability, the need for government oversight and auditing would be reduced by relying on the objectivity and analytical ability of public accountants and participants in the credit and stock markets. The need for burdensome form filing would also be effectively reduced.

An alternative, less burdensome goal for funding could be the liability for fully eligible and retired workers—that is, in FASB terminology, the minimum liability. With a fully funded minimum liability, the security of health benefits would be ensured for those most vulnerable to loss by virtue of their imminent or actual detachment from the work force. Although the accrued benefits of younger active workers would not be secured, it may be thought that fully funding the total accrued liability would be too heavy a burden to impose on employers, especially because at present little or no prefunding of benefit obligations exists. Another disadvantage of this approach would be the need to maintain two sets of liability calculations, one for accounting purposes and one for funding purposes.

Congressional concerns about fairness in the assignment of benefits could be addressed by the imposition of participation, coverage, nondiscrimination, and vesting standards.[9] At a minimum, requirements should be imposed that the terms of the retiree benefit plan should be made clear and permanent, so that workers can have a clear and confident understanding of the terms of their compensation. In response to this requirement, it is possible that companies would abandon the current ambiguous arrangement of giving retirees the same, but always evolving, benefits as are given to active workers, for the establishment of special retiree health plans. If companies continue the current typical arrangements, however, it is reasonable to require the continuation into retirement of the same benefit plan that the participants received just before their retirement.

Along these lines and more specifically, an important administrative issue in ERISA-fication is the exact type of benefit covered. There are three distinct possibilities.[10] In a defined health benefit plan—the type of plan currently most widely offered—a particular health plan is established. The employee vests in the provision of various kinds of health benefits, whatever their cost and rate of utilization. In a defined health benefit plan, however, certain administrative problems might arise related to any requirements of vesting and maximum benefit that Congress might impose. Because the concept of hospitalization, for example, although quantifiable in terms of value is not generally divisible, fine distinctions in the law or regulations in terms of vesting schedules and maximum benefits may be difficult to achieve. Hence, Congress would have to be satisfied with some fairly blunt and imprecise policy instruments. A defined health benefit plan, however, does have the substantial advantage to the retiree of imposing the risk of cost increases for health care on the employer.

A defined dollar health benefit plan is similar to a defined benefit pension plan, with this exception: in a defined dollar benefit plan, the amount accumulated must be used for the purchase of health insurance coverage. Although the administration of such a plan is considerably simpler than that of a defined health benefit plan, the retiree is left exposed to the risk of medical inflation. In addition, because the benefit is denominated in dollars, it might be difficult politically to prevent the money accumulated in the fund from being diverted from the purchase of health care.[11]

A defined contribution health plan is similar to a defined contribution pension plan, except that the amount accumulated must be used for the purchase of health insurance. The administration of such a plan is even simpler than that of a defined dollar benefit plan. In addition to disadvantages of the defined dollar health benefit plan, however, the retiree faces the risk of poor investment performance in a defined contribution plan.

The establishment of maximum allowable benefit levels in a scheme of ERISA-fication would accomplish two goals: the potential loss of revenues to the government would be somewhat limited, and a mechanism would be established whereby concerns about overinsurance and the resulting increase in health care costs could begin to be addressed.

The complete adoption of all features of ERISA to retiree health plans, however, is inadvisable. The establishment of a PBGC-like agency for retiree health benefits, in particular, would be very troublesome. Although most companies had already started funding their pension plans even before ERISA and the establishment of the PBGC, most retiree health plans are currently completely unfunded. When considered in conjunction with the deficit that the PBGC nevertheless accumulated over the years, the enormous exposure of the federal government implicit in the creation of a PBGC-like agency for retiree health benefits should certainly be avoided.[12]

Whatever the exact features of ERISA-fication, the most significant economic and political problem is the large loss of revenues to the federal government incurred when granting tax-favored status to a funded retiree health benefit plan. One way of financing this program could be the taxation at the household level of at least part of the premium paid for, or the actuarial value of, all health benefits provided by a current or former employer. As I have discussed above, two important goals in the creation of policy responses to the problem of retiree health benefits include the partial removal of the tax subsidy given to the health care industry and the internal consistency of the tax code for pension and retiree health benefits.

How does ERISA-fication fare in terms of the policy goals set out in the previous section? As is stated above, when combined with a proposal for the taxation of at least part of the value of benefits received by individuals, the goals of tax equity and consistency and of revenue neutrality are nicely met. Owing to mandatory prefunding, security of benefits is also achieved, although it would probably take at least two decades before full funding is reached for most plans. It is difficult to

135

judge, a priori, whether the appropriate balance is achieved in ERISA-fication between expanded coverage and containment of health care costs. If some companies would rather cancel their plans than begin prefunding, even on a tax-favored basis, coverage will be lost for some current and future retirees. But tax-favored prefunding may encourage the establishment of some plans, particularly by smaller companies. Prefunding may even lead to overinsurance, unless the maximum benefit rules are carefully designed. Probably the main drawback to the ERISA-fication policy option, no matter how carefully crafted and how reliant on accounting conventions, is the creation of an inevitably complex set of laws and regulations and of costly governmental intervention in the provision of retiree benefits.

This policy option has the political attraction of familiarity because it is patterned after ERISA. Moreover, aside from the problems of the PBGC and some employer dissatisfaction with its imposition of a not insignificant administrative burden, ERISA is generally thought to be a successful piece of legislation.[13] The political problem of financing ERISA-fication with the taxation at the household level of health benefits directly received by active and retired workers is no doubt a difficult one. The precedent of taxing employer-provided (life insurance) benefits in excess of certain amounts, however, has been recently established as a result of the Tax Reform Act of 1986.[14]

APPENDIX

Suggestions for Further Research

In the course of doing research for this book, I received many directions of analysis and data sources. I accepted some of the suggestions, and they are included in this book; I plan to follow up on others in future work. Some of the suggestions, however, while excellent and important, are beyond my capabilities to pursue. Furthermore, some of the suggestions require data that, while theoretically available, are in fact often out-of-date or otherwise unsuitable for use. This chapter briefly outlines these suggestions for further research and construction of data.

Concern has been expressed whether the high cost of health care in this country, especially because of the burden faced by many employers for retiree health benefits, makes American products more expensive and therefore less competitive in overseas markets. The logic behind this concern is threefold. As shown in figure A–1, statistics indicate that the United States spends more on health care as a percentage of gross domestic product than do other industrialized countries—even those with older populations. Second, health care is financed and managed by employers to a much greater extent in the United States than in other countries. Finally, obligations for retiree health care will now appear on financial statements, perhaps raising the cost of capital somewhat to some companies. Because of its relatively high cost, its private sponsor-ship, and its sudden appearance on financial statements, does the inclusion of health care in the total cost structure of the private sector make American products less competitive?

The answer to the concern will depend on several factors. Simple comparisons of relative private expenditures on health care are not sufficient grounds for drawing conclusions about relative competitive-ness. Wages in foreign countries may be higher to compensate workers for the higher taxes paid for government-sponsored health care. It is altogether possible, moreover, that because of the implicit burden of higher future taxes needed to pay for promised future health care in foreign countries, exchange rates have already adjusted to reflect the public promise for the provision of health care. Finally, viewed strictly from an economic viewpoint, higher corporate expenditures on health

137

FIGURE A–1
HEALTH EXPENDITURES IN SELECTED OECD COUNTRIES
AS A PERCENTAGE OF GDP, 1984

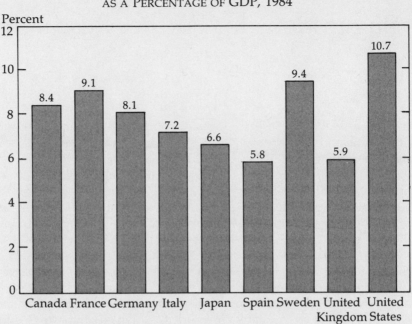

SOURCE: OECD.

care could produce a healthier, more satisfied, and therefore more productive work force. The relevance of these factors may be ascertainable by further research and analysis.

The unknown relationship between expenditures on health care and productivity and welfare more generally appears in other contexts as well. As is mentioned in chapter 7, one possible reason why improvements in medical technology are not currently accounted for in the construction of price indexes is precisely the lack of quantifiable knowledge about the relationship between more costly health care procedures and improved consumer welfare. Corporate and national decisions about the amount of resources to devote to health care are to a great extent not currently informed by specific knowledge about the relationship between expenditures on health care and the welfare of the consumers of health care. More research on this topic might prove beneficial to private and public policy makers.[1]

Returning to the specific topic of this book, current, publicly available information about the features of retiree health plans sponsored by specific corporations is difficult to find. While corporations are

138

required to file summary plan descriptions with the Department of Labor whenever changes are made to welfare benefit plans, such current information is generally not available in the public documents room of the Pension and Welfare Benefits Administration. Although the Bureau of Labor Statistics collects current information through the Survey of Employee Benefits about the features of many large plans, publishes aggregate statistics based on that information, and makes a computer tape of the survey available to researchers, the identity of the sponsors of plans is not made available to the public and no information is available about small plans.

Corporations are also generally required to file Forms 5500, available to the public, for welfare benefit plans containing information about the characteristics and finances of these plans. Because one Form 5500 is generally filed for many different types of benefits but more than one form may be filed for each plant within a corporation, it is generally impossible to utilize the Form 5500 for many research purposes—particularly regarding retiree health benefits sponsored by corporations. If a complete source of publicly available current information about health plans (specifically including retiree health plans) sponsored by corporations is desired, some thought should be devoted to the design of the Form 5500 and summary plan descriptions and to the processing of current information from that source.

Over the past decade, numerous theoretical and empirical studies have been conducted concerning the effect of pensions on labor and capital market conditions.[2] Although this book has addressed some of these issues in the specific context of retiree health plans, clearly more work can be done. In addition, it would be logical to repeat the pension studies *adding* relevant information about retiree health benefits. In particular, the following could be explored at the household or firm levels: measures of earnings replacement during retirement; factors relevant to the decision to retire; the relationship between pension and retiree health plans and the level and the age structure of wages; differences in the receipt of pension and retiree health benefits among segments of the population, such as among men and women, union and nonunion members, large and small firms, and so on; household portfolio composition and pension and retiree health plans; corporate finance and pension and retiree health plans; and pension and retiree health plans and employee turnover. Such studies would provide policy makers with more complete information concerning the economic status of the elderly and the functioning of labor and capital markets.

Commentaries

A Commentary by Mark Pauly

I learned a lot from Mark Warshawsky's study. I found myself going back to it to get useful information about estimates of the potential liability for health benefits for retirees, about the twists and turns of the legal views on this matter, and about the complicated attempts by the Financial Accounting Standards Board (FASB) to come up with something reasonable.

Giving an economist's view of retiree health benefits, I may say things that sound implausible but that are founded in economic theory. First, my main quibble with Warshawsky's assumptions is over the rate of growth for projecting future health care costs. My thought is that the value of premium payments in the future will obviously be related to the value of benefits, and the value of benefits will be driven not only by the CPI, a measure of price changes, but also by the quantity. The expected value of benefits is proportional to price times quantity.

If we extrapolate from trends as far back as we have data, we know that the rate of growth in health expenditures per capita, even after adjusting for demographics, has exceeded the rate of growth in the CPI, largely because of the intensity of care per person. If we assume roughly a 5 percent inflation rate and a 5 to 6 percent growth in real expenditures per capita, we come up with 10 or 11 percent growth in health expenditures.

As Mark Warshawsky mentioned, it is difficult to make people take these estimates seriously. One benefit of estimating future health care costs for retirees, or for the elderly population in general, is that it has persuaded actuaries of the existence of divine providence—because if God doesn't do something, we're in terrible trouble. So most people have assumed that there will be some change.

Nevertheless, past trends seem to show little behavioral change. Economists would like to see a behavioral model for future trends. As real health care costs rise, we have to believe that sooner or later demand curves slope downward and people react by doing less, by reducing the quantity.

143

There have been some attempts to construct such models, including one at the National Institute on Aging that I found interesting, but all of them suffer because we do not know how to model behaviorally the rate of technical change. That particular dinosaur keeps stomping through the forest at a rate of about 3 percent real growth a year, no matter what we do. If we did know that, we would have a better basis for projecting future costs.

While I find a lot that is meritorious, interesting, and challenging in this study, I have to ask what difference any estimate of future health care costs or liabilities makes. My professor in graduate school, James Buchanan, was fond of saying that cost is important only if it influences choice; if it does not influence choice, it is not really cost. He quoted his mentor, Frank Knight, who said that calling a situation hopeless is equivalent to calling it ideal. If we have already incurred a large liability that we can do nothing about, then in a sense it is not important what that liability is. From a broader policy perspective the rest of us perhaps need not care.

So the questions are, Why should it matter, and how should it matter? My thinking here is influenced by how I think of markets for employee benefits. I believe two things. First, benefit managers offer a benefit because they think it will lower the price of quality—the money wage cost of quality-constant labor. Either they will get better workers or they will be able to reduce the pay of existing workers by more than the expected cost of benefits. That is a rational model of benefit setting. The message it conveys is that one needs to look at the value of providing employee benefits in terms of whatever impact they might have on levels and rates of growth in money wages. I have been disappointed in this study and in other studies in seeing very little consideration of the impact health benefit costs have on the rate of growth in money wages. We can say money wages will be cut, but in an inflationary world they are likely to just grow a little less rapidly.

My other view is that I think of labor markets as competitive. Although there is unionization, only 16 percent of workers are unionized, and I will argue later that unions may make the labor market more rather than less competitive.

Two points that I want to talk about are, What should investors do, and what should the firm do? The policy question is, Why should the rest of us care?

One of the purposes of this study is to look at the effects of changes in the accounting standard on the valuation of stock. I believe in the efficient market hypothesis. If financial markets are efficient, the cat is certainly out of the bag by now, so the accounting standards should not change anything.

Holding meetings and writing letters to the FASB seem like a colossal waste of effort. If the market captures almost all of the information available at the moment, then the consequences of how that information is reported are relatively unimportant, as long as the experts who drive the marginal price in the market know what is going on. On the question whether a firm should report this liability all at once or spread it over several years, my flip comment is that I wouldn't worry about it if everybody already knows what the situation is.

There is a good bit of debate whether or not markets are truly efficient. I will hold to the efficient market hypothesis until I see people actually change their portfolios. At the moment, most of the information is already out there. Maybe FASB should have said it was going to promulgate the standard, calling people's attention to it and getting them all worked up, and then said, "We were just kidding." Then all the effort of calculating the numbers and defending them would have been unnecessary.

Mark Warshawsky's finding that about half of the liability is captured in current stock prices is interesting. It is hard to tell whether he is right and the market is wrong, or the experts in the market have different expectations from his about the future costs.

As for the consequences of promulgating these numbers on the benefits provided to retirees, let's look first at a nonunionized rather than a unionized firm. Should the firm change its benefits as a result of noticing these liabilities or having the liabilities publicized? It depends on whether the benefit package it was offering is the right one or not. That is equivalent to asking, Is the cost of the benefit to early or late retirees greater or less than the resulting reductions (or lower rate of growth) in what otherwise would be the level of money wages?

If in effect the employees pay for this benefit, it must be worth it to them and ought to be continued. If the benefit is too lavish—if, for example, they have no desire to buy Medigap benefits through the firm for those over sixty-five—then it should probably be eliminated. The issue for employers is to decide whether or not the benefits they are offering to workers are worth the cost. Since benefits for people who have already retired constitute a liability, the issue is whether or not the stock market has already capitalized it.

The stock market might seem to be capitalizing only half the liability of the expected costs of these benefits because it may also be capitalizing an expected reduction in the rate and growth of money wages of workers in firms that offer those benefits. The net effect may actually be 50 percent of the gross effect, and that may be what the market is measuring.

But should benefits be cut? The basic factor, as I said, is whether or not the right benefits are being provided. A worst-case scenario would

145

be a firm that promised a benefit but paid little attention to it. Employees from forty to fifty-five years old will cost the firm a lot. If workers nearing retirement have a clear understanding of these benefits, and if the firm, in a sense, has not already collected the value of the benefit, the trend of the rate of growth of money wages for them could certainly be lowered. Even if workers have not been well informed, there could be an adjustment in money wages to offset the cost of retiree health benefits after they are informed. That kind of labor market offset could happen.

Are there any advantages to the employer for offering Medigap benefits as a fringe benefit? It seems to me there are advantages. The firm can buy the insurance more cheaply as a group than individuals can, and it can get some tax benefits in the sense that the costs that are actually paid out are not treated as part of taxable income. From 70 to 75 percent of the elderly have Medigap. If they end up with it anyway, they might as well get it in the cheapest way, which for middle and upper income workers is likely to be as part of a fringe-benefit package.

The trick, again, is to make sure that money wages are adjusted to offset the cost of the benefits. My own public policy view is not to encourage Medigap coverage, but setting that aside, employers should be very leery of canceling or substantially reducing Medigap benefits.

What about unionized firms? My understanding is that unions know very well that wages and fringe benefits trade off against the total amount employers pay for compensation.

On public policy questions, a lot of the liability Mark Warshawsky measures, as he mentions, is for early retirees. We should seriously consider whether we are encouraging early retirement too much. Whether we want to fund retiree benefits through tax law changes depends on whether we think early retirement is a good idea. I think it may not be.

On the public policy question of Medigap, for a number of reasons I think it is socially undesirable to have Medigap coverage for middle and upper income retirees. Anything we can do to get rid of Medigap seems to me to be a good idea.

On the value of retiree benefits to workers, the issue is not the social value of this particular coverage, but rather that workers expect payment of their Medigap policy as part of the total income when they retire. Should that dry up, they will have to spend on Medigap the income they were counting on for other purposes. That pushes the question away from health and toward pensions, which, in a sense, is the main issue.

Do we want firms to have the flexibility to change their pension policies? There are arguments for limiting their discretion with regard to workers who may not be adept at sharing the risks. Firms are more adept than individuals at bearing the risk of future health care cost inflation. But what sort of guarantees do we want to offer, and what can

146

government do to enforce reasonable guarantees? Probably the most durable effect of the FASB flap is to force people to think about the demographic time bomb we are facing.

A Commentary by Olivia Mitchell

Let me start with some background on retiree health insurance. Almost a third of older Americans today rely on some kind of employer-sponsored health insurance—that is, from their previous employer. For folks under sixty-five, these plans usually represent the only source of health insurance; for people over sixty-five, employer insurance coverage provides a valuable supplement to Medicare benefits.

Although these benefits improve the well being of many older Americans, coverage for retiree health insurance is very uneven. Recent surveys show that something like half of all the workers in medium and large firms have some sort of retiree health coverage, but only 2 percent of workers in companies with fewer than twenty-five employees are offered such coverage. There are also big differences in the pre-sixty-five/post-sixty-five breakdown.

Not only is coverage uneven but it has been declining. That is why this book is so timely. Between 1983 and 1988, medium-sized and large firms reported a 15 percent decline in the number of workers below age sixty-five likely to be eligible for benefits after early retirement. And for workers sixty-five and older, the decline was about 20 percent in coverage over the same period. While some of this observed decline may be due to changes in the survey series used to track coverage, a part of the explanation for this big decline is that retiree health insurance has become very costly, as Mark Warshawsky has shown.

A related consideration is that companies have traditionally offered this coverage on a pay-as-you-go basis, in part because prefunded retiree health insurance was not afforded a tax shield that made benefits like pensions so appealing. Another factor is that retiree health insurance seemed very manageable back when the work force was relatively young and relatively healthy and had high turnover rates. This insurance has become a much more serious matter as the work force has aged and health care costs have increased.

Of course, one of the factors precipitating the interest in retiree health benefits is the change in the FASB accounting standards, as Mark Warshawsky has explained. Essentially, they require firms offering retiree health benefits first to measure and then to disclose publicly the magnitude of their underfunded retiree health obligations. This proposal has elicited consternation in some circles and sheer panic in others.

Against this backdrop Mark Warshawsky's book begins by charac-

147

terizing the current retiree health insurance field as "problem-stricken," a description that few would disagree with. Leading the list of problems are the inflation in medical care costs and the lack of prefunding of benefits and how these two problems interact with the problems in the Medicare and Medicaid system.

As a labor economist, I want to distinguish the factors that are critical in the retiree health insurance arena and to differentiate them from the general mess in the broader health insurance area. I believe that the retiree health insurance problem arose from a poorly specified labor contract. If the retiree health promise had been clearly specified to workers in advance, many of the problems would not have arisen. We have gotten into this mess precisely because the retiree health insurance promise has been so vague for so long.

Although it may seem odd that I emphasize a failure in the labor market driving a health insurance problem, I would argue that it boils down to two facts. First, many workers are very myopic about their future. Most people do not contemplate retirement until their fifties, and even when they do think about it, most of them seriously underestimate both their retirement income needs and their retiree health care needs. A second problem is that forecasting one's health care needs into the future is intrinsically difficult. These two problems, myopia and complexity, interact, so that workers really do not know what they are getting in retiree health insurance.

I can think of four ways that workers might have thought about the value of the retiree health promise. A simple approach is that retiree health insurance coverage was a claim on constant nominal dollar health insurance, that is, a fixed dollar contribution from when they retired until they died. I do not think that is what most people expected from retiree health insurance.

A more complex approach would have led them to expect a "defined-benefit" package; in other words, the same package from retirement until death. But that is probably not quite what people thought either. Another claim might have been on the best available medical care, including new technology and other new developments in the health field, regardless of expense from now until death.

A fourth view, embellishing on the others, recognizes that retiree health insurance is integrated with Medicare. In valuing the future promise of retiree health insurance, it would take into account what might happen to Medicare in the future, and how the retiree health program would interact with it. This method of valuing the benefit would require forecasting not only demographic change and what will happen to the company but also what will happen to Medicare.

These alternative views of retiree health benefits illustrate that valuing the retiree health promise is extremely difficult. They also show that the retiree health insurance problem faced today by companies and workers stems from the failure of workers to clarify the complex promise they have been buying into for the past thirty years.

But the blame should not be put totally on the workers. The people who design wage and benefit packages also bear responsibility. If human resource planners had been clear about the nature of the promise, they would have realized the importance of trying to value these benefits and how to pay for them.

While I do not have all the answers, I think this stance indicates where some solutions lie and where they do not lie. The right policy approach is to make clear the economic and legal format for a retiree health agreement. Then a company would know exactly what it would provide under what circumstances—and the worker would know what he or she is getting when a retiree health plan is promised.

This type of contract—call it, if you will, the full information contract—would require identifying what retiree health costs will be borne by whom, under what sets of risks, and who bears the risks under different scenarios. Under such a contract it would then be appropriate to let the freely contracting parties negotiate their own coverage patterns as they deem best. Of course, it would be necessary to have some legal recourse in the event that people actually break the contracts.

Against this backdrop, I approach Warshawsky's new book, which makes several contributions. It is the only source I have seen, for example, that presents a clear, comprehensive discussion from so many different fields—the accounting issues, the legal issues, the economic issues.

We disagree more over emphasis than economics. In a key section of his book, Warshawsky demonstrates that retiree health underfunding hurts firms' share prices. As Mark Pauly said, this analysis overlooks the fact that retiree health plans were designed, implemented, and adopted to influence compensation and human resource policy, that is, to attract and retain quality employees and then to get them to retire at the optimal point with sufficient income and economic security, to the mutual benefit of the firm and the worker. I would argue that unfunded liabilities of retiree health plans have serious consequences for workers and retirees, who are stakeholders in this contract and deserve more attention.

A related concern crops up in the policy chapter. Although I do not disagree with most of his policy goals, I wish he had gone further in trying to help clean up the mess. He suggested, for example, that the retiree health promise should not be rendered so fixed and rigid as to prevent the employer from responding to changing conditions. An even more valuable contribution would be to help people figure out how to value this risky element of the compensation package and to trace the various options.

On computations of simulated retiree health plan expenses and liabilities, I would have liked to see more sensitivity analysis. There is none, for example, with respect to costs once Medicare kicks in. This seems important because so much is driven by the existence of Medicare, which begins at age sixty-five. If that age is raised, what would happen to retiree health liability?

In conclusion, I would say that retiree health insurance should not be one of the main tools for fixing our chaotic and expensive health care problems. Retiree health insurance should be kept where it belongs, as an element of the compensation package, offered by some, but by no means all, firms as one of the benefits. Certainly, the nature of retiree health coverage will evolve as Medicare, tax policy, and other health policy evolve, but it should not be the tail that wags the dog.

In important ways, Mark Warshawsky's book is a valuable contribution to understanding retiree health. Restating my initial point, it focuses our attention on an important topic and should foster debate and research.

A Commentary by Eugene Steuerle

I, too, found this an excellent and thorough study of the many issues involved in financing post-retirement benefits. Part of the problem for reviewers and researchers alike is the complexity of the topic. Not only are we dealing with accounting, legal, and economic issues, but from a policy standpoint, we are asking questions dealing with labor policy, tax policy, retirement policy, health policy, and saving policy. All of them interact in this one topic.

Let me try to place this topic within the historical development of accounting systems along with the growth of the modern economy. One of the most important developments in the modern market system has been the parallel maturation of a modern accounting system. The latter has been led by the need to determine in a precise manner just how and where money within the firm should be allocated. Owners and managers of firms had to be able to make allocative decisions more effectively.

I believe, perhaps more than Mark Pauly does, that better accounting systems do guide choices and, therefore, do affect prices in markets. Information *is* power. I also believe—and this is very germane—that the determination of property rights is important for making allocative decisions.

I encourage those who do not believe that accounting systems or property rights make a difference to visit Eastern Europe, which is attempting a transition to a market economy without either institution being well established. Obviously, our economy is much further along in developing both concepts.

The issue of how to account for retiree health benefits fits into this framework by raising the question of how to ascertain more clearly and directly just what rights are available to people and the value of those rights.

There are many reasons why accounting systems are important. A large firm wants to know which parts of the firm are profitable, not just whether the firm as a whole is profitable. A manager should know which products have value in excess of the cash wages and fringe benefits of the employees that make them. The tax accounting system must be accurate if we want taxes to be fair and efficient. Both the financial and the tax accounting systems have a long and often tortuous history. There has always been much anguish whenever new rules have been adopted.

The new rules have moved in two directions in the past few decades: first, toward the greater assignment of income measured at the individual or subunit level; and, second, toward better and more thorough accounting and balancing of receipts and expenses or assets and liabilities. Over these decades we have seen more and more imputations of noncash transactions—promises, obligations, accruals—added to try to make a better accounting system. Special problems have always arisen when we went to a new accounting system and discovered an implicit imbalance in the old system, as when individuals supposedly had secured certain rights or assets but the liabilities were not recognized on the other side of the ledger.

Along with the assignment of income, assets, and liabilities, there also have been basic changes in the way firms operate and pay people. When capital expenses are more explicitly detailed, for instance, some firms move toward leasing assets that they had bought or, perhaps, vice versa. Better detailing of costs at different locations have led companies to move plants, sometimes across regions and sometimes across countries. With better inventory accounting came greater inventory control; with the assignment of pension rights came the gradual accrual of assets within separated funds, as well as shifts in the types of plans offered. The development of financial accounting standards for employee health benefits, it seems to me, represents another step along this road.

Let me state from the beginning that I am an unabashed fan of the FASB's decision to require accounting for retiree health benefits as a liability of the employer. The value of the promise may be very hard to measure, but it is clearly greater than zero in value. I prefer to use measures that may be highly uncertain, even inaccurate, but unbiased,

151

rather than use a measure such as zero, which is certainly biased. More elaborate and accurate accounting has reduced inaccuracies, inconsistencies, inefficiencies, and inequities before. Enactment of the new financial accounting standard cannot help but have real effects on the economy.

A special problem arises when assets and liabilities do not add up in an aggregate sense. Assessing the value of retiree health benefits can be thought of in this setting. It is a mistake, I believe, to think of these assets and liabilities as only those of the stockholders in the firm and the employees eligible for benefits. Our courts often assume this simple dichotomy when they try to assess rights between the employee and the employer. Mark Warshawsky had to grapple with this issue in trying to measure stock market valuation and the value of the rights of the employees versus the rights of the stockholders.

In the narrow accounting framework, the issue of how to attribute assets to covered employees and corresponding liabilities to the employer may be the correct one. But in a more dynamic economic setting, especially when the promise of health benefits may not be met (and that is always possible if they are unfunded), the assets or liabilities of a variety of groups are involved—bondholders, consumers, uncovered employers, taxpayers (who might have to help out or provide guarantees to lenders), and so forth. This was recognized by Mark Warshawsky when he said that some companies, previously unaware of the extent of their obligation, were reducing benefit levels, appealing for tax relief to prefund their obligations, and negotiating with unions on ways to control health care costs.

Firms that promise significant employee health benefits make commitments that depend on the availability of future funding, which means growth in the income of the firm itself. If that income is not forthcoming, then someone else will have to pay or the workers might lose their health benefits. In a monopolistic market, consumer prices might be raised temporarily, although eventually this creates threats to the firm from substitute goods. In other firms, wage levels might go down across the board, implying that junior workers have to pay for promises to senior workers. Finally, firms may have to downsize or even declare bankruptcy as a way of recognizing that potential or actual liabilities exceed assets. This is why relying solely upon a plan or a document to determine liabilities of employers is so tenuous. If the employer does not have the assets to cover costs, then the present value of the promise is clearly less than the fully funded cost of that promise.

Mark Warshawsky highlights the case of some coal companies that try to pass on cost to other companies within a multiemployer framework, but the other companies cannot bear the additional burden and remain competitive at the margin. In a highly competitive market, it may be impossible for an unfunded liability to be passed on to anyone, especially if labor is mobile and consumers can switch to producers of similar or substitute products.

Let me turn now to some of the policy considerations underlying the movement toward the booking of retiree health benefits. With regard to saving policy, I view the new standard as fairly positive—policy officials should be receptive to the new standard. Although I think the new standard will be only moderate in its effect on saving, funding of pensions and funding of retiree benefits is a major form of saving for most households. As a matter of saving policy, the government should react positively to the booking of liabilities.

With regard to retirement policy, I have a more mixed reaction. We now offer a quite large number of years in retirement. I have calculated that a typical couple retiring at sixty-two with a pension can expect to receive payments from that pension for close to a quarter century. Do we want additional subsidies or incentives to encourage even earlier retirement? Other needs of society appear to be even more in need of subsidy.

As a matter of labor policy, policy makers should have a mixed reaction. We should move towards divesting of rights. I am bothered by retiree health benefits that accrue only in the last year of employment; anyone who leaves a year before that loses the benefits altogether. This is not simply an issue of equity or of age discrimination; it provides firms with a powerful incentive not to hire older workers and to downsize when their labor force becomes elderly.

As a matter of health policy, I also have mixed feelings about how officials should react. Subsidies should not be provided to all forms of health insurance. When applied at the margin, these subsidies often drive up health care costs and raise the charges assessed by health care providers, without benefit to either employers or employees. The dollars spent on health policy are best spent where needs are greatest and where taxpayer support is needed because the private sector has not done an adequate job. I would much rather subsidize something like long-term care or health benefits needed by the older and poorer elderly, rather than for the early retirement of individuals who typically have a much higher income and less need.

Finally, this brings me to the tax issues. The tax issues, however, are mainly a subset of the saving, retirement, and health issues. Since the subsidization of health benefits is a cause of rising health prices, a significant share of the tax subsidy goes to providers of health services and is lost to employers and employees. If we allow early retirement health benefits to be nontaxable and also allow funds to be built up tax-free as we do for pensions, we would make retiree health the most

153

subsidized of all forms of consumption in the tax code. That may be going too far. At the same time, however, we do need to be more practical about tax policy and how it is administered.

In the treasury report on financing health and long-term care that I directed when I was at the Treasury, we concluded that payments toward retiree health might be accorded the same treatment as pensions, annuities, and other retirement income, but within the strict, combined limits.[1] When the payments were made to individuals, we argued, those payments should be taxable, again, like other pension and annuity payments. If taxpayers have high health expenses, they have recourse to the itemized deduction to take care of cases of extreme need. This is one way to deal with the policy dilemma of how to mix tax, saving, retirement, and labor policy.

Response by Mark Warshawsky

I appreciate these commentaries, and I have two quick reactions to them.

I strongly agree with Olivia Mitchell's observation—a big part of the problem is that benefit packages have, historically, been so misunderstood. That has engendered lawsuits because workers think they have the benefit as a guarantee, but employers believe they retain the right in all sorts of contingencies to cancel the benefit. There is obviously room for a lot of misunderstanding and ill will.

Just clarifying the promise, however, will probably not be enough. In fact, the Employee Retirement Income Security Act (ERISA) already requires a written document for welfare benefit plans. ERISA presumably required a written document to make sure everyone understood what was going on. It has failed because the Department of Labor Documents Room has not had current documents since about 1986. But the documents themselves are often not very helpful.

This, in turn, leads to the public policy question of prefunding. One advantage of prefunding is precisely how the power of money concentrates the mind. It is a question not just of paper but of actual assets going into the designated trust. It concentrates everyone's mind, both the employer's and the employee's, about the value of what is being set aside. That is a big advantage of prefunding.

A Commentary by Herbert Nehrling

Since public policy must focus in part on tax policy, my topic will be a corporate viewpoint on tax policy for employer-sponsored retiree health care. It should be understood at the outset that there is no monolithic corporate viewpoint on this issue. I am not speaking either for the

154

business community or for my former company. I will try to give a consensus view, to which most but not all major businesses could subscribe.

A company's viewpoint depends on the magnitude and form of its health care promises to retirees and future retirees, on the demographics of its retiree and employee populations, and, of course, on the strength of its balance sheet and income statement.

An obvious way for business to offset the adverse impact of the FASB standard would be to set aside funds to cover retiree health benefits, as we do for pensions. Because of revenue considerations, however, Congress will not permit tax-favored funding for retiree health care. The legislators have a dilemma here: they also worry that companies may not be able to keep their health care promises to retirees because funds have not been set aside.

Given tax incentives, corporations could go a long way toward resolving the dilemma. They could reduce their future FASB income statement charges and balance sheet liabilities, make their health care promises to their retirees more secure, and continue to provide high quality health benefits to future retirees. Although no one can be certain that corporations can solve the retiree health benefits problem given the proper tax incentives, we can be certain that they cannot solve the problem without such incentives. With such incentives, they have a good chance.

What incentives are needed? First, companies should be permitted to pay their retiree health benefits from so-called excess pension assets, either directly from their pension funds or from a separate fund, rather than from general corporate funds. The last Congress made a start, but the legislation contains so many constraints that most companies cannot use it. Not even improved legislation, however, would do the job over the long term.

Second, and more important, the same type of funding is needed for retiree health care as for pensions—that is, the continuing ability to prefund post-retirement medical benefits on a tax-favored basis.

In return, employers must be prepared to accept a retiree health equivalent of the Employee Retirement Income Security Act, ERISA. If the company elects to provide retiree health care, it would have to advance funds for the benefit. Further, it would have to meet vesting and participation standards in return for a tax deduction for the contribution and for tax-free accumulation of earning for the funds contributed.

Even with ERISA rules, however, the country's budget deficit would preclude tax-favored funding in the foreseeable future, because such funding would reduce tax revenues. To get such a funding vehicle—and we must ultimately have one—revenue must be raised to offset the revenue loss within a policy framework. This tax policy for retiree health care would be established in the context of a comprehensive national retirement income and retiree health care policy, which would recognize pensions and retiree health care as part of the same promise to retirees—that is, deferred compensation with the same legal obligation for providing it.

Under such a national policy, no corporate pension fund could have excess assets as long as the company had an unfunded obligation for retiree health care. Further, the policy would seek to spread the cost of retiree health care equitably across society—users, industry, and government. Retirees would have to pay a greater share of their health care benefits; industry would have to fund the benefit if it provides retiree health care; and government would provide tax-favored funding.

In addition to replacing the lost revenue, two other issues stand in the way. First, to achieve symmetry with the tax treatment of pensions and with generally accepted tax principles, many will insist that the value of health care benefits be taxable to retirees. This may be politically impossible. Second, without a national consensus on the future financing of total health care in this country, corporations will be reluctant to set aside substantial funds for retiree health care. They will want to know exactly what they are funding.

A tax policy like this will require tradeoffs by all parties. As the retiree health care problem shows, neither business nor labor nor government has sorted out its priorities in the total health care area. We all need to decide how much our society can afford, and who should pay for what.

If employer-sponsored retiree health care is deemed by all parties to have a high priority, a tax-favored funding vehicle will give business a chance to solve the problem. The terms and conditions of such a solution must result from compromises by all parties.

To summarize, the FASB standard will have such a severe impact on corporate earnings and liabilities that companies will have to find a way either of offsetting the FASB liability or of reducing or eliminating the retiree health care benefit.

The only way I know to offset the liability is to set aside assets to cover it. They can be either assets set aside for pensions but not needed for that purpose or new assets purchased through an advance funding vehicle. We must recognize that adequate retirement income and adequate retiree health care are part of the same promise and that no company can be considered to have excess pension assets as long as it has an unfunded health care liability. Accordingly, if assets set aside for pensions are not needed for that purpose, they should be used to satisfy retiree health care needs, and if retirement income warrants tax-favored funding, then retiree health care should receive the same treatment.

A Commentary by John Vine

Mark Warshawsky has done a wonderful job of analyzing a difficult problem. His is the first treatment I have seen of retiree health care from financial, legal, and actuarial perspectives. It is an enlightening manuscript.

From a legal perspective, there are some basic principles on retiree health plans that we all should keep in mind. One basic to the employee benefit plan system in the United States is that benefit plans are voluntary plans.

The principal federal law is the Employee Retirement Income Security Act, ERISA, and neither it nor any other federal or state law requires an employer to adopt an employee benefit plan. Particularly in the case of health benefits, neither it nor any other law tells an employer at what level benefits are to be provided. Some regulatory laws certainly do constrain an employer; the Medicare secondary payer provisions are relevant, for example, and age and sex discrimination laws are too. But employers are by and large free to decide whether or not to adopt a plan and what form that plan should take.

Another principle is that the benefits provided by the plan are governed by the plan document or plan documents. This is established by ERISA and the case law that has developed under it. The fundamental principle is that the benefits are governed not by what someone thought the plan said or what someone intended the plan to say, but by what the plan actually says.

The problem is that what the plan says often is not clear or is inconsistent. For that reason, courts have had to examine the expectations of the parties. But if the plan clearly documents that the employer reserves the right to amend or even to terminate the plan, for example, ERISA respects that provision, regardless of what might been have assumed about retirees' rights under the plan.

If an employer is accused of welshing on the deal, the question is, What was the deal? The answer lies, at least initially, in the documents governing the plan. If the employer was committed to providing lifetime retiree health care benefits without any limitation, that was the deal. If the employer described the benefits it was currently providing and reserved the right to change or terminate them, that is a deal of a different kind.

As Herb Nehrling mentioned earlier, the tax environment currently is hostile or at least inhospitable to prefunding retiree health obligations. An employer is severely limited in deducting contributions to prefund retiree health obligations or to accumulate funds free of tax.

The implications of these principles are important. If current law or future legislation makes it difficult for an employer to change or terminate its plan, employers will be less inclined to provide retiree health benefits. If an employer that provides any benefits is then irrevocably committed to providing them, employers will be reluctant to provide benefits in the first place. Employers are already examining whether to retrench on the benefits that they provide. If the law makes that more difficult, this will accelerate the pace at which employers retrench on their commitments to retiree health benefits.

Employers are already retrenching on those benefits. In part they are responding to FASB, and in part they are looking for ways to reduce costs. They are reducing benefits, raising the contributions that retirees are required to make, and increasing the deductibles and the copayment features of their plans.

Although better tax treatment for employers that provide retiree health benefits might seem attractive, it could raise other problems. As discussed, one is the revenue concern. Since tax benefits cost money, the question is, Where does the money come from? Or does it simply increase the federal deficit?

Another problem is that Congress is unlikely to confer more favorable tax treatment of retiree health benefits without imposing restrictions—nondiscrimination rules, for example, comparable to those provided for pensions. And the funds are likely to be restricted to providing retiree health benefits and nothing else.

Obviously, competing objectives must be accommodated, so the question is, Are those objectives reconcilable? I hope they are, and I think they are. I think incentives can be provided without so over-regulating employee benefits that employers are discouraged from providing them.

A virtue of our current employee benefit system is that it encourages flexibility, initiative, and diversity. They can be encouraged in the retiree health arena as well.

Employers may have to be more specific than many of them now are about what they are committing themselves to. That is not bad by any means. Employees may develop a better idea of exactly what they are being promised and what they are not being promised. Many employers may, of course, have to focus on that more than they do now.

In recent years, employers have shown greater interest in retiree health plans that quantify the employer's commitment in terms of a fixed dollar obligation. That concept has been used for years in pensions. It is a useful way of limiting the employer's obligation to something that can be quantified, and it communicates to employees in an understandable way exactly what they are being promised.

My last point is that retiree health benefits is an extremely important subject that merits a lot of attention. I came away from the book, however, feeling that it is a part—an important part, but only a part—of a much larger topic. That is, of course, the provision of health benefits to individuals generally. The question in my mind is whether a satisfactory approach toward retiree health benefits can be adopted without addressing the larger problem at the same time.

A Commentary by Anna Rappaport

A major contribution of Mark Warshawsky's book is in its information on the capital markets and on the modeling, areas in which there is a great deal of uncertainty. I would like to present a view from the trenches, from someone out there trying to help people decide what to do.

One concern is that our clients do not know the implications of these liabilities for their ability to borrow money or what they mean to the organization from a financial point of view. They see a tremendous issue in that they want to take care of their employees but they do not know whether the resources are there. They do not know how this change in measurement will affect the way they are perceived.

Most large companies have done at least one actuarial valuation that measures their costs and liabilities, and many of them have done more than one.

Companies with 500 to 1,000 employees have not done much yet. They face great difficulty with this problem. For many of them, the decisions they make will have a huge impact on the company's bottom line. There may be conflicts over the use of resources. There may be a need to change the culture of the company, which is very difficult. Any significant reduction in liabilities can have severe employee relations consequences. It may lead to litigation, to adverse publicity, to the formation of new unions, and to bad community relations. In many situations, the only choice will be between bad alternatives.

The people we work with want to take care of their employees, and they try hard to find ways to take care of them. They also recognize, however, that being strong and viable and able to raise capital over the long run is critical to the vitality of the organization. The employees are certainly not better off if the organization has no jobs for them. This is a difficult time, a time of struggle. That struggle may be hard to find in the literature but not out there in the trenches.

John Vine mentioned some changes that have been made to plans, and we are seeing many of them too. There are more deductibles, more copayments, more linking of benefits to age and length of service. Eligibility is tighter, with less support for dependents. The ways the plan is tied to Medicare are changing.

We are also seeing more radical changes. Preretirement employee contributions have been added, though in very few cases, including one that has been highly publicized. Defined contribution plans are being considered as a way to create funds, not to provide retiree health but to generate funds.

If employee money goes in before retirement, I see a policy problem relating to benefit security. If it is in a defined contribution pension plan, it is well protected; if it is not in a defined contribution plan, protecting it becomes an issue. Other policy options include the elimination of company support for retiree health, possibly combined with the provision of greater pension benefits or use of a defined contribution plan. We will see some use of the defined-dollar approach and some plans with choice. We may see a lot more of what could be called radical change.

Preferred provider organizations (PPOs), a managed care arrangement, have become much more common in the past two years. But people who think that managed care is a total solution are engaging in wishful thinking. There are real questions about how much can be saved and what can be done by managed care. There are also questions of opportunity. Because health care is a local business, there are very different opportunities in different locations. Certainly this is an important issue but one with limitations.

Although health maintenance organizations (HMOs) seem not to be used much for retirees, they can be an attractive alternative from a public policy point of view. If Medicare contracting became more attractive, employers would be willing to take advantage of it.

I have a few more comments. One of the chapters contended that the maintenance of effort provision showed that Congress intended retiree health to be vested. I would argue the opposite, because that was a two-year provision. And an observation was made that small employers are much less likely to offer coverage. I totally agree with that. In the marketplace today, very small employers as a practical matter probably cannot offer coverage. Many small employers that need insured rather than self-insured health benefits find that their coverage is canceled or their rates increased tremendously. To get coverage, they have to deal with a difficult marketplace. In the future, insurance carriers may not be willing to cover retirees from these companies. They are subject to an increasingly difficult insurance market, so it is virtually impossible for them to tell their employees they will provide health benefits for them in twenty years.

Taxability of benefits and individuals is becoming a hot issue. With regard to the ratios of FASB results to current pay-as-you-go, we have surveyed about 150 evaluations. For highly mature companies, the costs are likely to be about double after the rules are adopted; for mature companies, seven times; and for the immature, thirteen times or more.

I would like to see public policy focus on Medicare issues, as well as the other issues that have been raised, because the employer plan works with Medicare. Employers fear that Medicare will change, not in the ways it has been changing, making the employer's costs a little higher every year, but in ways that will make them radically higher, by changing the ages or by changing the way things are handled.

Another possible option is the former employee's right to remain in his or her employer's group policy at the employee's own expense.[2] An additional open issue is how funds that come from profit-sharing plans will be taxed.

And one final comment. Earlier, someone said that wages are adjusted when retiree health benefits are offered. Out in the trenches, though, there is far less of a tie between benefits and direct wage rates than is supposed by many economists.

A Commentary by Timothy Ray

Since my colleagues have discussed much of what I wanted to cover, it will be easy for me to keep my comments brief. As an employee benefit consultant, like Anna Rappaport, I see employers trying to grapple not only with issues of post-retirement health benefits but also with the larger issues of health care cost management in today's difficult environment.

FASB No. 106, as we all know, has brought the issue dramatically to the table in the past couple of years. It has been bad for many employers but very good for many employee benefit consultants. We have been involved continually in evaluation and plan design.

The decision-making process for many employers that I work with has changed dramatically over the past year in light of FASB. Instead of the traditional evaluation and planning process conducted in the human resources part of the corporation, it now includes much more significantly the chief financial officer and others with more of a focus on the bottom line of the corporation. As Anna Rappaport has said, those two parts of the employer's world have competing priorities, one trying to achieve a bottom line, the other trying to maintain a reasonable level of benefits for the employees.

There is significant concern in U.S. corporations about what is taking place in Medicare. We have seen a continual shift over the past ten years or so in public cost directed substantially at providers. As we all know, those providers, being rather bottom-line oriented, have spread those costs back to other plan sponsors, namely private and other nonpublic sources.

Watching Medicare is particularly difficult for U.S. corporations in that it appears that we are schizophrenic in how we develop Medicare policies. Let's keep in mind that just a few years ago we saw the first major expansion of Medicare, the Catastrophic Coverage Act. Just after employers had gone through the process of redesigning plans, complying with maintenance of effort provisions, and finishing with all the consulting work on plan changes, the bill went away. Then employers were faced with having to revert to the old Medicare program with all its problems.

We have seen the beginning of a significant shift in Medicare's primary responsibilities with the issuance of its secondary payer provisions. Since Medicare has begun making itself secondary to employer-sponsored plans, we are now seeing the enforcement of those provisions. Many of my clients have recently received notices from their insurance carriers that they owe Uncle Sam a substantial amount of money. To a General Motors, a Chrysler, a DuPont, or any other company with a comparable number of employees, those amounts will be significant.

My clients voice concern that some October when Congress finishes its work on the annual budget they will find themselves with a Medicare program that is secondary to all privately sponsored plans. My clients are moving to counteract that. They are also grappling with such things as union agreements. They are beginning to understand the effect of their retirement policies on their post-retirement health liabilities.

Many U.S. corporations went through a significant downsizing in the 1970s and 1980s and encouraged employees to retire early. Now we see that retirees between ages fifty-five to sixty-five, not yet eligible for Medicare, are considerably more costly to the employer than those aged sixty-five and older for whom Medicare is primary.

Our clients have begun developing complete benefit strategies, including the use of post-retirement health benefits and pensions. The entire retirement package is part of a benefit-planning process.

A Commentary by William J. Dennis, Jr.

Let me provide a few basic figures about smaller businesses. More than 99 percent of businesses with more than 100 employees provide employee health insurance, but only a third of those with 20 or fewer offer it. The comparable numbers for pension plans are 85 percent and less than 20 percent.

Urban Institute calculations cited by Mark Warshawsky indicate approximately 11 percent of employees retiring from firms with fewer than 20 workers provide some type of retiree health benefits compared with 65 percent among firms with over 1,000 employees. The figure of 2 percent has also been quoted and is probably closer.

Given these statistics, one can see that the immediate interest of small business is not in retiree health benefits per se. Rather, the interest is in the impact of retiree health benefits policy on the capacity of small business to purchase health insurance for current employees and their families and to provide a basic pension plan.

Even if tax law were to be changed to remove from pension plans the confusing and difficult nature of requirements for a 401(h) deduction (a Supplemental Health Account) the sequential manner of benefit introduction suggests that the number of beneficiaries tied to small businesses would rise modestly. Thus, of the five policy objectives set forth by Mark Warshawsky, small business is particularly interested in an appropriate balance between access to adequate and fairly priced health care and the containment of health care costs. The so-called promises issue, which is the heart of the current retiree health benefit debate, is very much subordinate.

The policy objective of small business is to squeeze health care prices. Prices cannot continue to rise as they have if smaller firms are to maintain their current health insurance effort, let alone increase it. Moreover, the fear larger firms have about the course of health care costs and their reluctance to promise retirees health benefits or more benefits is directly tied to prices and costs. If this problem is not resolved, the discussion of policies governing private retiree health benefits may become academic.

A discussion of retiree health care benefits usually rests on the assumption that these benefits will be financed through a public program (Medicare, for example), through an employer-based group, or through individually purchased policies. This locks us into dead-end thinking, particularly for those retirees not yet sixty-five.

We do not want to spend more on Medicare with our 32 million uninsured Americans under sixty-five and with a $300 billion deficit. Business, certainly small business, is not about to appreciably expand such an expensive and unpredictable benefit. The question is the extent to which they will contract it from a relatively small basis. The individual purchase of insurance for older Americans is often prohibitively expensive even when large deductibles and prior screening are included.

A major problem is that public policy has eliminated nonemployer-based groups. The reason is that the employer-based group receives a hefty tax subsidy that others do not. Usually, the tax subsidy issue is argued over purchase of health insurance or equity. Both are fair arguments and good reasons for change. But elimination of the subsidy or provision of the subsidy for everyone also releases the stranglehold on the employment-based group.

163

Nonemployment-based groups can provide individuals and employers, particularly small employers, greater flexibility in choice. The health care equivalent of a defined contribution plan, for example, becomes possible for many more small employers. Currently, the choice is to incorporate retirees into small employment-based groups, an enormously expensive and totally impracticable alternative for all but a few small business employers, or to provide some type of payment for individual purchase of health insurance. With equity in tax treatment, nonemployment-based groups can lower costs to levels of the employer-based group, provide a group affinity based on health care needs rather than on employment relationships, and be large enough to pool risks.

What distinguishes current employment retiree benefits is, of course, the issue of promises, and Mark Warshawsky also offers either the status quo or ERISA-fication as the policy alternatives. I have no difficulty with the idea, but employers should be required to honor promises made to employees. The ERISA experience, however, illustrates what can happen when good intentions run amok.

Mark Warshawsky hypothesized that small firms do not provide retiree benefits because employees believe the firm may not be around long enough to cash in on them. I disagree. In firms without the panoply of employee benefits, the first priority is to obtain the standard range of offerings. But among the businesses with the financial wherewithal to provide a full benefit package, I would make precisely the opposite argument.

Because small business management intends to be around for a long time, it cannot ignore the implications of expensive promises that extend well into the future. Accounting standards are a reasonably modest consequence in that regard. Short term management cannot ignore the implications, however, particularly when the price is labor peace and liabilities are not accrued. Thus, as long as retiree health costs are believed to be highly unpredictable and expensive, small business owners are unlikely to extend them, no matter what the accounting requirements or the tax implications.

We know that outside multiemployer arrangements, small business owners are much more likely to offer a defined contribution than a defined benefit pension plan. This suggests that should more small employers feel a need to provide retiree health benefits because of competition, they will probably use some type of defined contribution plan. This does not necessarily eliminate the promises issue for small firms, but it certainly reduces the magnitude.

I have not talked about either the financing problems or the tax implications. They have already been mentioned.

In sum, while I certainly do not wish to trivialize the retiree health care benefits issue, the primary small business interest in the issue as it is currently cast is in health care costs. The same should be true for most retirees. Thus, the most important step involves such issues as changes in the tax code, eliminating mandated service requirements, dissemination of vastly more information on costs and outcomes, and so forth.

A Commentary by Fred Van Remortel

Since the remarks I would have made have already been stated by others, let me make a few comments on what has been said.

The section in Mark Warshawsky's book on the valuation of the retiree health care liability itself, and the mechanics of it, concerns me because I think it is low by a factor of about 2.5 for 1991. For the past seven years or so, I have talked with about 280 of the Fortune 500 companies and seen much of the work done by Anna Rappaport's organization and other consulting actuaries, in addition to the valuation work that we have done internally. I come up with a liability in 1991 terms of about a trillion dollars.

To support that, as a matter of public record, the liability at General Motors is in excess of $10 billion. Its current period expense in 1990 was in excess of $1 billion. In 1993, it will have to add to its current-period service costs such things as interest expense, and it will have to begin recognizing or amortizing the accumulated benefit obligation, which was previously unrecognized. That pay-as-you-go or current-period expense will then become some six or seven times the current figure for General Motors.

For AT&T, again a matter of public record, 1990 was the first year it spent in excess of $400 million for retiree health care benefits. It has a present value liability in excess of $4 billion.

So when we add up that $10 billion and that $4 billion, together with the $2.6 billion loss IBM recently took and the hit of more than $1 billion to Alcoa's shareholder market capitalization—and understand that we have identified only four companies—we quickly blow through that $440 billion. Again, I submit, in 1991 dollars it is something closer to a trillion dollars.

Investment advisors around the country hold slightly in excess of $3 trillion in pension trust assets. Pension benefit promises are far more prevalent than retiree health-care-benefit promises. In some companies, though, the present value of the retiree health care liability is, in fact, approaching the present value of the pension benefit promise.

In respect to tax policy, from the time that corporations were allowed to take a federal income tax deduction for employee benefit promises, tax policy has in fact led benefit policy. From a public policy perspective,

165

which may well equate with tax policy, some serious questions have to be asked before 1996 or 1997, such as, Who will provide health care benefits in this country? What will be the role of the employer in providing those benefits? And how will trends be accelerated or decelerated by the federal income tax deductions allowed to corporations? If the employer is allowed to continue to take a federal income tax deduction for benefits paid in behalf of employees and retirees, clearly it is in their best interests to continue to be the provider because the employees certainly cannot take a commensurate deduction.

As was mentioned earlier, it is an anomaly that this benefit stream is nontaxable to the recipient. If we encourage the employer to provide the benefit and give the employer a tax deduction, we probably will see within four or five years an addition to the employee's or the retiree's W-2 form. Along with his pension benefit promise, we will see the value of the health care benefits the retiree is receiving, at least on an equivalent month-to-month premium basis.

Is that something that could be cranked through the back door of Congress, without a full analysis and study of its implications? Probably not. There are changes being made in the mechanics of the funding of retiree health care benefits, however, that are being made very subtly, without much public attention.

The 401(h) current period expense funding bill, for example, allows corporations to tap "excess pension assets"—five years of current expense funding plus the year of enactment, 1990, or *de facto* six years, if employers choose to pay the price. Some employers have decided that the vesting requirements, the maintenance of benefit levels, and so on are not a bad price to pay. Other employers have decided the price is too high.

Another issue I must address is that there are tax-efficient funding vehicles available today. They are reasonably lean and mean because they come with a minimum of regulatory constraints and requirements for vesting or the maintenance of benefit-level promises. The most common one is the collectively bargained Voluntary Employee Beneficiary Association, 501(c)(9) (VEBA).

The collectively bargained 501(c)(9) trust is a far superior funding mechanism for retiree health care benefits than any other. Most corporations with a significant number of represented employees are using that mechanism. The collectively bargained VEBA has none of the constraints imposed by the Deficit Reduction Act of 1984.

Where a significant number of employees are not covered by collectively bargained contracts, the standard or management VEBA, with the new generation of insurance contracts or triple-tax-exempt funds, is also an efficient funding mechanism. The contributions to the

VEBA in both cases are tax deductible and the earnings gains are tax free. That is the same as a 401(a) (structured pension fund provision of the tax code) pension trust offers, and it is not likely to be bettered—at least not in an environment with annual deficits exceeding $200 billion. I should also mention the Employee Stock Ownership Plan (ESOP) approach done a few years ago by Ralston Purina and the recent ESOP approach wrapped in a 401(h) done by Procter & Gamble. The latter may not be done again: the Internal Revenue Service did not seem to approve the mechanical structure Procter & Gamble put in place. But these examples do point out that many companies are taking their responsibilities seriously. The ultimate test of how seriously a company takes its retiree health benefit promises is, in my view, whether it is prepared to step up to the bar and fund.

From a Financial Accounting Standards Board point of view, paragraph 46 of rule 106 lists all the components of accrual accounting that must begin for fiscal years beginning after December 15, 1992, including many negatives—the current period service cost, the interest expense, and recognition of the previous Accumulated Budget Obligation (ABO). In that whole list in paragraph 46, the only one way to mitigate the impact of this benefit promise on the P&L or on the income statement is earnings gains on assets set aside that also meet the FASB plan asset test, segregated, restricted, et al.

Second Response by Mark Warshawsky

With regard to Mr. Van Remortel's comments, I was reluctant to mention specific companies because I was unsure of the appropriateness of singling out some companies without listing estimates for them all. Because Mr. Van Remortel has mentioned specific companies in arriving at his aggregate estimate of $1 trillion, however, it may be useful to indicate my estimate for one company—General Motors. Table 9–2 shows my estimates for GM in the columns labeled "Highest Expense" and "Highest Liability." The liability for GM in 1989, $29 billion, itself represents almost 7 percent of the estimated aggregate liability in the private sector—$426 billion. This is logical because of GM's size and the generosity of its health plans. It is, however, stretching a bit to think there are many GMs out there and therefore the aggregate liability is above $1 trillion.

One could arrive at an estimate higher than $426 billion by increasing the health care cost trend rate, as Mark Pauly has pointed out. I was reluctant to do this, however, because I'm already on the high end among the boys on the block, and I wasn't bold enough to go much higher. It is true, of course, that I have done the estimates only for the private sector. If one were to include the liabilities of the state and local governments and the federal government, one might indeed double the total accrued liability.

Notes

Chapter 1: The Problem of Retiree Health Benefits

1. Over the 1980s alone, employers' contributions to group health plans as a percentage of total compensation paid to workers increased from 3 percent to almost 5 percent, according to the Survey of Current Business.

Chapter 2: Benefits and Tax Considerations

1. Department of Labor, Bureau of Labor Statistics, *Employee Benefits in Medium and Large Firms, 1988,* August 1989, Bulletin 2336, pp. 36–74. Further details about the Bureau of Labor Statistics survey, particularly as it relates to retiree health benefits, will be given later in this chapter and in chapter 6.
2. A few retiree health plans are defined-contribution, and not defined-benefit plans. Under a defined-contribution arrangement, the employer agrees to pay a fixed dollar amount, which the retired worker then uses to purchase some sort of health insurance coverage. Adjustments for increases in premiums owing to inflation are not common in these arrangements.
3. A few plans reduce or cut off retiree health benefits upon the plan participants' eligibility for Medicare.
4. The information in this section is based on Health Care Financing Administration, *Program Statistics: Medicare and Medicaid Data Book, 1988,* HCFA Publication no. 03270.
5. Adjustments in the DRG payments are made, however, to account for differences in hospital cost structures owing to local wage differentials, to the type of hospital (teaching or not-teaching), and to the average number of poor patients treated. In addition, adjustments are made for large "outlier" costs.
6. S. DiCarlo, J. Gabel, G. deLissovoy, and J. Kasper, "Facing Up to Postretirement Health Benefits," Health Insurance Association of America, September 1989.
7. J. Dopkeen, *Postretirement Health Benefits,* Health Services Research reprint, vol. 21, no. 6, February 1987, p. 804.
8. Even prior to the passage of ERISA requirements for funding of pension plans, most companies at least partially funded their plans. Contributions to pension funds for the purposes of prefunding, however, were tax-deductible expenses to the employer for decades before the passage of ERISA, and no doubt these tax provisions made prefunding a more palatable business decision.

9. Employer contributions to provide retiree health benefits are deductible from corporate taxable income in the amount of the insurance premium or the cash paid by the employer on a pay-as-you-go basis when the coverage is provided to the former employee.

10. The information in the remainder of this section is based, in part, on the Joint Committee on Taxation pamphlet, *Present Law and Issues Relating to Employer-Provided Retiree Health Insurance* (JCT-15-89), June 12, 1989; and on M. Melbinger and S. Miller, "Maintaining, Funding and Terminating Retiree Benefits," *Benefits Law Journal*, vol. 1, no. 2 (Summer 1988), pp. 77–102.

11. The transfer provision allows corporations to gain access to excess pension assets on a favorable tax basis. Because the provision also disallows deductions from taxable corporate income in the amount of the transfer, federal taxes payable will be increased for those corporations employing the transfer option.

12. The UBTI can be avoided if the VEBA invests in corporate-owned life insurance (COLI) policies.

CHAPTER 3: STATUTORY REQUIREMENTS

This chapter was written with the assistance of Laura B. Warshawsky.

1. ERISA 3(1).
2. ERISA 402(a)(1).
3. Ibid., 402(b).
4. Ibid., 403(a).
5. Ibid., 403(c).
6. The Act addresses the obligation of the bankrupt employer to pay retiree benefits it undertook to provide; it is therefore distinct from the provisions of COBRA that address the requirement that bankrupt employers make available, at cost to retirees, continued health insurance coverage.
7. Senate Report 100-119 to accompany S. 548, "Amending Title 11, United States Code, the Bankruptcy Code, Regarding Benefits of Certain Retired Employees," July 21, 1987, p. 2.
8. *GF Corporation, Debtor,* Case nos. 490-00621, 490-00622, Bankruptcy Court for the Northern District of Ohio, June 7, 1990.
9. Of course, an alternative solution, not mentioned by the Court, would be to give retirees COBRA coverage and to reimburse them from any unencumbered assets that became available later. Health insurance coverage would not be cut off and the reorganization of the company could proceed more smoothly. In fact, as of April 1991, GF retirees were still without group health coverage.
10. *Chateaugay Corp.,* 12 EBC 1057 (Southern District Court of New York, 1990).
11. Senate Report 100-119, p. 4.

CHAPTER 4: RECENT COURT CASES

1. Because of ERISA's preemption of almost all state benefit laws, the appropriate venue for cases involving employee welfare benefit plans is a federal, not state court.

2. As the court cases have multiplied, so have the articles in law reviews, books, and professional journals. The following is a listing of some recent articles: G.P. Rogers, "Rethinking *Yard-Man*: A Return to Fundamental Contract Principles in Retiree Benefits Litigation," *Emory Law Journal*, vol. 37, 1988, pp. 1033–75; J. T. McNeil, "The Failure of Free Contract in the Context of Employer-sponsored Retiree Welfare Benefits: Moving Toward a Solution," *Harvard Journal on Legislation*, vol. 25, 1988, pp. 213–72; T. Lantry, "The End of Status Benefits? Will Traditional Contract Principles Prevail?" *American Business Law Journal*, vol. 26, 1988, pp. 363–72; M. Curto, "Legal Analysis," chapter 6 in *Retiree Benefits: The Complete Guide to FASB Compliance and Health Care Cost Control*, Washington, D.C.: Bureau of National Affairs, 1989; M. Melbinger and S. Miller, "Maintaining, Funding and Terminating Retiree Benefits," *Benefits Law Journal*, vol. 1, no. 2, Summer 1988, pp. 77–102; J. Hercenberg, W. Krasner, and others, "Legal Principles," chapter 4 in *The New Medicare Law: An Employer's Guide to Compliance and Health Plan Redesign*, Washington, D.C.: Bureau of National Affairs, 1989; K. Peter Schmidt, "Retiree Health Benefits: An Illusory Promise?" chapter 4 in *Retiree Health Benefits: What Is the Promise?* Washington, D.C.: Employee Benefit Research Institute, 1989.

3. M. Curto, "Legal Analysis." Unless the view of federal common law were invoked, most courts would probably allow such changes.

4. *UAW v. Yard-Man, Inc.*, 4 EBC 2109 (Sixth Circuit 1983).

5. *Yard-Man* at 2110.

6. *Ibid.*

7. *Ibid.*

8. *Ibid.*

9. *Yard-Man* at 2112–2113.

10. *Yard-Man* at 2113.

11. *UAW v. Cadillac Malleable Iron Co.*, 3 EBC 1369 (Western District Court of Michigan 1982).

12. *UAW v. Cadillac Malleable Iron Co.* at 1375.

13. *UAW v. Cadillac Malleable Iron Co.*, 5 EBC 1283 (Sixth Circuit 1984).

14. *Musto v. American General Corp.*, 6 EBC 2971 (Middle District Court of Tennessee, Nashville Division, 1985).

15. *Hansen v. White Farm Equipment Co.*, 5 EBC 2130 (Northern District Court of Ohio, Eastern Division, 1984).

16. *Musto v. American General Corp.*, 10 EBC 1441 (Sixth Circuit 1988).

17. *Musto v. American General Corp.*, 10 EBC 2328 (Supreme Court 1989).

18. *Hansen v. White Motor Corp.*, 7 EBC 1411 (Sixth Circuit 1986).

19. *United Paper Workers Local 1020 v. Muskegon Paper Box Co.*, 10 EBC 1329 (Western District of Michigan, Southern Division, 1988).

20. Other more recent cases decided, in part, using the principles of *Yard-Man* are *Smith v. ABS Industries, Inc.*, 11 EBC 2242 (Sixth Circuit 1989); *Hazel v. Curtiss-Wright Corp.*, 12 EBC 1809 (Southern District of Indiana, Indianapolis Division, 1990); and *Schalk v. Teledyne, Inc.*, DC WMich, Nov. 30, 1990. In the last case, the employer did not cancel benefits outright, but it did start charging retirees premiums and requiring the payment of deductibles and copayments. The court disallowed such actions. Hence, a court in the sixth circuit has apparently applied the principles of *Yard-Man* to the amendment, as well as to the cancellation, of retiree benefits.

21. *District 29, United Mine Workers v. Royal Coal Co.*, 768 F.2d 588 (CA4 1985).

22. In a 1988 case, *Trustees of the Graphic Communications International Union Local 546 Health and Welfare Fund v. Lith-O-Kraft Plate Co.*, the *Hansen* judge absolved Lith-O-Kraft of any responsibility for its retirees to the multi-employer trust fund because the contract between the company and the trust contained language expressly limiting the company's liability to the time period of the collective bargaining agreement. The judge additionally noted that the Multiemployer Pension Plan Amendments Act of 1980, imposing a withdrawal liability on companies formerly participating in a multiemployer pension plan, clearly did not apply to multiemployer retiree health plans. See *Local 546 H. and W. Fund v. Lith-O-Kraft Plate Co.*, 692 F.Supp. 782 (N.D. Ohio 1988).

23. *Moore v. Metropolitan Life Insurance Co.*, 9 EBC 2685 (Second Circuit 1988).

24. *Ryan v. Chromalloy American Corp.*, 11 EBC 1137 (Seventh Circuit 1989).

25. *Anderson v. Alpha Portland Industries, Inc.*, 9 EBC 1569 (Eighth Circuit 1988). *Howe v. Varity Corp.* is another recent case in the eighth circuit where the plan document was read narrowly. See *Howe v. Varity Corp.*, 11 EBC 2585 (Eighth Circuit 1990). In a very recent ruling in the ninth circuit on the issue, a magistrate in the district of Oregon ruled in *Chervin v. Sulzer Bingham Pumps* that retirees are not vested under ERISA with rights to health benefits where the plan documents reserve the right to the employer to terminate or amend benefits. See *Chervin v. Sulzer Bingham Pumps*, DC Ore, No. 89-1199-DA, Nov. 14, 1990.

26. In re *Robertshaw Controls Co. and United Steelworkers of America Local 1163*, 12 EBC 1889 (1989).

27. *Bundy Tubing v. UAW Local 1632*, 11 EBC 2775 (1989).

28. *Keffer v. H.K. Porter Co., Inc.*, 10 EBC 2413 (Fourth Circuit 1989).

29. *Sprague et al v. General Motors Corp.*, Complaint to Central District Court of California, August 8, 1989.

30. Statement of Patricia Malloy, spokeswoman for General Motors, quoted in "Benefits Battle Opens GM Front," *National Underwriter*, 1989.

31. Statements of GM retirees Wessinger, Bazinet, Opyr, and Francis in Appendix to "Plaintiffs' Brief in Opposition to Defendant General Motors Corporation's Motion to Strike Plaintiffs' 251 Declarations in Support of Plaintiffs' Cross Motion for Partial Summary Judgment," Case No. 90 CV 70010, *Sprague et al. v. General Motors*, Eastern District Court of Michigan.

CHAPTER 5: ACCOUNTING STANDARDS

1. This section is based largely on information provided in Financial Accounting Standards Board, *Facts about FASB, 1990*.
2. Apparently, the SEC can nullify the action of the FASB by declaring that a standard need not be applied in financial statements filed with the SEC. Such nullification, however, would require specific action on the part of the SEC. The FASB meets quarterly with the chief accountant of the SEC to discuss matters of interest to both parties.
3. Financial Accounting Standards Board, "Statement of Financial Accounting Standards No. 81: Disclosure of Postretirement Health Care and Life Insurance Benefits," Financial Accounting Foundation, November 1984, p. 7.
4. The FASB had apparently received many negative comments about the proposed standard for retiree health benefits.
5. FASB Statement No. 81, pp. 7–8.
6. A characteristic of a multiemployer plan is that assets contributed by one participating sponsor are not restricted to the provision of benefits to employees of that sponsor alone. Rather, all employees of all sponsors are covered equally by the plan. A multiemployer plan is usually administered by a board of trustees composed of union and management members and hence is sometimes referred to as a joint trust or union plan. Sponsors of a multiemployer plan are usually in the same industry, but they sometimes have only the bond of a labor union in common.
7. FASB Statement No. 81, p. 10.
8. Ibid., pp. 2–3.
9. Governmental Accounting Standards Board, "Exposure Draft: Proposed Statement of the Governmental Accounting Standards Board: Disclosure of Information on Postemployment Benefits Other Than Pensions by State and Local Governmental Employers," Financial Accounting Foundation, November 3, 1989.
10. Financial Accounting Standards Board, "Exposure Draft: Proposed Statement of Financial Accounting Standards Board: Employers' Accounting for Postretirement Benefits Other than Pensions," Financial Accounting Foundation, February 14, 1989. In this section, some quotes and definitions are taken from the exposure draft. Copyright by Financial Accounting Standards Board, 401 Merritt 7, P.O. Box 5116, Norwalk, Conn. 06856–5116. Reprinted with permission. Copies of the complete document are available from the FASB.

    Prior to the release of the exposure draft by the FASB, the Actuarial Standards Board, the rule-making authority for the actuarial profession, released a standard of practice for members of the actuarial profession on the issue of retiree health care. The actuarial standard is actually similar to the accounting standard, except that the actuarial standard allows the valuation actuary more discretion in the choice of allocation and amortization methods. See Retiree Health Care Committee, "Actuarial Standard of

Practice: Measuring and Allocating Actuarial Present Values of Retiree Health Care and Death Benefits," Actuarial Standards Board, October 1988.

11. Financial Accounting Standards Board, "Statement of Financial Accounting Standards No. 106: Employers' Accounting for Postretirement Benefits Other Than Pensions," Financial Accounting Foundation, December 1990, pp. 46–7.

12. Ibid., pp. 48–9.

13. Ibid., pp. 49–51.

14. Ibid., pp. 3 and 42–3.

15. Apparently only health and life insurance benefits figure in any significant way among retiree benefits other than pensions. Furthermore, for those companies in the sample described in chapter 9 that segregated the costs of retiree health from life insurance benefits, generally life insurance represents less than 10 percent of total retiree costs other than pension expense.

16. Ibid., p. 43.

17. Statement No. 87 was released in December 1985.

18. The exposure draft defines a fourth liability concept, the vested postretirement benefit obligation. The vested obligation is the actuarial present value of the benefits expected to be paid to retirees and active workers, assuming they retired or terminated immediately. It is similar to the minimum liability because only benefits to retirees and fully eligible active workers are valued. The vested obligation, however, may exceed the minimum liability because the present value of benefits to be paid immediately to active workers exceeds the present value of benefits to be paid to active workers at some time in the future. In deliberations following the release of the exposure draft, the FASB dropped this fourth liability concept from the proposed standard.

19. To the author's knowledge, only one life insurance company has written one contract defeasing the retiree health obligation of a plan sponsor. See Linda Koco, "Single-Premium Group Health Debuts," *National Underwriter: Life and Health/ Financial Services,* July 24, 1989, pp. 7 and 9.

20. This change, however, must be first offset against any unrecognized net loss.

21. In the final version of the standard issued in December 1990 the effective dates were postponed a year, and the minimum number of participants in nonpublic enterprise plans required for postponement of implementation of the standard was increased to 500.

22. See Diana J. Scott, "Other Postretirement Benefits: What the FASB Heard in Comment Letters and Public Hearings," *Status Report No. 206,* FASB of the Financial Accounting Foundation, November 27, 1989, pp. 5–7.

23. FASB Statement No. 106.

24. Ibid., paragraph 23.

25. Ibid., paragraph 25.

26. Ibid., paragraph 125.

27. Ibid., paragraph 130.

28. Actually, the concepts of vested and nonvested obligations are not stressed in the exposure draft and, indeed, recently have been deleted entirely. Apparently this company did not use the final version of the exposure draft for its accounting framework, but instead relied on earlier FASB discussion memorandums and analogized to concepts in pension accounting.
29. Coopers and Lybrand (H. Dankner, B. Bald, M. Akresh, J. Bertko, and J. Wodarczyk), *Retiree Health Benefits: Field Test of the FASB Proposal*, Financial Executives Research Foundation, Morristown, N.J., 1989; see, in particular, chapter 4.
30. Ibid., pp. 50–51.
31. Ibid., pp. 57–63.

CHAPTER 6: EXTENT OF COVERAGE

1. An alternative explanation of the reluctance of smaller employers to offer retiree health benefits relates to the difficult market for group health insurance many small employers face. It is reported that poor claims experience may cause huge increases in premiums or even cancellation of group coverage for a small employer. Because poor claims experience may be more likely among retirees, small employers do not want to risk the existence of group health coverage for their active workers by offering retiree coverage as well.
2. General Accounting Office, "Employee Benefits: Extent of Companies' Retiree Health Coverage," GAO/HRD-90-92, March 1990.
3. The tables were kindly provided to me by Sheila Zedlewski of the Income and Benefits Policy Center of the Urban Institute.
4. A. Monheit and C. Schur, "Health Insurance Coverage of Retired Persons," DHHS Publication no. (PHS) 89-3444, National Medical Expenditure Survey research findings no. 2, National Center for Health Services Research and Health Care Technology Assessment, Rockville, Md.: Public Health Service, September 1989.
5. Employee Benefit Research Institute, "Issues and Trends in Retiree Health Insurance Benefits," *Issue Brief* no. 84, November 1988.
6. The GAO estimated that about 30 million active workers are enrolled in company-sponsored health plans that cover retirees.
7. General Accounting Office, "Employee Benefits: Extent of Multiemployer Plan Retiree Health Coverage," GAO/HRD-90-132, July 1990.
8. The Urban Institute calculated that 14.335 million workers above age forty expected to be covered by employer-provided health insurance throughout retirement, while 5.303 million had the expectation that they would not be covered, and 7.948 million did not know or did not respond.
9. The NCHSR is now called the Agency for Health Care Policy and Research.
10. In its 1989 report, however, the NCHSR does not give any information from the NMES about cost-sharing arrangements between retirees and former employers. Such information is available in the CPS and is reported by the Urban Institute.

11. Actually, full payment of premiums and lifetime coverage are not independent events, because temporary COBRA coverage is almost always accompanied by the full payment of premiums by the retiree.

12. Department of Labor, Bureau of Labor Statistics, *Employee Benefits in Medium and Large Firms, 1988*, August 1989, Bulletin no. 2336.

13. Information from financial statements about the corporate sponsors of retiree health benefits included in a sample constructed specially for this book will be described in chapter 9.

14. In 1988, in the "old scope" survey in which service companies and many firms with fewer than 250 workers were excluded, 55 percent of participants had employer-financed retiree health coverage. This statistic further confirms the finding by the GAO that smaller companies and firms outside of the manufacturing and utilities industries are less likely to offer retiree health benefits.

15. Department of Labor, Bureau of Labor Statistics, *Employee Benefits in State and Local Governments, 1987*, Bulletin no. 2309, May 1988, table 48.

16. L. C. Bokemeier, R. P. Van Daniker, and S. R. Parrish, "Research Report: Other Postemployment Benefits in State and Local Governmental Units," Governmental Accounting Standards Board of the Financial Accounting Foundation, Norwalk, Conn., 1990, p. 17.

CHAPTER 7: UNDERLYING TRENDS

1. See Burma Klein, "Future Security of Retiree Health Benefits in Question," chapter 14 in *Retiree Health Benefits: What Is the Promise?* (Washington, D.C.: Employee Benefit Research Institute, 1989).

2. J. Faber, *Life Tables for the United States: 1900–2050*, Actuarial Study no. 87, Social Security Administration, Office of the Actuary, September 1982, Publication no. 11-11534.

3. R. Ransom and R. Sutch, "The Decline of Retirement in the Years Before Social Security: U.S. Retirement Patterns, 1870–1940," in E. Lazear and R. Ricardo-Campbell, eds., *Issues in Contemporary Retirement* (Palo Alto, Calif.: Hoover Institution Press, 1989) pp. 3–37.

4. I. Ford and P. Sturm, "CPI revision provides more accuracy in the medical care services component," *Monthly Labor Review*, April 1988, pp. 17–26.

5. Some proposed attempts at dealing with the problem of technological change in medical services are outlined in P. Armknecht and D. Ginsburg, "Improvements in Measuring Price Changes in Consumer Services: Past, Present, and Future," Bureau of Labor Statistics working paper, May 4, 1990.

6. M. Feldstein, "The Rising Price of Physicians' Services," *Review of Economics and Statistics*, vol. 52, no. 2 (May 1970), pp. 121–33; "Hospital Cost Inflation: A Study in Nonprofit Price Dynamics," *American Economic Review*, vol. 61, no. 5 (December 1971), pp. 853–72; "A New Approach to National Health Insurance," *Public Interest*, vol. 23 (Spring 1971), pp. 93–105; and "The Welfare Loss of Excess Health Insurance," *Journal of Political Economy* (1973), pp. 251–80.

7. R. Zeckhauser, "Medical Insurance: A Case Study of the Tradeoff between Risk Spreading and Appropriate Incentives," *Journal of Economic Theory*, vol. 2 (1970), pp. 10–26; and K. Arrow, "Optimal Insurance and Generalized Deductibles," *Scandinavian Actuarial Journal* (1974), pp. 1–42.

8. Feldstein, "The Welfare Loss of Excess Health Insurance," p. 252.

9. Bureau of the Census, *Statistical Abstract of the United States: 1990* (110th edition) and *Abstract: 1986* (106th edition) (Washington, D.C.: 1989 and 1985).

10. In addition to affecting retirees and employers, many attempts to control Medicare spending fall on health care providers.

11. A summary of the survey results is given in T. Leavitt, "Postretirement Benefits: What Do Retirees Want?" *Compensation and Benefits Management*, Spring 1989, pp. 215–25.

12. Other results of the survey are strongly supportive of Feldstein's theory that increased insurance coverage leads to increased health expenditures. In particular, the survey found that the incidence of out-of-pocket expenses was highest among households with company and private supplemental coverage. Those with substantial coverage tend to use health services more frequently.

CHAPTER 8: ACCRUED EXPENSE AND LIABILITY

1. The Group Annuity table is used instead of the U.S. Life table because group annuitants, who typically live longer than the general population, are probably representative of participants in retiree health benefit plans. See Committee on Annuities, "Development of the 1983 Group Annuity Mortality Table," *Transactions of the Society of Actuaries*, 1985, pp. 859–899.

2. According to Garfinkel, Riley, and Iannacchione, 1 percent of the population incurred health care charges of at least $8,744 in 1980, compared with median charges of $104, and this 1 percent accounted for about 30 percent of all charges incurred by the population. See S. Garfinkel, G. Riley, and V. Iannacchione, "High-cost Users of Medical Care," *Health Care Financing Review*, vol. 9, no. 4 (Summer 1988), p. 42.

3. Coopers and Lybrand, *Retiree Health Benefits: Field Test of the FASB Proposal* (Morristown, N.J.: Financial Executive Research Foundation, 1989), p. 54.

4. D. Waldo, S. Sonnefeld, D. McKusick, and R. Arnett, "Health Expenditures by Age Group, 1977 and 1987," *Health Care Financing Review*, vol. 10, no. 4 (Summer 1989), p. 117.

5. Garfinkel, Riley, and Iannacchione, p. 51. Using survey information is probably the best approach to estimating expenditures on health care by age. The most recent survey, however, the 1987 National Medical Expenditure Survey, is not yet available on a public access tape.

6. Another source of information about health care costs, although only suggestive, is the premium charged by Blue Cross-Blue Shield organizations for policies sold to individual households. In 1990, a major medical policy with a $500 deductible sold to a family headed by a fifty-five-year-old would

cost $3,240 a year. After adjusting for medical inflation, adverse selection, sales costs, and the higher deductible, this premium seems roughly comparable with an estimate of per capita cost of $1,500 for 1988.

These per capita costs represent nationwide averages. Medical costs vary not insignificantly by geographic region of the country, owing to variability in utilization rates and hospital costs. See Committee on Group Life and Health Insurance, "Sample of Group Hospital and Surgical Expense Insurance," *Transactions of the Society of Actuaries: 1974 Reports*, pp. 184–222. This variability of costs by geographic region is essentially ignored when the accrued expense and liability of retiree health benefits are estimated for individual companies.

7. P. Hutchings and R. Ullman, "Prepaid Hospital Care Age/Sex and Hospital Continuation Study," *Transactions of the Society of Actuaries*, vol. 35, 1983, pp. 623–56.

8. This pattern of claim costs by age is largely confirmed by an unpublished table furnished to the author by the Office of the Actuary of the Health Care Financing Administration, showing by age, utilization rates of hospital, skilled nursing facility, and home health agency benefits paid by Medicare in 1988. Another source largely confirming the pattern of health care expenditures by age is R.L. Brown, "A Demographically Neutral Comparison of Health Care Costs in Canada and the United States," Institute of Insurance and Pension Research, University of Waterloo, Research Report 89–02, February 1989.

9. A rate of medical inflation permanently higher than the general rate of price inflation is impossible, assuming the utilization of health care is not influenced by prices, because medical care would eventually constitute the entire GNP. In practice, however, high rates of medical inflation can be safely used in model simulations because in recent years medical inflation has, in fact, exceeded the general rate of inflation, and because the weight of value in present value calculations is on the near, not distant, future.

10. See Committee on Pension Actuarial Principles and Practices, *Pension Cost Method Analysis*, American Academy of Actuaries, 1985, all volumes. The age distribution of the retiree group used in the simulations comes from P. Doran, K. MacBain, and W. Reimert, *Measuring and Funding Corporate Liabilities for Retiree Health Benefits*, Employee Benefit Research Institute, 1987, pp. 90–93. The study by Doran et al. uses three of the demographic groups listed below to examine measurement and funding issues.

11. Committee on Pension Actuarial Principles and Practices, *Pension Cost Method Analysis: General Specifications*, American Academy of Actuaries, 1985, pp. 3–4.

12. If Group C had been used in the simulation instead of Group A, the accrued liability for 1988 would have been $445.9 billion. This latter estimate is virtually identical to the one the author made in an earlier, broad brush study of retiree health benefits. See M. Warshawsky, "Postretirement Health Benefit Plans: Costs and Liabilities for Private Employers," in D. Bartlett,

ed., *Corporate Book Reserving for Postretirement Health Care Benefits* (Homewood, Ill.: Irwin, 1991).

13. Office of Policy and Research, Pension and Welfare Benefits Administration, Department of Labor, "Employer-Sponsored Retiree Health Insurance," May 1986, pp. 73–9.

14. General Accounting Office, Human Resources Division, "Employee Benefits: Companies' Retiree Health Liabilities Large, Advance Funding Costly," June 1989, GAO/HRD-89-51.

15. Employee Benefit Research Institute, "Issues and Trends in Retiree Health Insurance Benefits," *Issue Brief* no. 84, November 1988.

16. Foster Higgins, "Survey on Retiree Health Care," 1988, p.10.

17. Three additional sources confirm to the author that his estimates are largely accurate. First, in the 1992 budget of the federal government, the Office of Management and Budget reported that for civilian federal employees, the pay-as-you-go cost for retiree health benefits was $3.6 billion and the accrued liability was approximately $130 billion. The implied ratio of liability to cost, 36 to 1, is clearly in line with the ratios implicit in tables 8–2 and 8–3. See Office of Management and Budget, *Budget of the U.S. Government, Fiscal Year 1992* (Washington, D.C.: U.S. Government Printing Office, 1991). Second, LTV reported in its 1989 financial statement an estimate of its accrued liability for retiree health benefits. The estimate produced by the methodology used in this book, as explained further in chapter 9, is nearly identical to the estimate reported by LTV. Third, Chrysler's health plan cost per capita for enrollees above age sixty-five was $910 in 1986. See Bater's Health Data Institute, *Chrysler/UAW Medicare Insured Group (MIG) Feasibility Study, Final Report*, November 1989. Assuming that its costs increased at the rate of medical inflation and that 70 percent of enrollees were spouses of retirees, Chrysler's cost per retiree above age sixty-five was $1,821 in 1988, somewhat higher than the author's estimate for the above-age-sixty-five population in 1988.

CHAPTER 9: ECONOMIC BURDEN AND MARKET RECOGNITION

1. Apparently Corporate Text contains the same set of documents and covers the same set of reporting companies as the data service SEC Online.

2. It was necessary to utilize a file containing the texts of annual reports and 10-Ks because Compustat, another McGraw-Hill CD-ROM product that is usually utilized in most financial analyses, contains only data variables and does not report any information about retiree health benefits.

    Excluding statements for utilities, not all 1989 statements had yet appeared on the November 1990 CD:

3. In a survey of employee benefits provided by major corporations, 820 firms reported that they extended some form of retiree medical coverage. See Hewitt Associates, "Salaried Employee Benefits Provided by Major U.S. Employers in 1989," 1990. The difference in coverage may owe partially to the inclusion of NASDAQ-listed companies and of mutual and nonprofit

organizations in the Hewitt survey. It is also possible that some companies responding to the Hewitt survey did not disclose either the existence of retiree health plans or the pay-as-you-go costs of such plans in their annual reports because of immateriality.

4. The most significant case, in dollar terms, of early adoption of the proposed FASB standard was a steel company in reorganization. This company apparently was taking the opportunity of reorganization to release "bad" news and perhaps to bolster its position in negotiations with unions, various creditors, and government agencies.

5. An artificial ticker symbol is created by Compustat when the company has been delisted for any reason. Otherwise, the actual ticker symbol defined by the stock exchange is used.

6. Department of Labor, p. 1.

7. In an attempt to get better information about the active and retired demographic mix of retiree health plans, the author asked the Department of Labor if it would be possible to match information from Forms 5500 for welfare benefit plans (containing some elementary demographic information) and the Employee Benefit Survey for 1988 (containing information about plan provisions, as described in chapter 2). A sample match was attempted under the supervision of William Wiatrowski of the Bureau of Labor Statistics and Dan Beller of the Pension and Welfare Benefit Administration. Owing to the fact that most Forms 5500 included information about many types of benefits and plans in aggregate, while the EBS was careful to distinguish among plans, the sample match was deemed not successful. More generally, Forms 5500 for welfare benefits plans are not audited and the data tapes are not cleaned, and hence they provide the researcher with little information at great effort.

8. No relationship of cause and effect between offering retiree health benefits and the size or profitability of the corporation can be inferred or is intended here.

9. This section draws upon joint work the author has conducted with Professor Fred Mittelstaedt of Arizona State University. See F. Mittelstaedt and M. Warshawsky, "The Impact of Liabilities for Retiree Health Benefits on Share Prices," Finance and Economics Discussion Series working paper no. 156, Federal Reserve Board, April 1991. Definitions of variables used in the empirical work may be found there.

J. Grant, "Liabilities for Non-pension Retirement Benefits—Impact on Firm Valuation," Ohio State University working paper, July 1990. Her study is discussed later in this section.

10. M. Feldstein and S. Seligman, "Pension Funding, Share Prices, and National Savings," *Journal of Finance*, vol. 36, no. 4 (September 1981), pp. 801—24.

11. W. Landsman, "An Empirical Investigation of Pension Fund Property Rights," *The Accounting Review*, vol. 61, no. 4 (October 1986), pp. 662–91.

12. Circumstantial evidence supporting the supposition that the market is knowledgeable about the corporate obligations for retiree health benefits includes research papers circulated by investment banks among clients in

this period. See for example, D. Zezulin, "Post-Retirement Health Benefits," J.P. Morgan Investment, August 1988, and L. Bader and H. Rodgers, "Retiree Medical Benefits in Transition," Salomon Brothers Asset Allocation Group, January 1989. It has been reported, however, that in a survey of twenty-five security analysts, none was conversant with corporate liabilities for retiree health benefits. See K. Ambachtsheer, "Employee Benefits as Corporate Debt: What Investment Professionals Should Know," *Financial Analysts Journal*, March–April 1989, pp. 5–6. Other circumstantial evidence favoring the theory of the lack of complete knowledge includes press accounts in the late 1980s that retiree health benefit plans acted as a deterrent in some proposed mergers. In general, corporate raiders and other merger seekers search for undervalued firms as takeover targets. Apparently in certain instances, the raiders thought they had found such targets, until such time as the retiree health plans were evaluated. That the raiders then declined to take over the target would seem to indicate that the target firms were not, in fact, undervalued, and were even perhaps overvalued.

13. An alternative explanation for the higher coefficient on the retiree health variables in the 1986 equation than in 1987 and 1988 is statistical. In the 1986 equation, the coefficient on book value liability is also higher than in 1987 and 1988. Indeed, when comparing the coefficients in each year, the coefficients on retiree health liability are *uniformly* half of those on book value liability.

14. Moody's, the other major credit-rating agency, later announced it would follow Standard and Poor's lead.

CHAPTER 10: POLICIES AND POLITICS

1. The information in this section is partly based on the following sources: J. Hercenberg, W. Krasner, and others, *The New Medicare Law: An Employer's Guide to Compliance and Health Plan Redesign* (Bureau of National Affairs, 1989), pp. 27–61; J. Dopkeen, A. Rappaport, and L. Bergthold, "Crisis or Opportunity? Medicare's New Provisions Could Offer Employers Positive Change If Companies Assess Obligations," *Business and Health*, November 1988, pp. 24–9; M. Melbinger and T. O'Donnell, "The Medicare Catastrophic Coverage Act of 1988 and Its Impact on Employer-Sponsored Retiree Medical Plans," *Employee Relations Law Journal*, vol. 14, no. 3 (Winter 1988), pp. 399–406.

2. The Secretary of Labor's Advisory Commission on United Mine Workers of America Retiree Health Benefits, *Coal Commission Report: A Report to the Secretary of Labor and the American People* (Washington, D.C.: November 1990).

3. Ibid. Statement of the minority.

4. With the revelation of the burdens shouldered by many companies for retiree health benefits, support for another policy option—national health insurance—may begin to build. National health insurance has taken many forms in industrially developed countries (see Organization for Economic

Cooperation and Development, *Financing and Delivering Health Care: A Comparative Analysis of OECD Countries*, 1987). Implementation of most of these forms of a government-sponsored program would have a radical implication for retiree health benefits—namely, their complete elimination. Universal coverage would obviate the need for employer-provided coverage to those under age sixty-five, and full payment for medical services would obviate the need for supplemental coverage to Medicare. Indeed, the elimination of retiree health benefits may be one of the underlying reasons for the support given to national health insurance by one auto manufacturer burdened by a relatively large population of retired workers.

I have not considered national health insurance as a policy option, however, because it clearly and massively violates my fifth policy goal, the minimization of government intervention. Other broad proposals for reforming the health care system—the Enthoven and Heritage proposals—are more market-based than national health insurance and seem to support prefunding the obligation for retiree health benefits. See Alain Enthoven, "Retiree Health Benefits as a Public Policy Issue," chapter 1, in *Retiree Health Benefits: What Is the Promise?* (Washington, D.C.: Employee Benefit Research Institute, 1989), p. 12; and Peter Ferrara, "Health Care and the Elderly," chapter 4, in Stuart Butler and Edmund Haislmaier, eds., *A National Health System for America* (Washington, D.C.: Heritage Foundation, 1989), p. 83.

5. The argument made by Professor Mark Pauly that companies will not change retiree health plans in response to the new FASB standard depends heavily on the assumption that managers, investors, and workers have been and are currently completely and fully informed of the extent of companies' obligations for retiree health benefits. I disagree with the assumption for the following reasons. As is shown in chapter 9, the stock and credit markets are apparently not completely aware of the extent of companies' obligations for retiree health benefits. Hence investment decisions are being made, in part, on the basis of incomplete information. When more complete information is disclosed, either some of those investment decisions will be changed or companies will reduce benefits. Furthermore, if investors—generally thought to be very sophisticated—are not perfectly informed, it is highly unlikely that workers are fully aware of the extent of value in their future retiree health benefits. Hence Professor Pauly's argument that the operation of labor markets has already caused wages to be lower in the amount of the actuarial value of the accrued benefits for the employees of those firms giving retiree health benefits is somewhat farfetched. Stated another way, the operation of labor markets is highly unlikely to be close to the ideal required for companies not to cut benefits because wages are already lower in the exact amount of the value of benefits.

At least some of the controversy, publicity, and effort expended in persuading the FASB to alter the accounting standard for retiree health benefits can be explained by the entirely rational view that implementation of a new accounting standard will reveal new information and have a real impact on decisions. In particular, a reasonable view of human behavior is that the larger the controversy related to a proposal to reveal new information, the larger the surprise contained in that information and the larger the impact on decision making. Finally, even before the final adoption of the new FASB standard, but in anticipation of the revelation of reduced earnings, a few companies in 1989 and 1990 have reduced, capped, or canceled retiree health benefits. See M. Pauly, "Book Reserving for Retiree Health Benefits: Economic Issues," in D. Bartlett, ed., *Corporate Book Reserving for Postretirement Health Care Benefits* (Homewood, Ill.: Irwin, 1991).

6. As is explained in chapter 2, the transfer of excess pension assets cannot serve as a method of prefunding retiree health benefits. Furthermore, because of the many requirements imposed on those utilizing the transfer option, it may not be too attractive to many corporations.

7. A brief description of ERISA is contained in M. Warshawsky, "The Institutional and Regulatory Environment of Defined Benefit Pension Plans" and "The Adequacy of Funding of Private Defined Benefit Pension Plans," chapters 3 and 9, respectively, in J. Turner and D. Beller, eds., *Trends in Pensions* (Department of Labor, Pension and Welfare Benefits Administration, 1989). A fuller treatment is given in D. McGill and D. Grubbs, *Fundamentals of Private Pensions*, sixth edition (Homewood, Ill.: Irwin, 1989).

8. It is interesting to note in this regard that the public report recently issued by the PBGC listing fifty underfunded pension plans utilized adjusted accounting, not regulatory, statistics.

9. A practical political constraint on the imposition of detailed nondiscrimination and participation requirements for health plans, however, is the experience of Congress concerning the passage and repeal of the Section 89 requirements on health plans.

10. See Joint Committee on Taxation, pp. 25–29.

11. A hybrid defined health benefit–defined dollar plan that avoids some of the problems listed here was described in chapter 2.

12. If all plans were fully funded with a diversified portfolio of assets, there would be no need for a PBGC-type of agency, except to ensure against the extreme events of the theft of funding assets or the wholesale collapse of asset values.

13. For a considerably more skeptical view of the effectiveness of ERISA, however, see R. Ippolito, *The Economics of Pension Insurance* (Homewood, Ill.: Irwin, 1989). Ippolito views the underfunding of pension plans as an effective means of disciplining the demands of aggressive labor unions by combining the specter of bankruptcy with the loss of pension benefits. Moreover, Ippolito views the establishment of the PBGC as an effort by certain ailing industries and unions to gain a taxpayer bailout in the form of pension insurance. Apparently, in Ippolito's preferred world, pensions (and by logical extension, retiree health benefits) should be considered a type of profit-sharing plan and not a type of deferred compensation. Moreover, according to Ippolito, the possible loss of benefits by retirees who no longer have any input in unions' demands or the management of the

plan's sponsor is apparently an acceptable price to pay for the discipline the threat of loss brings to management-labor relations.

14. Another possible advantage of ERISA-fication, not part of the policy goals specific to health care but nevertheless significant, is an increase in the savings rate resulting from the prefunding of benefits. Some researchers found an increase in the savings rate resulting from ERISA, and owing to the logical similarity, an increase in the savings rate might also be expected from ERISA-fication. See A. Munnell, "Pension Contributions and the Stock Market," *New England Economic Review*, Federal Reserve Bank of Boston, (November/December 1987).

APPENDIX: SUGGESTIONS FOR FURTHER RESEARCH

1. A survey of time-series and cross-sectional studies failed to discern a strong relationship between the quantity of health resources expended and improvement of health status. The studies did not consider other measures of well-being, however, such as reductions in pain and suffering. See Alan Monheit, "Returns on U.S. Health Care Expenditures," *Journal of Medical Practice Management*, vol. 6, no. 1 (1990), pp. 7–13.

2. The National Bureau of Economic Research published four volumes on pensions in the 1980s under the editorship of Professors Zvi Bodie, John Shoven, and David Wise.

COMMENTARIES

1. Department of the Treasury, *Financing Health and Long-Term Care: Report to the President and to the Congress* (Washington, D.C.: Department of the Treasury, March 1990).

2. This provision, which was established by the Consolidated Omnibus Budget Reconciliation Act (COBRA, PL 99–272, 1985), currently allows a former employee, with some restrictions, to remain in the employer's group health policy for up to three years.

Bibliography

Ambachtsheer, K. "Employee Benefits as Corporate Debt: What Investment Professionals Should Know." *Financial Analysts Journal*, March–April 1989, pp. 5–6.

Armknecht, P. and D. Ginsburg. "Improvements in Measuring Price Changes in Consumer Services: Past, Present, and Future." Bureau of Labor Statistics working paper, May 1990.

Arrow, K. "Optimal Insurance and Generalized Deductibles." *Scandinavian Actuarial Journal*, 1974, pp. 1–42.

Bader, L. and H. Rogers. "Retiree Medical Benefits in Transition." Salomon Brothers Asset Allocation Group, January 1989.

Baxter's Health Data Institute. *Chrysler/UAW Medicare Insured Group (MIG) Feasibility Study, Final Report*. November 1989.

Bokemeir, L.C., R.P. Van Daniker, and S.R. Parrish. "Research Report: Other Postemployment Benefits in State and Local Governmental Units." Norwalk, Conn.: Governmental Accounting Standards Board of the Financial Accounting Foundation, 1990.

Brown, R.L. "A Demographically Neutral Comparison of Health Care Costs in Canada and the United States." Institute of Insurance and Pension Research, University of Waterloo, research report 89–02, February 1989.

Bureau of the Census. *Statistical Abstract of the United States: 1986*. 106th ed. Washington, D.C.: 1985.

———. *Statistical Abstract of the United States: 1990*. 110th ed. Washington, D.C.: 1989.

Committee on Annuities. "Development of the 1983 Group Annuity Mortality Table." *Transactions of the Society of Actuaries*, 1985, pp. 859–99.

Committee on Group Life and Health Insurance. "Sample of Group Hospital and Surgical Expense Insurance." *Transactions of the Society of Actuaries: 1974 Reports*, pp. 184–222.

Committee on Pension Actuarial Principles and Practices. *Pension Cost Method Analysis*. Washington, D.C.: American Academy of Actuaries, 1985.

Coopers and Lybrand (H. Danker, B. Bald, M. Akresh, J. Bertko, and J. Wodarczyk). *Retiree Health Benefits: Field Test of the FASB Proposal*. Morristown, N.J.: Financial Executives Research Foundation, 1989.

Curto, M. "Legal Analysis," in *Retiree Benefits: The Complete Guide to FASB Compliance and Health Care Cost Control*. Washington, D.C.: Bureau of National Affairs, 1989.

Department of Labor, Bureau of Labor Statistics. *Employee Benefits in Medium and Large Firms, 1988*. Bulletin 2336, August 1989.

―――. *Employee Benefits in State and Local Governments, 1987*. Bulletin 2309, May 1988.

Department of Labor, Office of Policy and Research, Pension and Welfare Benefits Administration. "Employer-Sponsored Retiree Health Insurance." May 1986.

Department of the Treasury. *Financing Health and Long-Term Care: Report to the President and to the Congress*. Washington, D.C.: Department of the Treasury, March 1990.

DiCarlo, S., J. Gabel, G. deLissovoy, and J. Kasper. "Facing Up to Postretirement Health Benefits." Health Insurance Association of America, September 1989.

Dopkeen, J. *Postretirement Health Benefits*. Health Services Research reprint, February 1987.

Dopkeen, J., A. Rappaport, and L. Bergthold. "Crisis or Opportunity? Medicare's New Provisions Could Offer Employers Positive Change If Companies Assess Obligations." *Business and Health*, November 1988.

Doran, P., K. MacBain, and W. Reimert. *Measuring and Funding Corporate Liabilities for Retiree Health Benefits*. Washington, D.C.: Employee Benefit Research Institute, 1987.

Employee Benefit Research Institute. "Issues and Trends in Retiree Health Insurance Benefits." *Issue Brief*, no. 84, November 1988.

Enthoven, A. "Retiree Health Benefits as a Public Policy Issue." In *Retiree Health Benefits: What Is the Promise?* Washington, D.C.: Employee Benefit Research Institute, 1989.

Faber, J. *Life Tables for the United States: 1900–2050*. Actuarial Study no. 87, Social Security Administration, Office of the Actuary, September 1982.

Feldstein, M. "Hospital Cost Inflation: A Study in Nonprofit Price Dynamics." *American Economic Review*, December 1971, pp. 853–72.

―――. "A New Approach to National Health Insurance." *Public Interest*, Spring 1971, pp. 93–105.

―――. "The Rising Price of Physicians' Services." *Review of Economics and Statistics*, May 1970, pp 121–33.

―――. "The Welfare Loss of Excess Health Insurance." *Journal of Political Economy*, 1972, pp. 251–80.

Feldstein, M., and S. Seligman. "Pension Funding, Share Prices, and National Savings." *Journal of Finance*, September 1981, pp. 801–24.

Ferrara, P. "Health Care and the Elderly." In Butler, S., and E. Haislmaier, eds. *A National Health System for America*. Washington, D.C.: The Heritage Foundation, 1989.

Financial Accounting Standards Board. *Exposure Draft: Proposed Statement of Financial Accounting Standards: Employers' Accounting for Postretirement Benefits Other Than Pensions*. Norwalk, Conn.: Financial Accounting Foundation, February 14, 1989.

———. *Facts About FASB*. Norwalk, Conn.: Financial Accounting Foundation, 1990.

———. *Statement of Financial Accounting Standards No. 81: Disclosure of Postretirement Health Care and Life Insurance Benefits*. Greenwich, Conn.: Financial Accounting Foundation, November 1984.

———. *Statement of Financial Accounting Standards No. 106: Employers' Accounting for Postretirement Benefits Other Than Pensions*. Norwalk, Conn.: Financial Accounting Foundation, December 1990.

Ford, I., and P. Sturm. "CPI Revision Provides More Accuracy in the Medical Care Services Component." *Monthly Labor Review*, April 1988, pp. 17–26.

Foster Higgins. "Survey on Retiree Health Care." 1988.

Garfinkel, S., G. Riley, and V. Iannacchione. "High-Cost Users of Medical Care." *Health Care Financing Review*, Summer 1988.

General Accounting Office. "Employee Benefits: Companies' Retiree Health Liabilities Large, Advance Funding Costly." GAO/HRD-89-51, June 1989.

———. "Employee Benefits: Extent of Multiemployer Plan Retiree Health Coverage." GAO/HRD-90-132, July 1990.

———. "Employee Benefits: Extent of Companies' Retiree Health Coverage." GAO/HRD-90-92, March 1990.

Government Accounting Standards Board. *Exposure Draft: Proposed Statement of the Governmental Accounting Standards Board: Disclosure of Information on Postemployment Benefits Other Than Pensions by State and Local Government Employers*. Norwalk, Conn.: Financial Accounting Foundation, November 3, 1989.

Grant, J. "Liabilities for Non-Pension Retirement Benefits—Impact on Firm Valuation." Working paper, Ohio State University, July 1990.

Health Care Financing Administration. *Program Statistics: Medicare and Medicaid Data Book, 1988*. Publication no. 03270.

Hercenberg, J., W. Krasner, and others. *The New Medicare Law: An Employer's Guide to Compliance and Health Plan Redesign*. Washington, D.C.: Bureau of National Affairs, 1989.

Hutchings, P., and R. Ullman. "Prepaid Hospital Care Age/Sex and Hospital Continuation Study." *Transactions of the Society of Actuaries*, 1983, pp. 623–56.

Ippolito, R. *The Economics of Pension Insurance.* Homewood, Ill.: Irwin, 1989.

Joint Committee on Taxation. *Present Law and Issues Relating to Employer-Provided Retiree Health Insurance.* JCT-15-89. June 12, 1989.

Klein, B. "Future Security of Retiree Health Benefits in Question." In *Retiree Health Benefits: What Is the Promise?* Washington, D.C.: Employee Benefit Research Institute, 1989.

Koco, L. "Single-Premium Group Health Debuts." *National Underwriter: Life and Health/Financial Services.* July 24, 1989.

Landsman, W. "An Empirical Investigation of Pension Fund Property Rights." *The Accounting Review,* October 1986, pp. 662–91.

Lantry, T. "The End of Status Benefits? Will Traditional Contract Principles Prevail?" *American Business Law Journal,* vol. 26, 1988, pp. 363–72.

Leavitt, T. "Postretirement Benefits: What Do Retirees Want?" *Compensation and Benefits Management,* Spring 1989, pp. 215–25.

Malloy, P. "Benefits Battle Opens GM Front." *National Underwriter,* 1989.

McGill, D., and D. Grubbs. *Fundamentals of Private Pensions.* 6th ed. Homewood, Ill.: Irwin, 1989.

McNeil, J.T. "The Failure of Free Contract in the Context of Employer-Sponsored Retiree Welfare Benefits: Moving Toward a Solution." *Harvard Journal on Legislation,* vol. 25, 1988, pp. 213–72.

Melbinger, M., and S. Miller. "Maintaining, Funding, and Terminating Retiree Benefits." *Benefits Law Journal,* Summer 1988, pp. 77–102.

Melbinger, M., and T. O'Donnell. "The Medicare Catastrophic Coverage Act of 1988 and Its Impact on Employer-Sponsored Retiree Medical Plans." *Employee Relations Law Journal,* Winter 1988, pp. 399–406.

Mittelstaedt, H.F., and M. Warshawsky. "The Impact of Liabilities for Retiree Health Benefits on Share Prices." Finance and Economics Discussion Series working paper no. 156, Federal Reserve Board, April 1991.

Monheit, A. "Returns on U.S. Health Care Expenditure." *Journal of Medical Practice Management,* vol. 6, no. 1, 1990, pp. 7–13.

Monheit, A., and C. Schur. "Health Insurance Coverage of Retired Persons." Department of Health and Human Services Publication no. 89-3444. National Medical Expenditure Survey Research Findings 2. Rockville, Md.: National Center for Health Services Research and Health Care Technology Assessment, Public Health Service, September 1989.

Munnell, A. "Pension Contributions and the Stock Market." *New England Economic Review.* Federal Reserve Bank of Boston, November/December 1987.

Office of Management and Budget. *Budget of the U.S. Government, Fiscal Year 1992.* Washington, D.C.: U.S. Government Printing Office, February 1991.

Organization for Economic Cooperation and Development. *Financing and Delivering Health Care: A Comparative Analysis of OECD Countries.* 1987.

Pauly, M. "Book Reserving for Retiree Health Benefits: Economic Issues." In Barlett, D., ed. *Corporate Book Reserving for Postretirement Health Care Benefits.* Homewood, Ill.: Irwin, 1991.

Ransom, R., and R. Sutch. "The Decline of Retirement in the Years Before Social Security: U.S. Retirement Patterns, 1870–1940." In Lazear, E., and R. Ricardo-Campbell, eds. *Issues in Contemporary Retirement.* Hoover Institution Press, 1989, pp. 3–37.

Rogers, G.P. "Rethinking *Yard-Man*: A Return to Fundamental Contract Principles in Retiree Benefits Litigation." *Emory Law Journal,* vol. 37, 1988, pp. 1033–75.

Schmidt, P. "Retiree Health Benefits: An Illusory Promise?" In *Retiree Health Benefits: What Is the Promise?* Washington, D.C.: Employee Benefit Research Institute, 1989.

Scott, D.J. "Other Postretirement Benefits: What the FASB Heard in Comment Letters and Public Hearings." *Status Report no. 206.* Financial Accounting Standards Board of the Financial Accounting Foundation, November 27, 1989.

The Secretary of Labor's Advisory Commission on United Mine Workers of America Retiree Health Benefits. *Coal Commission Report: A Report to the Secretary of Labor and the American People.* Washington, D.C.: Department of Labor, November 1990.

Senate Report 100-119 to accompany S. 548. "Amending Title 11, United States Code, the Bankruptcy Code, Regarding Benefits of Certain Retired Employees." July 21, 1987.

Waldo, D., S. Sonnefeld, D. McKusick, and R. Arnett. "Health Expenditures by Age Group, 1977 and 1987." *Health Care Financing Review,* Summer 1989.

Warshawsky, M. "The Adequacy of Funding of Private Defined Benefit Pension Plans." In Turner, J., and D. Beller, eds., *Trends in Pensions.* Department of Labor, Pension and Welfare Benefits Administration, 1989.

———. "The Institutional and Regulatory Environment of Benefit Pension Plans." In Turner, J., and D. Beller, eds. *Trends in Pensions.* Department of Labor, Pension and Welfare Benefits Administration, 1989.

———. "Postretirement Health Benefit Plans: Costs and Liabilities for Private Employers." In Bartlett, D., ed. *Corporate Book Reserving for Postretirement Health Care Benefits.* Homewood, Ill.: Irwin, 1991.

Zeckhauser, R. "Medical Insurance: A Case Study of the Tradeoff between Risk Spreading and Appropriate Incentives." *Journal of Economic Theory*, vol. 2, 1970, pp. 10–26.

Zezulin, D. "Post-Retirement Health Benefits." J.P. Morgan Investment, August 1988.

A Note on the Book

This book was edited by Cheryl Weissman
of the staff of the AEI Press.
The figures were drawn by Hördur Karlsson.
The text was set in Palatino, a typeface designed by
the twentieth-century Swiss designer Hermann Zapf.
Publication Technology Corporation, of Fairfax, Virginia,
set the type, and Edwards Brothers Incorporated,
of Ann Arbor, Michigan, printed and bound the book,
using permanent acid-free paper.

The AEI PRESS is the publisher for the American Enterprise Institute for Public Policy Research, 1150 17th Street, N.W., Washington, D.C. 20036; *Christopher C. DeMuth,* publisher; *Edward Styles,* director; *Dana Lane,* assistant director; *Ann Petty,* editor; *Cheryl Weissman,* editor; *Susan Moran,* editorial assistant (rights and permissions). Books published by the AEI PRESS are distributed by arrangement with the University Press of America, 4720 Boston Way, Lanham, Md. 20706.